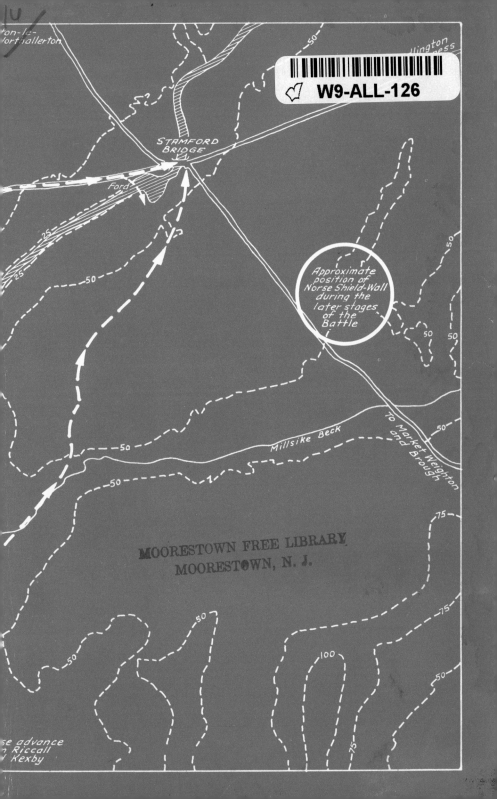

STAMFORD
BRIDGE

Ford

Approximate
position of
Norse Shield-Wall
during the
later stages
of the
Battle

Millsike Beck

To Market Weighton
and Brough

1066

THE STORY OF A YEAR

Denis Butler

G. P. PUTNAM'S SONS
NEW YORK

FIRST AMERICAN EDITION, 1966

ACKNOWLEDGEMENTS

My gratitude is primarily due to those whose co-operation and encouragement enabled me to bring the work to its conclusion. My particular thanks are owed for their inspiration and enthusiasm to my agent, Kenneth Ewing, and my brother, David Butler; for their assistance in the labours of the last years to Miss Sheila Garland and Miss Elizabeth Craddock; and for their faith and forbearance to my publisher, Anthony Blond, and my wife, Nan Butler.

Many people eased my search for the information on which the book is based. Of these, I must particularly mention Dr. Roy F. Leslie, who provided me with many of the original texts, including a new translation of the *Carmen* of Guy of Amiens; Miss Marie Penrose, who prepared for my purposes a new translation of the *Gesta Willelmi* of William of Poitiers; William Godfrey, who supplied a new translation of the relevant passages of the *De Inventione* of Waltham Abbey; and Captain G. P. D. Hall, R.N., whose estimates of sailing times and rates, etc., in the eleventh century were invaluable. I must also acknowledge the unstinted help which I have received in the solution of sometimes peculiarly esoteric problems from the staffs of the Reading Room of the British Museum and of the Reading Public and University Libraries.

A special debt is owed by me to Miss Hope Muntz, authoress of *The Golden Warrior*, whose critical interest throughout the composition of *1066* forced upon me a steady attention to detail in the justification of the theories on which the work depends.

for my father

CONTENTS

vii

Contents

Contents

1066

ENGLAND UNDER EDWARD THE CONFESSOR

IN extent, the kingdom to which Edward returned in 1042 after nearly thirty years of exile differed more from the realm inherited by his grandfather, Edgar, than from the England we know today. From Land's End to the North Foreland, from Wight to the Holy Isle, Britons, Teutons and Norsemen acknowledged the sovereignty of the English king. Westward, the Welsh march ended at Offa's Dyke, running south along the Cambrian foothills from Rhuddlan to the Wye, and from the Wye to the Bristol Channel at Chepstow. The northern border had changed many times since in the west the Scots had first thrust south through Cumberland, and in the east the great earldom of Northumbria had sprawled from the Humber to the Forth. It would change again; but eighty years before the coming of Edward, Edgar had ceded Lothian to the king of Scots, and more recently the Northumbrian Earl Siward had driven the Scots from Cumberland and now ruled north to the Tweed and the Solway Firth.

The resemblance ends with a statement of the frontiers; the land within, the languages, even the people would be unrecognisable to a traveller from the twentieth century. Almost a third of the country was covered by dense forest; marshlands, heaths and moors abounded; much of the arable land lay yet untouched and uncultivated. A hundred miles of fen cut off East Anglia from the midland shires of Mercia; marshes made Glastonbury and Athelney practically inaccessible, and Ely an island. The citizens of London chased wild boar in the woods of Hampstead, and in the northern forests wolves prowled. The open land was rich; but even in the more settled regions of the south-east, across the rolling downs of Wessex, a chapman might journey a long afternoon without sight of human habitation. The cities and citadels of the Roman legions were gone, even the sites of many forgotten, swept over by the tidal waves of the Teutonic and Scandinavian invasions; and the hamlets and towns of Anglo-

Saxon England were little more than centres of trade and fortresses in times of trouble, few and widely scattered. Between the lost cities the Roman roads still ran, but they were falling now into disrepair, cracked and split by grass and ling and the spreading roots of the forest trees, oak, ash, birch and pine, and here and there so overlaid as to seem no more than long-trodden folkways.

The forests had grown since the legions left. They gave the merchant much of his goods and the builder most of his material. Not till the Norman came with his buttressed keep and high-vaulting church was the art of building in stone practised in England by more than a few, and these were taught by foreign masters. The forests had spread and thickened. They determined the movement of trade and the march of armies. When, less than a year after the death of Edward, William of Normandy landed at Pevensey, two routes only could lead him to London and the centres of English power. In the west, his way was blocked by the Sussex marshes, and to the north, by the Andredsweald, the forest of Andred, stretching through the present counties of Hampshire, Surrey, Sussex and Kent, almost from Winchester to Canterbury. One route penetrated the forest, the narrow road down which Harold would march to death at Senlac. The other followed the coast to Folkestone and Dover, then turned northwest to Canterbury, rounding the eastern limit of the Andredsweald; and this was the route that William, fearing ambush on the forest road, would take after Senlac.

Isolated farms, cultivated or grazed by one family, scattered pockets of a rude civilisation over the land, particularly in the north and west; but more commonly, several households were gathered in a group, for mutual help and protection. These groups formed the nuclei of villages and towns; and although many hamlets consisted of no more than four or five families, where the sites were naturally strong, or lay at the meetings of ways, the manories and market-towns of England grew. They did not grow far, however, by present standards, since with few exceptions they were dependent for subsistence upon the tillage and grazing of the common fields about; and when in 1085 the commissioners of the Norman king surveyed England, only twenty towns had populations of more than a thousand. There were 'cities' in England; but the term was merely a corruption of the Latin 'civitas', and meant little more than that once a Roman town had stood on the site. Worcester was referred to as a 'city' in 803, but it was still only vaguely settled when the Mercians raised a fortress there in 900. In 1085 there were eight towns in England with more than three thousand inhabitants, York and Lincoln in the north, Norwich, Thetford and Ipswich in the east, and Oxford, Winchester and London in the south. They had their own markets and mints, their cathedrals and courts of justice. They were centres of commerce and administration, and the greatest by far was London.

London was not included in the Domesday survey and no contemporary document lists its population; but comparative estimates suggest that it supported between fifteen and twenty thousand inhabitants. Then as now it must also have housed within its walls and in the new suburbs beyond the walls a large, but constantly varying, floating population, merchants and tradesmen, foreign as well as national, clerks and seamen, the retinues of the king and his witan, and of visiting notables. In the wake of the first Norman invasion that followed peacefully the accession of the half-Norman Edward came, in 1051, Duke William himself, to receive a dubious promise of the succession from his royal cousin in his new palace of Westminster. Until the coming of the Angevins a century later, the seat of government was the court of the king, wherever he might be, and London was therefore not a 'capital city' in the modern sense, but the title fitted it more closely than any other city in western Europe at the time. Westminster was the favourite residence of the king and the principal meeting-place of the *witenagemot*, the gathering of the 'wise men', the king's advisers. The city itself contained many churches including the great minster of St. Paul, and, before the death of Edward, on Thorney Island just beyond the west gates would rise the new minster of St. Peter to challenge the glory of the older church and testify the piety of the dying king. In twenty mints dispersed through the city the coin of the realm was struck, and three specialised courts, the folkmoot, the husting and the wardmoot, dispensed the justice of the king and of the common law of London itself. The docks and wharves of the port of London carried the major

3

part of the foreign trade of England, with the Rhine and the Hanse, with Normandy and Lombardy, with the ports of the Mediterranean and, through these, with the Far East; and the merchants of London formed the first English trading association, the guild of *cnihts*.

Winchester, like London, was excluded from the Domesday survey, and its population is also unknown. It had declined from its earlier importance as the centre of Wessex and the seat of power of the first English kings; but it was probably still the second largest city in England, with market and minster, courts and mints, challenged only by York, with over eight thousand inhabitants, and Norwich, with over six thousand. Kings would no longer be crowned there, but the royal traditions were strong and would be long in dying. It was the administrative capital of the premier earldom, and the official residence of the queen, the 'Lady' of England. Emma of Normandy, mother of Edward and widow of Ethelred, lived there after the death of her second royal husband, Canute; and when Edward expelled Earl Godwin and his sons in 1050, he sent his queen, Edith, the daughter of Godwin, to exile in the nunnery of Wherwell near Winchester, and she returned there after the death of Edward himself. Most of the other major towns depended for their growth on foreign trade. York had established commercial links with Frisia as early as the eighth century. The populations of Norwich and Lincoln were larger than could have been supported by English traffic alone. Regular exports and imports flowed between Ireland and the western English ports, Bristol and Chester.

The Anglo-Saxon *tūn* was surrounded by gated walls or earthen ramparts, and through the gates the roads ran to the open square of the market, to the church, the mint, where coin was manufactured under licence, and the town-hall, where the townsfolk gathered in times of danger, debate or celebration, and where the shire and hundred courts met. In the larger towns there might be several markets, fish, poultry, cattle, vegetable and dairy produce, tools and handicrafts. A diocesan cathedral might administer several lesser churches within the same town walls. York possessed ten mints and Lincoln five. Clustered about and among the public spaces and buildings were the residential areas, divided into enclosed holdings or *hagae*, hedged

4

or fenced plots, each with a house and vegetable garden, and perhaps a pig-sty and a grazing strip for a goat. As the town grew in importance, the hagae tended to spread beyond the walls and to shrink within them. By the ninth century, town planning had already become an urgent necessity in most towns, and a Canterbury charter of 868 provides that new building must leave two feet between houses as 'eavesdrip'. As well as being in itself a strategical, commercial and judicial centre, the town formed part of an agricultural unit. The leading inhabitants shared ownership of the fields, meadows, woods and marshes that lay about the town, and frequently town houses were attached to rural manors. The rent, or 'landgable', of a haga was paid not only in money, but in services, most commonly rendered in the landlord's fields. The houses themselves varied more in size than in quality, from the one-roomed hovel of the slave to the many-chambered, barn-like hall of the thegn. Only the few sought more than a rude comfort; and with wood as the main building material, construction could not but be limited in scope and diversity. None of the wooden houses of the period has survived, but it is probable that the largest was built on a single level and consisted of a great hall from which radiated smaller, interconnected chambers, with rush-strewn, earthen floors, ventilated by open doorways and windows, curtained or tapestry-screened, fired only in the earthen hearths of the great hall and kitchens, and lit at night by burning rushes.

Despite the richness of the land, and the long peace that began with Canute and ended only with the death of Edward, life was harsh, and there was little place and little hope of survival for the weakling. The Anglo-Saxon was forced into maturity, married, bred and died young, and, though this restricted national expansion and held the population down to little more than a million, it meant that the nation was young, virile and vigorous. The eulogists of William of Normandy have pictured him rescuing the English from a slough of decadence, bringing Norman light to the Anglo-Saxon darkness. This could scarcely be further from the truth; in the art of building the Normans were more advanced, but in practically every other sphere of human activity the changes they introduced were retrograde. They did not endure: in 1075 it seemed that the Normans had

5

conquered the English; two centuries later it was more easy to define who were the conquered, and who the conquerors. Much of the strength and heritage of the English lies in the fact that they are one nation but not one race; even today regional differences can be discerned, but they are blurred and diffuse, and frequently more a matter of accent than of character. The blending of the centuries had only begun in Edward's day, and in Cornwall and Cumberland, Kent, Wessex and Mercia, East Anglia and Northumbria, the subjects of the West Saxon king still retained and maintained their separate folk-identities. East and North, in the Danelaw, the most recent arrivals, the Scandinavian pirates who sailed with Swegen Forkbeard, father of Canute, waged precarious peace with the earlier settlers, Angle and Saxon. The Kentish Jutes, the dark changelings of England, held to folk-ways and customs shared with no other known peoples. In the far west and north-west, the last of the Cymri struggled to wrest survival from fields of stone and meadows of bracken; and here and there, in the remote hearts of the upland moors, lived yet the remnants of an even older race, squat and dark, the first inhabitants, dying slowly but surely, and leaving no trace except in legends of dwarf and troll.

Socially, the peoples of England were divided into three main classes: thegns, ceorls and slaves. Divisions between the classes were not distinct, however, and intercourse and movement, upwards and downwards, were more fluid than would be possible under the Norman and mediaeval monarchies. A merchant who financed three successful voyages was raised automatically to the status of thegn. A thegn who failed in his duties to the king could become a slave. In general, the determining qualification was the tenure of land. There were two types of tenure: folk-land was land which had been held by a family from ancient times, and the title was recognised as the property of the family; book-land was land granted to the tenant by a superior for services rendered, or for rent or future services, and full title was not held by the tenant. The slaves were men without possessions; mainly prisoners taken in foreign raids or in war, they were wholly dependent upon their masters, and though they had certain rights in law, these rights were few and difficult to maintain. Many slaves were freed by the wills of their owners, and these formed an intermediate class of the landless freeman between the slave and the ceorl. The only legal hope of survival for such a man was 'commendation': he commended himself to a lord, and as a vassal was given land and protection in return for services in peace and war. The ceorls combined the peasantry and the middle classes of Anglo-Saxon England. They were the yeoman and the townsman, the small farmer, the chapman, the tradesman and the merchant. Peasant land was usually folk-land, but the feudal tendency was powerful, and many ceorls commended themselves to thegns, giving up their land, to receive it back as book-land from the lord, together with his protection in times of trouble and want. The thegns were the nobles, and ranged from the squire of a country manor to the most powerful earl. The patent of nobility came generally from personal service to the king, and though the privileges of the thegn were many his duties were demanding and without appeal. He ruled the land, but he was responsible for the well-being of the humbler people in his demesne. He administered justice, 'with sake and with soke, with toll and with team, and with infangentheof', but that justice was subject to the scrutiny of the king and of the royal agents. When his attendance on the king was required, only severe illness could justify his absence. Over all, and solely charged with the welfare of all, was the king himself.

The heart of England was the court of the king; but, although the organisation of the state was increasingly more feudal, the rule of even the stronger kings was less centralised and less rigid than under the system developed generally in western Europe, in the fragments of the Frankish Empire. The Englishman was freer than he would be again through six centuries; and the Englishwoman enjoyed a respect and independence she would not regain for a millenium. Kingship was elective, and restricted to the descendants of Alfred only by the choice of a tradition-minded people; neither the tradition nor the choice was unalterable, and Harold and William were not less truly kings of England for their lack of the royal blood. The king was chosen by the witenagemot, the council of the English magnates, the royal family, the earls, the thegns and the bishops, and, anointed and crowned, he governed the realm through the same body. The witan themselves had no hereditary rights of title or position, for the appointments of earl and bishop were grants of the crown, and the most powerful magnate could be broken by a determined king. Less the precursors of parliament than of the Privy Council, the witan were in law no more than advisers to the throne; under such a king as Edward they ruled England.

The earls were the regional viceroys of the realm, and in the eleventh century four earldoms controlled most of the country: Wessex in the south, East Anglia in the east, Mercia in the midlands, and Northumbria in the north. Of these, the largest in territory was Northumbria, but the most populous and the most potent was Wessex. The earldoms were divided into shires, corresponding more or less to those of today, and the shires were further divided into hundreds. The earl administered in the king's name; he kept the royal peace and dispensed justice; he determined and imposed the taxes that maintained his own and his master's states; he commanded the troop-levies of the earldom, and represented its interests in the witenagemot. As well as administrator, however, the earl was of necessity also courtier and statesman, and his position at court demanded frequent absences from his earldom; in the last fifteen years of Edward's reign the government of the nation passed effectively to the Earl of Wessex, and both Godwin and his son and successor, Harold, were involved continuously in national rather than regional affairs. The routine business of the shire was carried out by another royal appointee, the shire-reeve, or sheriff. Not yet as powerful as he would become, he was nevertheless of considerable consequence, and seldom either the villain or the fool that later legends would portray. He administered the royal demesnes and collected the royal dues, enforced the customs and the laws, presided in the shire court in the absence of the earl and gave judgment in the lesser hundred courts, maintained the police system of the time and commanded the troop-levy of the shire. In the larger towns, an equivalent royal appointee, the portreeve, administered the affairs and courts of the town. Minor appointments in earldom, shire and town, the selection of subordinate officials and officers, were made by the earls and the reeves directly.

The routine of the court and of national government was attended to by the king's private household, under the direction of a secretariat that travelled with the king, the *scriptorium*. This was staffed by priests from the royal chapel, supervised by an official who was chancellor in all but title, and was responsible to the king for the maintenance of the machinery of his state and for the clear interpretation of his laws. The scriptorium prepared judgments in legal cases brought before the king, drafted laws and charters approved by the witan, drew up appointments of earls, bishops and other royal officials, made out titles of estates gifted to the king's servants, and issued summonses and tax-impositions. It also acted as a central intelligence office, ensuring that information of importance reached the king and witan, and that governmental decisions and directives were issued promptly to the provinces or individuals concerned.

Christianity was the official religion of England, and the ecclesiastical authority of the bishop of Rome was generally recognised; but the influence of the older, Celtic church was still strong. This gave to English Christianity a sturdier and more independent outlook than was usual on the continent, and this was reflected in everyday life: the Anglo-Saxon would accept from Rome an interpretation of the gospels, but, peasant, thegn, or for that matter bishop, he would resist a dictated application of that interpretation to his own life; canon law was studied and quoted, but disregarded where it clashed with folk-law. It is certain, too, that Christian observance was not practised exclusively; paganism was still common, and harvest offerings were given as bountifully to the old gods as to the new. There were only about four hundred churches in all England, or less than one place of Christian worship for every two thousand of the population, and this suggests that the believers in Tiū, Odin, Pan and Mithras were more numerous than official history will allow. Church organisation followed the European pattern, with two arch-dioceses at Canterbury and York and lesser sees serving the country from Crediton to Hexham; each bishopric had constituted originally a single parish, but by the reign of Edward most had been divided into minor parishes, administered by parish priests. The apparent co-ordination of religious activity was, however, illusory: even the primacy of Canterbury was no more than a convenient fiction, without papal sanction, but accepted by virtue of the location of the see. The jurisdiction of the primate was itself illusory, and he exercised little control over his theoretically subordinate bishops, for they owed their preferments and returned their allegiance directly to the king. Equivalent difficulties faced the bishops in the administration of their own dioceses : many churches were founded independently of the diocesan chapters, and the lay founders tended to regard these chapels as private possessions and parts of their private demesnes.

The *fyrd*, the army which marched with Harold to Stamford Bridge and Senlac, will be discussed in detail later; but it was essentially a synthesis of the forces that had followed Edmund Ironside, the eldest son of Ethelred, and Canute, fifty years before. Among the separate elements that made up the fyrd, weapons and armour varied rather in quality than in nature : protection was given by broad, hide shields, kite-shaped, or in the older form circular, and thick leather *byrnies*, or jerkins, the heavier types reinforced with metal studs or rings; offensive weapons included throwing lances, hatchets, and hammers, long, broad-bladed swords and two-handed axes. The more powerfully armed men, the housecarls and thegns, normally rode to battle, and they were capable of service either as heavy infantry or as cavalry. The housecarls were mercenaries, frequently Scandinavian, and were bound by duty and personal advantage to their employers; in battle they formed both the principal shock troops and the last line of defence. Their traditions of loyalty, courage, ferocity and skill made them the most feared and honoured soldiery in England, if not in Europe, and defensive tactics were built around the 'shield-wall' of the housecarls. The thegns were equivalent to feudal knights, trained warriors, and second only to the housecarls in fighting ability. The mass of the army was made up of the shire-levies : normally called upon only for local service, the levies were peasant in origin, lightly armed, and employed generally as skirmishers, archers and support troops. The machinery of the army, however, was cumbersome and ill-designed for rapid or protracted warfare. The summoning of the fyrd took time, and only the housecarls could be depended on for continued service.

The standard naval vessel of the period was the longship, fast and manoeuvrable, single-decked and single-masted, with one large, square sail and raised bow and stern, and guided by a steering-oar. It was manned by oarsmen who were more marines than sailors; and though some ships were fitted with rams, and fire-ships were occasionally used, a naval battle was commonly decided by boarding and hand-to-hand fighting. The English fleet had originally been maintained by a system of land-levy like the army. Thus, in Warwickshire, every three 'hundreds' were required to supply one warship with sixty men, or one man for every five 'hides' of land, the area of a 'hide' varying in different parts of the country from forty to one hundred and twenty acres. This sea-fyrd, however, was now obsolete, for certain south-coast ports had contracted to provide a fleet in return for the profits of their courts. Such profits were normally payable to the exchequer, but could be alienated by the king; and the incomes of many towns, religious foundations, and magnates of the state and church were augmented by fines and fees awarded in the courts under their jurisdiction. The contract with the south-eastern ports was a profitable one for the crown. It increased the efficiency of the fleet and strengthened the naval defence of England. It could do little, however, to diminish the problems of supply to a fleet in service, and nothing to lessen the dependence of the seamen upon favourable winds.

The economy of England was largely agricultural, and, though tin and other metals were mined in alluvial deposits and veins near the surface, the principal exports were animal and dairy produce. Anglo-Saxon art-work was also in high demand in Europe, and a lesser, but significant, export trade had grown in illuminated manuscripts and gold embroidery. On the west coast a darker trade was strongly developed, the transport of slaves from Bristol for sale in Ireland. Imports were many and varied : in a writing of the time a merchant is asked, 'What do you bring to us?' and he replies, 'I bring you skins, silks, costly gems and gold, besides garments, pigments, wine, oil and ivory, with brass and copper, and tin, silver, and suchlike'. There were skins, ropes and ship-masts, and iron and steel from Scandinavia; marten skins from Ireland; iron-work from Liège; butts of wine and vinegar from France; gloves and fine cloth from Lombardy; pepper and other spices brought by caravans to the eastern shores of the Mediterranean. The English farm-animals were, as now, cattle, sheep, pigs and goats. Fish were plentiful, and salt was obtained from brine springs and by the distillation of sea-water. The imported French wines were expensive and strange to the palate of the average Englishman, and the main beverages, apart from water, were milk and the local brews of mead and ale. The basic unit of the coinage was the silver penny, two hundred and forty of which were minted from the pound of silver, while increasingly common was the Scandinavian mark, valued at one hundred and sixty pennies.

The general structure of English law has already been indicated. It was a simple, but effective system, and the time would shortly come when men looked back with nostalgia to 'the good laws of Edward the Confessor'. The shire-court met twice a year and was attended by the earl or sheriff, the bishop, thegns representing the townships and the hundreds, and the litigants; the court could try all civil and criminal cases, except those concerning thegns, which were reserved for the judgment of the king and the witan. The hundred court met every month and was attended by the sheriff, the priest of the hundred, four men from each township, and the suitors, who were known as 'hundredors'; judgment could be given in most local civil actions, but only on the lesser, unreserved criminal charges. The major reserved, or crown, cases were treason, murder, coining, arson, attacks on houses, open theft and persistent robbery, and these were punishable by death; the minor reserved cases were homicide, rape, mayhem, wounding, disobedience of a royal command and dereliction of a duty to the crown. The decision of the court was customarily the verdict of the sitting judge or judges, but in special circumstances trial by ordeal could be authorised. The juridical rights of a thegn over his demesne consisted of the seeking out of truth and the summoning of manor courts, 'sake and soke', the imposition of taxes and the allocation of duties, 'toll and team', and the summary hanging of a thief taken in the act, 'infangentheof'; only in this did the lord hold any power of life and death over his people. Every life had value, and the value of every life was established by law. The value varied with the social status of the subject, as did the worth of his peace and of his oath, but the laws were clear and definite, and the value of a slave was as closely determined as that of an earl. Accidental or unintentional killing might be compounded by the payment of a 'weregilt', but the retribution for proved murder was death.

This, then, was the England of Edward the Confessor : a land of great potential wealth, scarcely tapped as yet; a nation de-centralised and unfashionably loose in social structure, but young, vigorous and lively. This was a nation with a history of battle, and a memory of war longer than its history; the heirs of Cerdic told the legends of Arthur and sang proudly of their own most bitter defeats, yet, though the battles of Arthur were named, the sites were already lost and Camelot itself lived only in myth. This was a land of deep forests and wide marshes, of primitive farms and rude townships, of wooden churches and wooden halls, but this England of the ox-yoked plough and the twin-bladed axe was much more. The mingling of bloods, of the dark imagination of the Celt with the clear vision of the Saxon, of the solid tenacity of the Angle with the berserker ardour of the Dane, would lead eventually to a culture and a civilisation that would shape the face and the history of the world, and the first shoots of this culture had already flowered. There was in Anglo-Saxon England a tradition of literature in the vernacular unequalled elsewhere in Europe, and in the making and copying of books the pre-eminence of the English monastic craftsmen and of their illuminated scripts was recognised. Though most pictorial art was religious and dedicated to the glory of God, and little has survived the depredations of later ages, the sculptures of the English stone-masons were prized in the churches of Normandy and Rome. Harold's great abbey of Waltham would be trun-cated, desecrated, and reshaped by vandals, the gold stripped from its pillars and its stones used for the building of dykes, but enough remains to show the nobility of the original, its beauty and its power.

JANUARY

THE first day of the new year was a Sunday. Across the broad lands of England, in the narrow-streeted cities, the fortress burghs, and the villages and hamlets, wherever communities had grown, behind earthworks and walls or palisades of stone or wood, or clustered about the little churches in the open fields, on the downs, in the river-valleys, on the reclaimed fens, in clearings of the old forests, from wooden halls and wattled hovels, the bells called the English to mass. Earl and thegn, merchant and trades-man, farmer and labourer, they made their way through the dark, winter morning to the minsters and the chapels to give thanks by candlelight for another day and another year, with prayers and psalms, on this eighth day of the Feast of Christ's Nativity. In the abbey-churches and monastery-chapels monks and nuns had been already at their devotions for several hours. All over Christian England it was a time of rejoicing, but in the palace on the island by the Thames voices were muted and foot-steps hesitant, for in an inner chamber of the palace the Christian King of England was dying. He lay on a narrow couch, richly canopied and ornamented with carvings, the long, thin hands pale and translucent against the covers of fur, silk and linen, resting back against an embroidered pillow, the breathing weak and shallow, the hair and beard milk-white about the wasted cheeks that in health had been full and ruddy.

Edward was now over sixty years old and had reigned for more than twenty-three years. He had not ruled in the sense that Canute the Dane had ruled before him and William the Norman would after him, but he had looked like a king, of outstanding height, fair and noble in appearance, and dignified, but amiable in bearing; and through the years of his reign, apart from the border wars that had punctuated all the history of the kingdom and would continue to do so for another five centuries, England had known peace. The desolation of the Danish wars had passed into memory, and the land was more prosperous than it had

15

been even in the days of Athelstan. Edward had looked like a king and he had lived like a king, graciously and richly; but for the last few months, since the autumn hunting had been interrupted by rebellion in the north, and the king had been called back from the forests of Hampshire to give reluctant assent to the outlawing of his last favourite, Tostig, Earl of Northumbria and third son of the great Earl Godwin, his strength had failed. Tostig had left England, and Edward had sickened; and on the 26th of December he had finally surrendered to the fever that had gripped him intermittently since late October. Despite the messages of cheer which he sent to the court, it was evident to those close to him that the king was dying. The principal work of his reign, the great Abbey-Minster of St. Peter on Thorney, only a little way to the west of the palace, was consecrated in his absence on Holy Innocents Day, the 28th of December, in the presence of the Queen, Earl Harold, *dux et subregulus*,[1] the nobles and the high clergy of England, while Edward lay on his couch, consumed by the fire of the illness.

The Christmas witenagemot, the meeting of the great council of England, took place normally at Gloucester; but in December, 1065, it met in London, or more probably in the West Palace on Thorney Island, between the arms of Tyburn River and the Thames, some two miles from the west gates of the city, and there the king wore his crown at the feasting on Christmas day and on the earlier part of the following day. The particular reason for the change of venue was the forthcoming hallowing of the new West Minster, but it seems likely that, after the fall of Tostig, Edward lost all will to live. The mental disorder that the court had witnessed before, after the return of Godwin in 1052, overtook him again, and his horizon narrowed to Thorney Island, and his purpose to the completion of the abbey-foundation he had vowed to St. Peter. In the palace he may himself have built, he waited only for the fulfilment of his vow, and thereafter only for release. The weakness of the mind accentuated the weakness of the aging body, and, although Edward had led an active life that continued to within three months of his death, when the final disease struck there was neither power nor desire to resist it. The great church had been built and blessed, and now there was no purpose left, and the king gave himself into the hands of the ministers of the faith he had served so long and so assiduously, if on occasion with a certain degree of self-interest.

The magnates of England were on Thorney Island, or in the neighbouring city : the archbishops, Stigand of Canterbury and Eldred of York, the bishops and many of the lesser clergy; the earls, Harold of Wessex, Gyrth of East Anglia and Leofwine of Essex and Kent, the sons of Earl Godwin, Edwin of Mercia and Morkere of Northumbria, the grandsons of Earl Leofric and the Lady Godiva, and Waltheof of Northampton and Huntingdon, the son of Earl Siward, the royal officials and the thegns of the shires about London. The three great earls who had ruled England in the first years of Edward were gone, but the earldoms were still held by their descendants, and one of these would soon hold all England.

There was little to choose, except perhaps ecclesiastically, between the two archbishops in 1066. Both were statesmen, counsellors and administrators of the first order, and neither was particularly noted for holiness, and if Eldred's canonical position was more secure than that of Stigand, this was rather a matter of fortunate timing than of innate worthiness. Intelligent and forceful, subtle and opportunist, Stigand seems to have strayed into eleventh-century England from the Renaissance, an intellectual and political realist in an age of anti-realism. His ability must have been noted early, but even more significant was the evident power of his personality, and those who have defamed him throughout succeeding centuries have largely ignored the fact that he made himself necessary to at least four kings of England, covering a span of fifty years, and that his power was still a reality to within two years of his death, more than half a decade after the crowning of William of Normandy.

The battle of Assandun in 1016 gave the English kingdom to Canute, and in 1020 he had *a church built there of stone and lime for the men who had been killed in the battle, and he gave the church to his personal priest, whose name was Stigand.*[2] This is the first mention of Stigand in history, and the last for twenty years, but it is clear that during those years he remained in close contact with the Danish royal family, exerting a particular influence over Emma, wife of the king and mother of Edward by her first royal husband, Ethelred. Stigand's rise to power, once started, was meteoric : in 1037 he was still no more than an unconsecrated priest; fifteen years later he was archbishop of Canterbury. The rise began when he was appointed to the bishopric of Elmham in East Anglia at some time between 1038 and 1040, but most probably on the accession of Harthacnut, Emma's son by Canute, in midsummer, 1040. Twice deprived of the see, Stigand was twice restored, and by the end of 1044 his position was established. In 1047 he was translated to the royal diocese of Winchester; and in 1052, following the outlawry and banishment of the Norman favourite, Robert of Jumièges, forced upon Canterbury by the king in the preceding year, he was appointed to the archiepiscopate. That Stigand was capable of the position is beyond doubt, and that his appointment was legal is equally beyond doubt, for in England the ties between church and state had been for many years closer than was general on the Continent. To Rome, however, the expulsion of the Norman was uncanonical, and for six years Stigand was an archbishop without the pallium, the vestment-symbol of papal recognition; during these years, for ceremonials, he used the pallium abandoned by the fleeing favourite, and he received his own at last from a pope, Benedict X, who, within a few months of his election, would be himself pronounced schismatic and deposed. These circumstances, coupled with his continued holding of Winchester in plurality, formed the basis of the ecclesiastical attack upon his authority.

The rise of Eldred, if less spectacular than that of Stigand, was ultimately more secure, although for a time, in 1061, it seemed that both Canterbury and York would be administered by archbishops without the pallium. First reported as a monk at Winchester, Eldred later became abbot of Tavistock, and in 1046 was consecrated bishop of Worcester. From 1056 to 1060 he held Worcester and Hereford in flagrant plurality, administering also Ramsbury from 1056 to 1058, and gave up Hereford only on his elevation to the archbishopric of York in 1060, still retaining, however, his holding of Worcester. It was a matter of some scandal that when, as bishop of Worcester, he rebuilt the abbey-church of St. Peter at Gloucester he transferred several estate-revenues of the abbey to episcopal use, and that later, as archbishop of York, he added a large share of the estates of Worcester to his archbishopric, while throughout both his episcopate and his archiepiscopate he kept some of the lands of his former abbey at Tavistock. In 1061 the new archbishop went to Rome to obtain the pallium, but the uncanonical nature of his last appointments, together with the reports of his various depredations, caused a papal reaction that led to Eldred's withdrawal from Rome in confusion : not only was he refused the pallium, but his preferments were taken from him. Only after the forceful intervention of Earl Tostig, who had accompanied Eldred on the visit to Rome, did Pope Nicholas II grant the pallium, and only then on the condition that Eldred surrendered immediately the see of Worcester.

The sharpness and self-seeking of Eldred should not obscure his high qualities as a statesman, nor the importance of the final recognition by Rome. He was possibly the best negotiator of his age, both in peace and in war, and was entrusted by Edward and the witan with the leadership of most of the important embassies of the last twenty years of Anglo-Saxon rule. Able and energetic, he led the troops of his diocese against the invading Welsh in 1049, and travelled more widely than any other known Englishman of the period, visiting all western Europe and Italy, eastern Europe, Byzantium and Jerusalem. He reformed radically the administrations of both his bishopric and his archbishopric, and built generously in honour of his faith. If he was scarcely a subject for canonisation, his private life was blameless, and his gaining of the pallium gave official sanctity to his later actions, which were to include the crownings of two kings.

Little is known of the lesser earls present at the great gemot of Christmas, 1065. To some extent, their qualities and characters can be estimated from their recorded activities, but they remain shadowy figures. It has been said that the grandsons of Leofric inherited envy of the children of Godwin, but the envy between Leofric and Godwin is itself a supposition, with small evidence to support it. Some historians have held that the events of 1066 were dictated by the isolationism and separatism of the North, but again the evidence is ambiguous, and if Edwin and Morkere came tardily to the aid of Harold, there is no proof that this was deliberate treason instructed by jealousy. That the North had an innate tendency to independent thought and action is true; the tendency still exists, but it would be dangerous to suggest that the Northerner is less an Englishman because of it. Of Gyrth and Leofwine, Edwin and Morkere, and Waltheof, it is in any case necessary to know no more than that they were the sons of their fathers, and that they held the earldoms they held, when the mass-bells rang at the third hour of the morning on January 1st, 1066.

The first two days of the new year were uneventful. It was a hard winter, as indeed most had been since the turn of the century, when the mild weather of the early decades began to harshen, but no more so than most. What records there are, indicate a cold, dry period, and certainly without the severity of the early months of 1047, when winter came *with frost and snow, and with all kinds of tempestuous weather, so that there was no man then alive who could remember another so severe as this was.*[3] In the hearths of the West Palace the logs burned and men walked softly over the rush-strewn floors as the whispers spread that the king's life was now very near its end. In the early hours of Tuesday, the 3rd of January, Edward passed into a coma, and during the next two days or more the few words he spoke were the unintelligible mutterings of fever. On the morning of Thursday the 5th, however, this stage of the disease ended, and the sick man's movements became so violent that the priests in attendance were terrified and wakened him. Though too weak to raise himself, the king now seemed calm and at rest, and his speech was lucid. He caused to be summoned those members of the witan presently in the palace, and other members of the court.

They stood about the bed, Earl Harold and Archbishop Stigand, the witan and the courtiers, except for the queen, who sat on the floor at the end of the couch, warming her husband's feet in her lap, and Robert fitzWymarc, the staller or steward of the palace, and a kinsman of possibly both the king and Duke William of Normandy, who stooped to raise Edward and support him against the pillow. The king spoke clearly and eloquently, and his first words were of prayer: 'Eternal God', he said, 'if those things which now have been revealed to me originate from You, grant me strength to relate them. But if they are no more

THE ENGLISH EARLDOMS AT THE BEGINNING OF 1066

(OSWULF)

NORTHUMBRIA
(MORKERE)

MERCIA
(EDWIN)

(WALTHEOF)

EAST ANGLIA
(GYRTH)

(SYRTH)

ESSEX
AND
KENT
(LEOFWINE)

WESSEX
(HAROLD)

than phantasies, let my past sickness burden me at Your pleasure.' For a little his strength seemed to be restored, and Edward turned to those who stood about him.[4]

'Just now,' he continued, 'two monks, whom I knew well in my youth in Normandy, very holy men and long since taken from the cares of this world, came to me with a message from God. "Since", they said, "those who have reached the highest positions in the realm of England, the earls, the bishops, the abbots and all in holy orders, are not what they seem to be, but are on the contrary ministers of the devil, God has given this kingdom, within a year and a day of your death, under His curse into the hands of enemies, and fiends shall pass through the whole land and harry it with fire and sword." Then I said to them, "Under the will of God, let me show these things to the people, and if they will repent God will have mercy upon them. He showed mercy to the people of Nineveh, when they heard the divine wrath and repented." "They will not repent," they said, "nor will the mercy of God come to them." "Then what", I asked, "will happen? And when can a remission of this terrible sentence be hoped for?" "In that time", they answered, "when a green tree, cut down in the middle of its trunk and carried three furlongs from its roots, shall be joined again to the trunk, without the help of man, and begin once more to put forth leaves and bear fruit from the union with its first love, than can a remission of these great evils first be hoped for".'

The king's voice died away and there was silence in the chamber. The listeners were afraid and speechless, awed by a prophecy that promised only despair and a seemingly impossible hope of redemption. How long the silence lasted is not recorded, but the first to regain his balance was Stigand, perhaps, because of his calling, experience and intellect, less liable to the disturbing effects of superstition in a superstition-ridden age. While the others were still stupefied, the archbishop leant over to Harold and whispered that the king was worn out by age and sickness and did not know what he was saying. It is possible now to interpret the prophecy of the green tree, to link it with the uniting of the blood of Cerdic to the Norman stock, with the coming of the Angevin, Henry II, great-grandson of William of Normandy and a descendant, through his grandmother, of Edward's own father. The whisper of Stigand has echoed down the centuries, damning further a reputation already damned by the monastic sycophants of the Norman, but his reaction was at least rational and practical.

The weakness of the king was increasing now, and those about him wept openly. Edward spoke again, telling them not to weep, but rather to pray for him, and then he turned to the queen. 'May God be gracious', he said, 'to my wife, for the constant vigilance of her service. She has tended me devotedly, and has stood always by my side as a dearest daughter.' He turned from her, and now, at last, he spoke the words that the men about the couch had waited to hear : stretching out a hand to Harold, son of Godwin, brother of the queen, earl of the West Saxons, and underking of England, Edward said, 'This woman and all the kingdom I commend to your charge; serve and honour her faithfully as your lady and sister as long as she lives, and do not rob her of any honour received from me'. The kingdom was committed and the heir recognised, and the words which followed emphasised the unreserved finality of the dying king's choice : 'I also commend to you those men who have left their native land for love of me, and who have served me loyally; accept their fealty if they wish to give it, and keep and protect them, or if not, send them, under your protection, to their own homes with all they have acquired by my favour'.

In the reported words of Edward, the commendation of the kingdom, the act by which the king nominated his successor, is confused with the committal to Harold's care of his sister's future. It is none the less clear and unequivocal, and it is recorded as clearly and unequivocally in the chronicles. The report was written in a work dedicated to the queen, and which might, therefore, be expected to stress her interests, and it was written after the death of Harold himself and within a year or so of the seizure of power in England by one who counted himself the true, designated successor of Edward. It was a time for circumspection in Anglo-Saxon England, and while the biographer of Edward might be driven by his convictions to condemn Stigand, he could not with safety provoke the uncertain temper of King William by asserting loudly the legitimacy of King Harold. Eighty years later the dynasty of William would be established and secure, and an Englishman might write of the last English king freely and without fear, but not in the first years of Norman rule, when effectively that rule extended only over the south-eastern parts of the realm, and north and west resistance and rebellion loomed. In this same period the Saxon designer of the Bayeux Tapestry would be forced to like subtleties and evasions in his telling of the story of Harold and Duke William; commissioned by Normans to create for Normans a work based on a Norman history, he would follow his commission faithfully, but by careful emphasis and symbolic usages, insertions and omissions, and by realignments of scenes, he would point the English history for Englishmen to come.

The winter morning was lightening, and in the king's chamber the speculations of the witan were stilled. The last act of kingship was completed, and Edward's thoughts turned again to the well-being of his soul. He asked that his grave might be prepared in the place already chosen in the West Minster of St. Peter, and that the announcement of his death be prompt, so that the devout might intercede for him with the Almighty. The queen was still weeping ceaselessly, and Edward tried to comfort her : 'Fear not,' he said, 'I shall not die now, but by God's grace I shall regain my strength.' The end was near, however, and the last rites had still to be observed, the viaticum and the unction still to be given. The king took the eucharist, possibly at the hands of Stigand, for whatever the rights and wrongs of his archiepiscopate he was a consecrated priest, but more probably from his handpriest, or personal chaplain, or from Edwin, abbot of Westminster and Edward's friend for many years.[5] The king's breathing fell away and he lay as if asleep. His cheeks flushed like a rose, framed by the gleaming, lily-white beard, and the long, thin hands lying by his sides whitened, and the last king of the line of Cerdic, Alfred, Athelstan and Edgar was dead.

Edward had reigned for just over twenty-three and a half years. Twenty-eight years of his earlier life had been spent in exile and idleness, until a year before his accession with no expectation of a crown. He had come to the throne a foreigner, with little knowledge of England, with alien concepts and ideals, alien obligations and friendships, and with his experience of kingship restricted to the observation of an alien rule. Speaking

Norman-French with more ease than his native tongue, with little learning or intellectual power, and with a training concerned chiefly with hunting and the practices of the Norman court, he sought at first to re-create around him the world he knew and loved. He could not displace the English magnates, but the court was his, and the benefices of the church were largely in his gift. From Normandy came courtiers and ecclesiastics, and when in 1051, in a brief access of power, Edward rid himself of Godwin, Earl of Wessex, who had made him king, the young Duke William himself came to London. Out of that visit came probably the later tragedy of England, for it seems likely that at this time Edward nominated, at least to William's satisfaction, the Norman duke as his heir. It was the promise of a king who had been an Englishman for less than a quarter of his life, and in the following summer Godwin returned. English rule returned with him, and the Norman bishops and courtiers were banished. The years passed and the memory and significance of the promise faded, and in the end, on Edward's death-bed it was revoked; but it had been given, and in Rouen it was not forgotten.

The group in the royal chamber began to break up, for there was urgent business to be done. As the king had commanded, the news of his passing would soon be spread throughout his kingdom and beyond, and, though many would pray for the safety of his soul, there would be others more concerned with the disposal of his heritage. There could not be two kings in England, and until Edward was buried his successor could not be crowned; and until the succession was established and the crown bestowed, there could be no security in the land. The witan present debated with the king-designate. The details of the funeral were arranged, and the body was taken from the palace to the monastery to be prepared for burial. The councillors left, but it seems probable that Harold remained behind, perhaps to attend to the business of the court and the chancellory, or to prepare himself for the long day that would follow this, or possibly to give what comfort he could to his sister.

The character of the Lady Edith, widow of Edward and sister of Harold, is misted by the passage of time, and the little we know of her is complex and contradictory. Possibly the eldest child of Godwin, she was married at about the age of twenty-five to Edward, then a little over forty. The marriage lasted more than twenty years, but was childless. The cause of this is unknown: the hagiographers claimed that the saintly king lived, by deliberate choice, a life of chastity, *dedicated to God in true innocence*,[6] but that argument was essential to their subject's claim for canonisation; at the same time Edith was unlikely to deny the legend, for as queen and wife it was more acceptable to have been celibate than barren. It has been alternatively suggested that Edward was impotent, but there is clear evidence that he was not, or at least that he was not thought to be: Leofric, a priest and an old friend of the king, by his name an Englishman, but who had known Edward in exile, and who came to England with him, wrote of him in words that appear to deny both impotence and celibacy; another writer reports two earlier, if irregular marriages of the prince before his union with Edith, and though the source is tainted and the statements untrustworthy,[7] their existence denies any universal *knowledge* of the chastity, or presumably of the incapacity of the king. The most probable explanation of the barrenness of the marriage is that either Edward or Edith was sterile. It may not be significant, but it is interesting to note that none of the sons of Emma, wife of Ethelred and Canute, produced offspring. On the other hand, it seems likely that, in 1051, during the exile of Godwin, Robert of Jumièges, the Norman archbishop of Canterbury, proposed a royal divorce, in an age when one of the few possible grounds for divorce was the sterility of a queen.

Edith was described by her admirers as beautiful, intelligent, accomplished and modest. Her conduct exemplary, her piety humble, in her relations with her husband she was faithful, solicitous and circumspect, looking up to him as a second father and anticipating his every need. She gave generously to the church and supported zealously the purposes and actions of the worthy. Living the life of an unsullied virgin, and exciting the enmity of none, she was kind, gentle and tender in her affections. Her voice in council was listened to, with respect. She was also accused of adultery in her husband's lifetime, and of inchastity after his death. Her support for monastic claims and suits, like that of the king, could be bought, with suitable gifts, and her own claims might similarly be mitigated. It is stated without equivocation, by the most trustworthy of the later chroniclers,[8] that at the Christmas feast in 1064 she ordered and had carried out the killing of Gospatric, a Northumbrian thegn who had quarrelled with Tostig, her favourite brother. Her actions in the nine months of her brother's reign are unrecorded; but she was the first of the national figures to submit to William, and she earned the dubious honour of the praise of the most violent of the Norman partizans, as one who wished to see the Norman duke, lord of the English. It is impossible to say now whether the Norman calumny was justified; the little that is known of her later life, of her continued holding of Winchester and the constant respect with which she was treated after the deaths of her brothers, indicate that it may have been. In her love of Tostig, she may have seen William as his avenger against the other brother who had first expelled and then destroyed him. If she was guilty of treason, its effective extent could only have been slight, with little influence upon the events that were to shape the future of England.

While the prayers and psalms rose up about the body of Edward, and Harold waited, the recalled witenagemot assembled. With the death of the king expected daily, few would have left after the consecration of the new minster, and most would be still on Thorney, or in neighbouring manors or villages, or in London. By late morning or early afternoon the witan were in session, the earls, the bishops, the thegns and the substantial citizens of London, to choose a king. The choice was little more than a formality, and unlikely to be long delayed. It is possible that isolated voices spoke for Edgar Atheling, the nearest to the throne in blood, or for William of Normandy, the earlier nominee of Edward, or even for Harald Hardraada, King of Norway, successor of Magnus, heir by treaty to Harthacnut. If they spoke it was without force or conviction. Edgar was a child, and this was not a time for a child-king; the nomination of William had been cancelled by the dying Edward himself; the claims of Magnus and his heirs had been denied before. One candidate remained. Harold Godwinsson could show relationship with both royal houses of England, by marriage, with Edward and the West Saxon kings, and by blood, with Canute and the

Danish kings; and if the kinship claim seemed tenuous, it was little more so than that of the Norman duke who would succeed him. More importantly, Edward had commended to him all the kingdom, and the allegiance of his subjects. The final step in the justification of Harold's candidature was now to be taken : the confirmation by the witan of the king-designate as king-elect. The choice was made, and the magnates of all England voted the election of Harold, son of Godwin, king of the English.

In 1042, before the burial of King Harthacnut, the witan had gathered hastily to elect his successor. Then, there was the threat of Scandinavian invasion to be countered, and the country could not be left in safety without a king; but Edward had come to England a year before as the recognised heir of his half-brother, and his election to the throne was largely formal. In 1066, the situation was strangely parallel : the witan met before the burial of Edward, and there were now twin threats of invasion; and, although there is no trustworthy record of any earlier recognition of Harold as heir to the throne, there is about his election the same sense of formality that marks that of Edward. It may in truth have been as purely nominal, and the unique and curious titles Harold bore in the last years of his predecessor, duke of the English, and underking, may signify more than mere adulation. In a Life of Harold, written many years after his death and notoriously corrupt and misinformed, it is reported that the witan elected him king, apparently in the lifetime of Edward. The story is linked with other circumstances which will be discussed later, and its central statement is obviously impossible, but it may contain an essence of fact : that in an unrecorded gemot, probably in 1064, Harold was recognised as heir-apparent. This would explain the rapidity with which the events of the 5th and 6th of January, 1066, took place, and the seeming, immediate lack of opposition to the accession of Harold.

The body of Edward was prepared for burial. The crown was taken from the head and replaced by a closely fitting cap, and while the priests chanted and prayed, the servants of the monastery stripped from the royal corpse the robe the king had worn in his last hours of life and wrapped the body in another, rich and lined with fur. Meanwhile, in a chamber of the palace the king-to-be awaited the decision of the witan. At moments like this, problems are magnified and urgent, and it is impossible to doubt that the thoughts of Harold now were clouded with anxiety and uncertainty. Within and without, dangers would threaten his rule, and although, as king of a united realm, the soldier who *came with watchful mockery through all ambushes*[9] would scarcely fear the inroads of foreign adventurers, he could not yet be certain of the whole support of the nation. His royal connections were distant : through his mother he was great-great-grandson of a king, but of a foreign king, Harald Blatand of Denmark, grandfather of Canute. Never before had the crown of England been offered to a subject, or to one so distantly royal, while his enemies were independent princes, though the Norman duke owed nominal fealty to a French king whose power was less than his own. In time Harold could weld the English to him, but he could not be sure that he would be given that time. If he accepted the crown, it was almost certain that he must fight to hold it; if he did not accept it, anarchy would follow in England, and the likelihood of invasion would be increased. In the difficulties that faced him, and which he must face to survive, he was involved not solely as a statesman, but also as a man and as the head of his family. Whatever came of this day, among those who challenged his honour and his safety would be the one of all most nearly kin to him : across the Channel lay Tostig, less than half a year before, closest subject to the king and ruler of one of the greatest earldoms in England, and now landless and exiled, brotherly rivalry transformed to enmity, and respect to hatred. Harold could be sure of his other brothers, Gyrth and Leofwine, but the loyalty of the earls of Mercia and Northumbria, the brothers Edwin and Morkere, was questionable. He might secure their allegiance by marriage with their sister, Alditha, widow of Gruffydd, the North Welsh king, but without guarantee; and, in an age when marital fidelity was more the rule than the exception, the continuity of marriage and allegiance would require the putting from him of the woman he had loved for many years, mother of his children and possibly his handfast wife, Eadgyth Swanneshals, Edith of the Swan's Neck.

It has seemed certain to all who have written of this time that over Harold's thoughts one shadow must have brooded more darkly than any other: in 1064 Earl Harold rode from court to his manor at Bosham, and from the little port on Chichester harbour he set sail for Normandy and the court of Duke William; when he returned, after a stay of several months, he had sworn an oath to William, and that oath, two years later, would give ground to one of the most potent of the Norman claims to the English throne. The origin, nature, implications and effects of the oath will be discussed later; at this point in the narrative of the year, 1066, it is sufficient to state, or perhaps to emphasise that the Norman challenge had not yet been issued. That William would challenge the succession, Harold knew; the bases of the demand he might estimate, but he could not know. We can believe that thoughts of the oath, made under other circumstances and in another land, troubled him; to what extent they seemed significant, or influenced Harold's decisions and plans in the first days of his rule, we cannot even estimate.

The election of the witan had been made, and had now to be announced to the king-elect. From the body of the council, two of its members were delegated to carry the decision to the waiting earl. The names of the delegates are unknown. They were lay-men and of high rank, presumably among the highest in the land; it can be argued that they were the brothers of Harold, or the senior earls, Gyrth and Edwin, but further than this, identification cannot go. The crown that had been taken from the head of the dead king, and the great, ceremonial axe of authority were given to them, and they went to Harold. He met them at the door of his chamber, and they told him that the witan had recognised and obeyed the will of the dying Edward, and they held out crown and axe to him. He may have hesitated, in one last moment of indecision; but then he took the symbols of power, and entered into his kingship. The short, winter day, the day when Edward, King of the English, was alive and dead, darkened into early evening. Fresh candles were lit, and in the palace, after the waiting silence of the past week, there must have been bustle and noise, as the court and the royal servants prepared for the ceremonies that would begin before dawn on the next day. In the monastery, the devout still prayed and sang about the body of the dead king, and their intercessions continued throughout the night.

*   *   *   *   *

The sky was still dark on the morning of the Epiphany, Friday the sixth of January, when the business of the day began. On the ninth day after its hallowing, the great minster that Edward had chosen as his place of burial was to receive his corpse, and immediately afterwards it was to witness the anointing of his successor. Until the king was buried, the king could not be crowned, and by custom the office of the coronation took place during a festival of the church, when the time was holy, and the witan were gathered to debate the effairs of state. This was the last day of the Christmas feast, and before it ended, for the safety of the kingdom, Harold must sit securely and consecrated on the throne of England. The coronation rites were lengthy, and exhausting, and the king-to-be fasted until he had received communion in the mass which ended the ceremony. If the burial of Edward seemed hurried, there was reason for haste; and it is clear that, in the yellow glow of the torches that lit his last journey, all honour was shown to the dead king, his weaknesses and his follies forgotten, and his subjects wept as he was carried to his grave.

They gathered in and before the monastery, the great and the humble; and the body of Edward, dressed in royal robes beneath the shroud that now wrapped him from head to foot, was lifted to the bier and laid under the cross-embroidered pall. Eight bearers, laymen and presumably nobles, raised the two poles that supported the bier, lengthwise below the pall, to their shoulders, four in front and four behind, and the funeral procession formed. Behind the torchmen came the bearers with their burden. On either side of the bier walked acolytes of the abbey ringing bells, and behind the bearers were the clergy, tonsured and led by a churchman of high rank, carrying his crozier. Neither archbishop, Stigand nor Eldred, he may have been Abbot Edwin, Edward's friend and beadsman. Among the lesser religious who followed him, some carried prayer-books or missals, and some sang. Others may have sung too, moved by the occasion, amidst the laymen who came to witness the laying to rest of their king, and to walk in his procession. Solemnly and slowly they went from the old abbey to the west porch of the new minster. They passed in through the porch and the doorway and along the eight bays of the nave, wide and high under the wooden roof, to the presbytery and the vaulted apse. At the entrance to the apse stood the altar of St. Peter, the high altar of the church dedicated to the apostle, and before the altar the stones had been raised from the floor of the presbytery and the tomb prepared. Gently the bearers lowered the bier, and the funeral service began. When it ended, Edward lay in the grave he had chosen himself, and the long legend of miracles would begin. Later chroniclers would write of the healing of the sick, the returning of sight to the blind, and other wonders that took place at the tomb of the royal saint. The chroniclers of Edward's own time wrote not of miracles, but of a righteous soul, a gracious ruler and a blameless king, ever full of cheer, noble and upright, and they closed their panegyric with these lines.

> *Yet did the wise ruler entrust his realm*
> *To a man of noble rank, to Harold himself,*
> *The noble earl, who all the time*
> *Had loyally obeyed his lord's commands*
> *In word and deed, neglecting nothing*
> *To meet the need of the national king.*[10]

The mourners of Edward dispersed, and gathered again to acclaim Harold. The priests were ready and the mass had begun. In the coronation rites, Eldred of York would give the unction, the crown and the blessing, for although Stigand might assist his brother archbishop in the ceremony, he would not perform the central acts that would change a subject into a king. The magnates of England could not risk the accusation that the ruler they had chosen had been anointed by a primate whose election was uncanonical, and whose recognition was schismatic. That accusation would be made, and repeated through nine hundred years after the crowning of Harold; but it had been anticipated in the debate and preparations of the previous day, and the possible recusancy of Canterbury gave precedence to the conse-crated grace of York. It may be that the suggestion that he with-draw from the highest office of his primacy came from Stigand himself, for if the heterodoxy of the prelate was a matter of argument, the devotion of the priest to the family of Godwin was beyond question, and recorded in the chronicles. Now the family reached up to the summit of power; and the bishop who had wept at the exile of the great earl, and the archbishop who had leant across the death-bed of Edward to reassure the son of the earl, was unlikely to insist on rights that might endanger that power. Stigand cannot have stepped down gladly in favour of Eldred, but it cannot have been without good will.

While the abbey workmen relaid the pavement-stones before the altar of St. Peter, Harold had waited with his witan in the great hall of the palace. The morning sky was still grey when the coronation procession left the palace. The two archbishops led the king-elect, dressed now in royal robes, to the minster and to the high altar. As they came, the choir sang, their anthem praying that the hand of the king might be made strong and his power exalted, and that justice and wisdom might be the foundations of his throne, mercy and truth going before him. Harold prostrated himself in front of the altar, humbling himself for the last time as a common man, a sinner and unconsecrated, before the seat of holiness. Eldred moved up to the altar, and the choir sang again: 'Te Deum laudamus, Te Dominum confitemur'; 'Thee, God, we praise, Thee, Lord, we acknowledge'. When the hymn had ended, the king-to-be rose and turned to his people. Chosen by Edward and recognised by the witan, he now faced the supreme election, before the coronation altar, by the assembled clergy and the whole *folk* of England. Nine centuries later, the great election would shrink to recognition, the ritual mouthings of a ritual assembly, but now the people spoke their will, and they spoke it loudly. In a clear voice Eldred asked the English, the Angles, Saxons, Jutes and Danes, if it was their wish that the Earl of Wessex be their king; tumultuously, they shouted their assent.

Harold turned again and mounted to the altar. He set his hand on the sacramental book, the century-old manuscript of the gospels that had been made for Athelstan, and that now lay upon the high altar of the new minster, and he swore his oath of service to his subjects. Loudly, and in the full sight of the people, he swore to preserve peace and concord in his realm, to the Church of God, the clergy and the Christian people of England. He swore to prohibit under law the evil actions of all men in his kingdom, of whatever rank and condition. He swore to uphold equal and rightful justice in all his dooms and judgments, and to leaven retribution with mercy, as he prayed that God might show mercy to him. The coronation-oath had been given, and the people cried, 'Amen!' and Harold drew back from the altar and knelt. The supporting bishops prayed for divine guidance in the rule of the king chosen by all, for peace under his sovereignty, and for his welfare in life and after death; and then Eldred spoke alone over the kneeling earl. In the solemn stillness before the high altar, the archbishop reached out his hands above the king-elect and prayed that the one, omnipotent, eternal God might bless with grace and strength the king chosen to reign over the Anglo-Saxons. He prayed that Harold might nourish and teach, fortify and instruct his church and his people, protecting them through his power and majesty against all enemies, visible and invisible, and that he might never fail the royal throne and sceptre of the Angles and Saxons; and finally he prayed that Christ Himself would sanctify the anointing of the king.

The time of the unction had come now, and the earl was disrobed. As Saul and David had been anointed with oil, and the priests and prophets of the Hebrews, so too were the Christian kings of the English. This was the central rite in the making of the king, the hallowing, the symbolic giving of the grace and divinity of royalty; and in these moments the man who knelt before the archbishop would become the consecrated ruler of his people. Eldred raised the cruse and poured the holy oil on the head of Harold Godwinsson, and, as he did so, the voices of the choir rose again, triumphantly, singing now the anthem of the anointing of Solomon, son of David, by Zadok the priest and Nathan the prophet. The sacrament was given, and the echoes of the anthem died away. Eldred prayed that, with the sanctified oil, holiness might descend and penetrate to the heart of the anointed sovereign; and Harold was king of England.

The supporters of the king raised him, and dressed him in the coronation vestments. They put on him the colobium, a sleeveless surplice of fine, white cambric, and drew over it the super-tunica, a close surcoat of thick, gold cloth, richly ornamented with gold brocade. They fastened the coat about his waist with a gold-buckled belt of cloth of gold, with runner, tab and hangers for the sword of state. Next came the dalmatica, a loose, three-cornered mantle in the fashion of a cope, and lastly the stole, again of heavily embroidered cloth of gold, fastened with double ribands at each end above and below the elbows. Dressed now as a consecrated sovereign, Harold took from their bearers the insignia of his sovereignty. First the sword was given into his hand, with the prayer that through the power of the Holy Spirit the king might resist and cast out his enemies and the adversaries of the Church of God. The sword was fastened to the hangers of the golden belt, and Harold bowed his head. Eldred took from its cushion the crown of Edward, the imperial crown of England, and raised it up before the people. He prayed that with the crowning might come justice and glory, and he lowered the gold circlet with the *fleur-de-lys* rising from it, and placed it on the anointed brow of the king. The sceptre was brought then, and the rod of Edward, crested with the holy dove, while the prayers continued, invoking the blessing of the Almighty on the symbols and realities of the reign that was beginning that day, and imploring, for the newly crowned monarch, the intercession of the Virgin, St. Peter, St. Gregory, the apostle of the English, and all the saints. The investiture was completed, and the nobles who had supported the king through the ceremony led him to the seat of royalty. He gave the dove-crested rod to one and the sword to another, and turned to face his people. The crown of Edward on his head, the sceptre in his right hand and the orb in his left, Harold, King of the English, sat on the throne of England.

Small blessing was to be given to the reign to come, and Harold was to meet *little quiet while he ruled the kingdom,*[11] but on this day, Friday the 6th of January, 1066, the son of Godwin was king of England, by right and by law. Already designated, elected and acclaimed, he now sat anointed and crowned, but if those who knew the storms that threatened the realm had listened with a deeper solemnity to the prayers that preceded the unction, none realised more clearly than Harold himself the difficulties and perils of the months that lay ahead. Able and prudent in both statesmanship and war, and lacking even the momentary rashness of temper and temperament that flawed the character of Tostig, Harold accepted the throne knowingly, trusting his own safety and the safety of England to the love of his pledged people, and to their courage and strength. For the past thirteen years he had been protector and war-leader of the realm of Edward, and he knew the quality of the men he had led, the housecarls, the thegns, and the men of the shire-levies. Now he was king, and the allegiance of all men was bound to him.

The coronation ceremony was ended, and after the prayers and collects of the solemn mass that followed the acclamation of the crowned monarch, and the taking of communion by the king, Harold and the witan and the burghers of London returned in triumphal procession to the palace. The king still wore the ceremonial robes in which he had been dressed after his anointing, and he continued to wear them through the day, together with the crown, in full royal state. The afternoon and evening were given up to feasting and celebration, and throughout the hours of revelry King Harold sat in glory at the high table in the great hall of his palace on the isle of Thorney.

*   *   *   *   *

The new reign began uneventfully. The work of government went on, but Harold had been so long *de facto* ruler of England that the change of title involved, in these first days, little change of position or policy. The one great alteration that might have been expected in the political structure of the country, the re-allocation of the southern earldoms, did not take place. No realignment of appointments followed the elevation to the throne of the Earl of Wessex, and the king kept, in his own hands, authority over the province he had governed since the death of his father. The general business of state was directed and administered by the royal chancellery, and the lesser members of the witenagemot almost certainly left Thorney within a day or two of the coronation, but it seems reasonable to assume that the senior witan, the archbishops and the earls, remained with the king, temporarily at least, to form what was in effect a provisional privy council to deal with the more urgent problems raised by the accession of Harold. Among those who may have left early in the year were the Lady Edith and Bishop Wulstan of Worcester, the most venerated of the English bishops, and the close friend and confidant of the new King. There is no direct evidence of the departure of the queen, but it appears probable that, soon after the burial of her husband and the crowning of her brother, she withdrew from court to the royal demesne of Winchester, then traditionally the dower-portion of the queens of England. Her influence gone, and her sympathies more disposed to the enemies of her country than to her nearest brother, the king, Edith would have little cause to stay at court; and, if there is truth in the implications of the chroniclers, though he did not despoil her, Harold cannot have wished her near to his council. In the case of Wulstan, there is again no direct evidence of a return to Worcester after the ceremony in the West Minster, and it might even seem unlikely that the bishop did leave, but, either later in the month, or in early February, it is reported that Harold called Wulstan to him, in such a manner as to suggest that the summons was issued at a distance.

Happenings in England between Epiphany and Easter, 1066, can only be dated very generally, through the relating factors of cause and effect, and all the accepted datings are suspect. The description of the entire reign of Harold is complicated, too, by the fact that most of the major, or primary authorities for the period are unreliable, their chronicles being written to the greater glory of a king whose rule was founded on the destruction by arms of his anointed predecessor, whose claim was shadowy, and whose possessing fear was the recognition by the English of a legitimate pretender. At the same time, none of these 'authorities' can be neglected, for each on occasion writes non-polemically, and each contains something of value. Harold is accused of almost every imaginable crime, including some that he could not have committed in the circumstances of the time, and some contradicted directly by existing documents. Among the crimes laid to the charge of the last Anglo-Saxon king is the seizure of lands by him after his accession, and this indeed appears to be supported sporadically by the Domesday Survey. There are occasional reports in the lists of holdings in Hampshire, Norfolk and elsewhere, that estates were taken from their holders by Harold, *in the time when he reigned*. In most cases, however, the estates

36

'usurped' were held either of the king, or of the family of Godwin, and the transactions are, therefore, to be described more accurately as repossessions from Harold's own tenants, than as spoliation. The causes of repossession are in all cases unknown, but there is no reason, other than tendentious, to assume that they were not wholly legal. Further, the lands seized by Harold were not returned to their 'rightful owners' by his successor.

Harold's first aim was to secure his position in England. As ruler of a disunited kingdom he would have little hope of beating off his foreign enemies, and although the magnates of all England had sworn without dissent to uphold his sovereignty, he could not yet be sure of the allegiance and support of the lesser nobility and commoners of the more distant parts of his realm. Since discontent could only provoke the disunity he feared, and arbitrary injustice would ensure it, he gave his immediate attention to law, and to government. Laws which were unjust he revoked, and he replaced them with equitable ones. He issued orders to his officers, and to the representatives of the royal authorty, to arrest all disturbers of the peace of the kingdom, and wrongdoers were treated with the utmost severity. At the same time, he upheld the forces of order in the country : he reverenced the clergy, and patronised churches and monasteries; and he showed himself *pious, humble and courteous to all good men.*[12] It must have been towards the beginning of the reign, too, that the coinage of Harold was designed and first minted : on one side was a portrait, in profile, of the crowned king; on the other was the single word 'PAX'.

The support of the Church was essential to Harold's security. Its influence was powerful and pervasive, and the king had, therefore, the strongest possible political motive for keeping its interests welded to his. It was, moreover, in a sense that it would not be again for five centuries, a national church. Nominally under the authority of Rome, the English Church had inherited much of the independence of spirit of its Celtic predecessor, and most of Stigand's troubles, for example, arose from this independence. Unlike their Continental contemporaries, the English prelates were more closely committed to the national state than to international Catholicism, and more concerned with the affairs of the people of England than with those of the bishop of Rome.

Theirs was a special independence, too, for even within the state they were to a certain extent not of it; alone in England, they could appeal to an authority higher than the king, and their powers were not limited by secular statutes. When Harold was still Earl of Wessex, Bishop Duduc of Wells died and bequeathed to his see certain private lands gifted to him by Canute. Duduc was foreign, a Lotharingian, and left no blood-heirs in England, and the estates were forfeited by the earl, in whose fief they lay. It seems probable that, under English law in that age, this was a legitimate proceeding: that, in circumstances such as these, gifts of the Crown reverted to the Crown on the death of their recipient. The successor to Duduc, however, Bishop Gisa, opposed the seizure so strongly that at one time he considered the possible excommunication of the Earl of Wessex. In the event, the anathema was never pronounced, and the dispute dragged on till after Harold's accession, when the king promised, as perhaps the earl could not, the restoration of the tenures to Wells; but the threat of religious outlawry, uttered by a newly made bishop against the most powerful noble in the realm, is a significant measure of the moral strength and political emancipation of the Church in late Anglo-Saxon England.

Despite the evident motive, however, there is little doubt that Harold's devotion to clerical interests was not determined wholly by political necessity. In the previous reign, King Edward's rebuilding of the abbey on Thorney was paralleled by the raising by the Earl of Wessex of another minster, also in the Norman style and of comparable size, in the forest settlement at Waltham. Referred to in the royal charter of confirmation as a 'monastery', it was, in fact, a secular college of canons, and the new church was consecrated in the late spring of 1060. It was dedicated to the Holy Cross of Waltham. The cross had been discovered, shortly before or after the accession of Edward, just beneath the top-soil on a Somerset estate belonging to a thegn, Tofig the Proud. It was of great size, hewn from black marble and embellished with silver and precious stones, and it was credited with miraculous powers. Tofig transported the rood to his Essex estate of Waltham, and there he built a small chapel for its reception and endowed two priests to watch over it. After the death of the proud thegn, the estate was forfeited to the

Crown, and it was granted by Edward to Harold. Waltham became one of the earl's favourite estates, and the Holy Rood, an object of his special veneration. He adopted as his battle-cry, '*Holy Cross!*' and began the enlargement of Tofig's original foundation, possibly in thanksgiving for his recovery from an illness contracted during the Welsh campaign of 1055. By the charter, drawn up in 1062 and signed by the king, the queen, the earl himself, most of the high clergy of England and many nobles, Harold endowed the minster with the revenues of no fewer than seventeen manors to support the dean and twelve canons whom he gathered there. The bounty of the earl did not end when he became king: apart from the manors listed in the charter, he gave to the foundation many riches, shrines and altars of gold and silver, with many holy relics, crucifixes, censers, chalices and candelabra, again of gold and silver, vestments and books of Holy Writ, ornamented with precious metals and gems, bells, phylacteries, pitchers, dulcimers, saddles and a silver wine-horn. Waltham was the principal object of Harold's largess, but not the solitary object: the abbey of Peterborough, for example, the 'Golden Borough', is known certainly to have been gifted estates, or estate-revenues by the earl; the one extant writ of his reign confirms the disputed diocesan rights and possessions of the pugnacious Bishop Gisa; Abbot Athelwig of Evesham *obtained from him whatever he wished*.[13] The devotion of the king to his clergy was reciprocated: Gisa of Wells might want generosity of spirit, but, both before and after the coming of the Norman duke, many of the English churchmen would prove that the king's trust was not ill-placed.

In general the Church supported Harold: the allegiance of his lay subjects was much less certain. A century and a half before, at the death of Alfred the Great, it was written in the Chronicles that he had been *king over all England except that part which was under Danish domination*, but, in effect, Alfred was born a prince of Wessex and he died king of Wessex. His greatness, indeed, lay in his preservation of the independence of the southern kingdom, and it was left to his son and grandson to extend the hegemony of the royal house of Wessex over all England. Both Edward the Elder and Athelstan inherited the military genius of Alfred, and the former was perhaps a greater captain than his father. When Edward died he bequeathed to his son a realm reaching from the Channel to the Trent, and Athelstan pushed the frontiers of the kingdom northwards into southern Scotland. There was, however, a significant difference, unrelated to territorial advancement, between the rule of Athelstan and that of his predecessors : brought up in Mercia under the care of his aunt, Aethelflaed, Lady of the Mercians, his West Saxon origins were obscured, and he was, in a sense that neither Alfred nor Edward could have been, an English king. The unity of the kingdom of the English was organised under Athelstan, and established under his son, Edgar, and it remained a political reality through the Danish conquest and beyond, to the death of Edward the Simple in January, 1066. The accession of Harold reversed the slow process of unification. Once again all England was given into the hands of a West Saxon, and this time to one who could not even claim descent from the kings of Wessex. The new ruler kept the territories of the old southern kingdom as a personal fief, and Mercia and Northumbria became again dependencies of the West Saxon throne, as they had not been for over a hundred years.

There was no reasonable alternative to the retention by Harold of immediate control over Wessex. The success or failure of any attack against the kingdom would be determined by the fate of the south. Invasion from Normandy must necessarily be directed against the southern shires, and, if Duke William could establish himself in south and east England, he would hold a strongly defensible base, linked by the shortest possible lines of communication with the continental centre of his power; at the same time, the establishment of such a base would imply the previous destruction of the main English strength, and of the national potential of resistance to his further advance. A Norwegian attack would come almost certainly in the north-east, and Hardraada might take Northumbria and even Mercia; but he possessed neither the genius nor the might of Canute, and the opponent he faced was not Ethelred; while the richer and more populous south remained beyond his grasp, his occupation of the north could be in the end only transitory. In the military preparations that began immediately after Harold's accession, therefore, the preparedness of Wessex was a central necessity,

40

and any change in the administration of the earldom could only confuse and disrupt the organisation of the defence of southern England. There were, indeed, no substitute claimants to the earldom : the adult males of the three great houses that had ruled the country for twenty-five years were already provided for; and no other Englishman, or, more particularly, West Saxon, had raised himself to such an eminence that he might claim eligibility by personal merit. For almost half a century, Godwin and Harold had administered Wessex, and the loyalty of the West Saxons to the house of Godwin had been demonstrated and proven. It would have been impolitic, to say the least, for the king to endanger that loyalty; and the territorial division of the kingdom was such that he could not appoint a tried representative of his own house to the vacant earldom without seriously disturbing the balance of power in the country as a whole.

The south of England was secured to the king, under Harold himself and his brothers, Gyrth and Leofwine; the earldoms they had held under Edward covered the southern shires from Cornwall to Kent, and reached north to Oxfordshire centrally, to Radnor and Hereford in the west, and to Norfolk and the Isle of Ely in the east. The midlands and the north, east and west, were held by the grandsons of Leofric, Edwin, Earl of the Mercians, and Morkere, Earl of the Northumbrians, and it was upon these brothers that Harold must depend for the defence of his kingdom against the Norsemen. The attitudes and actions of the remaining earls, Waltheof and Oswulf, were of relatively little importance : the territories of the former, the son of Siward, were restricted to Northamptonshire and Huntingdonshire; the latter, the son of an earlier Northumbrian earl murdered by Siward, administered only the north-eastern fragment of the great province of Morkere, and was titled more by courtesy than by right. It has already been suggested that, at the beginning of his reign, Harold kept about him a council of the senior witan, and this suggestion was founded, not on evidence, of which there is none, but on plausibility. Whether or not the council was formed and met as such during those first days, it can be taken as certain that the Mercian and Northumbrian earls gave their assent to the continued holding of Wessex by Harold, just as they had concurred before with his election to the throne. Many reasons have been given to explain the acceptance by Edwin and Morkere of a political arrangement that, on the surface at least, could be felt to reduce the status of their earldoms. It may have been that this suited their own purposes: they may have considered that a king who chose to exercise the local, provincial authority of a subject, chose also to be less elevated above themselves than his crowning allowed; or they may have believed that the preoccupation of Harold with Wessex would distract his attention from the realm as a whole, and increase their own autonomy; or they may have aimed at a division of the kingdom between the families of Leofric and Godwin, and hoped that this action of the son of Godwin would provoke such a division. It is equally possible that they recognised, as clearly as Harold did, the military necessity of the arrangement, and wished the king nothing but well. Again there is no evidence, but some things are sure: England was threatened, both north and south, and the king must face the nearer danger himself, leaving the farther to those who ruled in his name; Harold had no alternative but to command in Wessex, to place his fullest confidence in Edwin and Morkere, and to entrust the north to their care.

The days passed, and the couriers rode out from the palace of Thorney to all parts of the kingdom, to the sheriffs and the port-reeves, to the towns, the great manors and the religious houses, to bring them word of the passing of the king and the crowning of the king, and to bid them look to their allegiance and their defence. The king may have remained in the palace, or he may have moved for a little to his manor at Waltham. The first business of the reign was completed and the rest could be left with safety to the chancellery. It is probable that as yet the officers of Edward remained as the officers of Harold: the stallers, Robert fitzWymarc, Bondig, Ansgar and Eadnoth, Hugolin, the treasurer, and Reginbald, the chancellor. The business was completed, and the couriers rode out, and, among the many, one at least took ship and crossed to Normandy.

* * * * *

The death of Edward had been expected in the Norman court,

for the seriousness of his illness had been known for some time, and there can be no doubt that Duke William awaited only the passing of his cousin to press his claim to the vacant throne. Even so, when the news came at last, it came suddenly and as a surprise, and unquestionably as an unpleasant one: in the same breath that told him of the death of the king, the duke learned that the throne was no longer vacant, and that it had remained so less than a day. Probably within hours of the crowning of Harold, the messenger who would carry the tale of events to Rouen had ridden out of London, or perhaps from the palace itself. By the bridge that crossed to Southwark, or by the old Roman ford from Thorney, he passed the Thames and rode south, swiftly, for the one who sent him had impressed on him the urgency of his mission: he must find the duke and tell him, at once and alone, of the happenings in England. The name of the informant is unrecorded, but that informant may have been closer to the king than we can now know: there were many Normans still at the court of Edward, and not all the witan could have favoured without reserve the election of the West Saxon earl. It is certain, however, that whoever sent the message occupied a position of both authority and power, for the courier was a serjeant, a man-at-arms, and, it may be, himself a Norman. The choice and detailing of such a message-bearer narrows considerably the search for the author of this first treason against King Harold: the possible disaffection of the Lady Edith has been remarked upon already.

The messenger rode for one of the Sussex ports gifted by Edward to the Norman Abbey of Fécamp, Rye or Winchelsea, Ramsey or even Steyning, where the Norman monks had settled under the casual patronage of Harold. In a small ship, lightly crewed, in the heavy January seas, the direct sea-passage from London to St. Valery in Ponthieu or the mouth of the Seine would have been long and hazardous; both distance and danger were halved by the sailing from a south coast port, where a ship could be held in instant readiness without exciting overmuch comment or unwelcome attention. The messenger arrived and went on board, and without delay the little ship set sail.

*　　*　　*　　*　　*

It was, perhaps, four days after the crowning of Harold. The Christmas festival was over, and in the palace on Thorney the king debated with his ministers the defence of England, and he may have discussed with the earls of Mercia and Northumbria the question of an alliance between their houses, cemented by marriage : it was time the king took a wife, a suitable consort, who would produce a legitimate heir to a union sanctioned and hallowed by the Church; and Alditha, the widowed sister of Edwin and Morkere, languished in a northern borough, ripe, but without sons. In the farthest parts of England now, the English villagers were hearing of wonders wrought already at the tomb of King Edward, who, a sleep before, they had not known was dead. In Normandy, in the streets of Rouen, men had talked with the English sailors lately arrived, and a rumour was spreading, that boded no joy to the stern duke whose hall lay close by; but, in the ducal park of Quevilly near the city, under the cold light of a winter morning, there was no rumour, no murmuring, but only the high laughter and the loud, gay chatter of men alert for the chase, for the Norman courtiers were making ready for a day's hunting. They thronged about Duke William, the knights, the esquires and the pages, excited and expectant, for the duke was a skilful and an eager huntsman, and those who accompanied him could be sure of sport, in the open parkland and in the adjoining forest. William had finished stringing his bow, a powerful, long-ranged, hunter's bow that few could bend, and he had given it to the page who would attend him in the chase, when a man-at-arms, bearing the stains of travel, appeared at the park-gate. The serjeant paused, searching for the duke, and when he had found him he picked his way, drab among the gaily accoutred courtiers, to William, saluted, and drew him out of earshot of the attendants. Quietly and briefly, he gave the duke the message he had brought from England : Edward was dead, and Harold reigned in his place. The duke listened intently, questioned the messenger shortly, then dismissed him and turned abruptly away. It was clear to those about him that his earlier mood, the hunting mood had passed, and that he was possessed by a cold and deadly rage. He tied and untied his mantle, nervously and without conscious purpose, then turned again and left the hunting party and the park, suddenly and without speaking, and no one of the companions of his erstwhile merriment dared to address him. The travel-stained serjeant had slipped away, and none had thought to question him. Silent, and engrossed in his anger, the duke was rowed back across the Seine, and he went from the boat directly to his hall.

William entered the hall and sat on the end of a bench next to a pillar. At first, he turned restlessly from one side to the other, but at length his emotions quietened. He drew his mantle about his face, rested his head against the pillar, and sank into a deep study. When it was clear that the duke would not return, the disappointed courtiers had straggled back to the hall, and now they stood about, agitated and distressed, watching the duke anxiously. Although none had the courage or the foolhardiness to interrupt his thoughts, they murmured wonderingly among themselves. Time passed, and still the duke sat immobile and silent, until at last there arrived one of the few men in Normandy who might, with some degree of safety, deal bluntly with William. He was the namesake of the duke and his distant cousin, William fitzOsbern, lord of Breteuil and seneschal of Normandy, and had been for many years one of the most intimate friends of Duke William. That morning he had ridden to the hunt, and when the duke left the park the seneschal also returned to the ducal hall, but, instead of crossing the river by boat, he rode back through Rouen itself, talking now and then to the townspeople as he went. He came into the hall and passed close by William, affecting not to notice the duke and humming a tune as he walked. The nervous courtiers clustered about fitzOsbern, asking him what had happened, and what ailed the duke. He answered them brusquely, telling them that they would learn in good time, and he spoke loudly enough to catch the ear of William. The duke drew away from the pillar and straightened, lowering his mantle, and fitzOsbern went to him. He told his master that it was purposeless to try to hide the information that he had been given : concealment could do only harm. The secret William was guarding so carefully was already discussed all through the city : it was common knowledge in the streets of Rouen that King Edward was dead and that Earl Harold had seized the throne.

William relaxed a little. He grieved, he told fitzOsbern, for Edward, his cousin, and for his death, and for the wrong that Harold had done Normandy. The seneschal had never been noted for timidity, and he was not given to introspection. Grief could be assuaged by action, and he told the duke so : if Harold had been disloyal to Normandy, then let Normandy avenge the injury. What a bold man began, he should carry through, or abandon for ever. If only by arms could Duke William take what he considered his by right, then let him call his vassals to him and put down the usurper with the might of Norman chivalry.

The courage of the duke was not less than that of the seneschal : they had passed through too many hazards and trials of battle together for fitzOsbern to doubt it. But if William of Normandy was bold, he was also cautious; and there were years of his life that he could not have survived, if he had not known instinctively when to be politic. Daring he had shown often, but never reckless daring; and as much of his power had been earned by craft, as had been won on the fields of war. It seems certain that from the beginning, from those moments in the park when he listened to the messenger from England, the duke must have known that only by invasion, with all the force he could muster, could he hope to challenge the rule of Harold in England; but he did not rush to arms, and when his initial anger had subsided, his thoughts turned to diplomacy. William and his advisors knew well that the strength of Normandy alone was not sufficient to their purpose; but if invasion could be made a crusade, with the plunder of a kingdom the reward for holy zeal, the duke would gather under his banner half the adventurers in Europe, the condottieri, the landless knights, the younger sons of impoverished princedoms, and face the English king with an army that, with the aid of God, might destroy him. There were no illusions in Normandy about the quality of the enemy : William and Harold had campaigned together, and the Normans knew the military skill, the personal bravery and the inspiring leadership of their past comrade-in-arms; the strength of the old Norse and English shield-wall was famous throughout Europe and beyond, and Norse mercenaries, the cousins of the English housecarls, formed the Varangian Guard of the Emperor in Byzantium. The duke debated with his coun-

sellors for several days before a decision was reached; and it was
on, or about the 15th of January that the first Norman embassy
left Rouen for England.

The embassy was an act of war. It has been suggested it was
the sincere appeal of a legalist seeking to avoid unnecessary
bloodshed. There is little evidence that William was tender-
hearted, and much that he was both realistic and ruthless,
wherever and whenever it proved advantageous to be so, while
nothing in his history indicates a studied avoidance of bloodshed, particularly if the blood was not Norman and shed in his
own cause. It may well be that, even in diplomacy, the duke was
frequently sincere, but in this case he patently was not. William
of Normandy was an astute and experienced leader of men,
trained not in mock battle or the tourney, but in field campaigns
where defeat and capture would have meant certainly his imprisonment, and probably his death. Ruling a people who had
been called 'a nation of pirates' less than a century before, a
quality essential in his character was the ability to read and
understand the hearts of men; and he had known Harold
Godwinsson. The conclusion is inescapable : knowing Harold,
William could not expect the embassy to succeed; therefore he
intended it to fail. The emotional disturbance that shook him
when the English messenger arrived may have been, in part,
grief for the death of Edward, but its principal cause was the
realisation that Harold had chosen to reign without reference to
Normandy, and that, whatever might have passed between them
two years before, there was now no possibility of a peaceful alliance between himself and the English king. In failure, the
purpose of the embassy was threefold : it served notice to Harold
that his 'usurpation' would not go unchallenged; it gave to
the English supporters of William a tool in the development of
a subversive movement within England; it could be adduced
later as semi-legal support for further action against Harold,
as evidence before the courts of Europe, and in particular of
Rome, that the duke resorted to trial by battle only when all
other attempts to establish his 'rights' had been formally defied
by Harold.

The name of the ambassador is not recorded in either the

English or the Norman sources. He may have been a churchman, but there is a greater likelihood that he was a layman, and one of the senior Norman knights. Since it would be of obvious advantage, to both William and Harold, that the leader of the embassy be a man of high rank known to both, of proven fidelity to Normandy, yet not unwelcome in England, the list of possible emissaries is short, and in that list one name stands out commandingly. William Malet, lord of Graville in Caux, was closely in the confidence of the duke, and his principal estate lay less than twenty leagues from Rouen, yet his ties with England were almost as strong as his ties with Normandy. The son of an English mother, and possibly married to an English wife, he was related by blood and marriage to at least one great house of England, and he may have been the grandson or great-grandson of an English earl, Thored of East Mercia. The putative relationships of William Malet are too confused and too conjectural to be discussed here in detail; but it seems likely that he was the nephew or great-nephew of Godiva, Countess of the Mercians, and, through a later linking of the families, he may have been the uncle of the earls Edwin and Morkere, by the marriage of his sister with Aelfgar, the son of Godiva. More importantly, he knew Harold, and he may have known him well, for they had stood godfathers together at a christening, and nine months after the sailing of the embassy, nine months perhaps to the day, William Malet would render a last service to Harold, on the windswept cliffs of Fairlight above the Hastings shore.

The message carried by the embassy was brief and uncomplicated : Duke William required Earl Harold to fulfil the terms of the agreement between them, by the oath he had made.

* * * * *

There is a footnote to the history of the time which hints that, at his accession, or perhaps even while Edward yet lived, Harold tried to buy a few days of security by the sealing of the English ports opposite Normandy. It can be no more than a footnote, for it was an endeavour without hope of success. The wealth of the island kingdom hung upon trade, and upon the free movement of shipping; and very soon the news from England was spreading across Europe, carried by seamen and other travellers, spies and merchants, the official and unofficial couriers of the lords of England and Europe, well-wishers and ill-wishers. In some courts it was received calmly and without rancour, and Swegen Estrithsson, who might have claimed the throne, slept no less tranquilly in the royal bed of Denmark because his cousin had been crowned king of the English; to others it brought anger and trepidation, that a subject could become a king, and, in some of these, the fear it bred would conjure aid to the Norman duke in the months to come. There was in the Europe of 1066 no comprehension of the forces and processes that had raised Harold to the throne of a kingdom even less akin to 'the continent' than it is now. There were other enemies of the English king whose cause was more immediate, sworn enemies nearer even than Rouen; and it cannot have been more than a day or two after the meet in the park of Quevilly when the news reached Flanders, and Tostig learned that the brother who had voted his outlawry a quarter of a year before, now ruled all England. On his expulsion from England at the beginning of November, 1065, the banished earl had sailed with his wife, Judith, their children, and their supporters to the territories of his brother-in-law, Baldwin V, count of Flanders, and the winter of their exile had been passed in the court of Baldwin at St. Omer.

Tostig's situation was impossible : related by blood to the kings of Scandinavia, brother to the king of England, and uncle by marriage to the duke of Normandy, for Duchess Matilda was the niece of Judith, he was virtually a man without a future, a man for whom there was no place in the world of his time. A few months previously the ruler of a vast earldom, the favourite of a king, and richly endowed with private estates, he was now powerless and landless, a pensioner of his wife's brother. He might by humble suit regain the lost estates, but humility was not part of his character : violent and tempestuous, he could return in triumph, or not at all, and land was valueless without position. There was no possibility of his restoration in Northumbria while Harold reigned : Tostig had shown himself unfit to govern the northern province; the Northumbrians themselves, in open rebellion, had demanded his removal; and the dispossession of Earl Morkere would mean, almost inevitably, civil war and the end of the Anglo-Saxon kingdom. Equally, Harold could not entrust the vacant earldom of the West Saxons to his wayward brother : civil war would again be the likely result of the appointment, for the political balance was critical; and it was essential that Wessex be held in dependable hands, under a government that was stable, and mindful more of the duties of authority than of its privileges. While Edward had lived, Tostig could hope : the old king had a stubborn will and a long memory, and the third son of Godwin had stood high in his esteem. Now hope was gone : barred from eminence, and incapable of accepting less, of living in retreat as a private landowner, only by armed treason to his native land might he regain his lost power, and, even if treason should succeed, he would hold what he won only by oppression, and in constant vigilance against the axe of rebellion and the assassin's knife.

Four choices lay before Tostig : he could settle in Flanders and continue the life he had begun in November; he could try to find in Europe, or even beyond Europe, what he had lost in England; he could fit out ships and so harass England with piratic raids that Harold might be driven to take him back; or he could ally himself with an enemy of the English king, and sell his allegiance for a share in the plunder of his brother's kingdom. It is doubtful, if, even momentarily, the first and second alternatives were considered. It has already been indicated how far the former was divorced from the character of Tostig, and the latter would offer little hope of success and much difficulty and danger. The third alternative was more promising : during the banishment of Godwin and his sons, in 1052, Harold himself, with Leofwine, had sailed from Dublin against England with nine ships, and had spilt British blood at Porlock; Aelfgar, the father of Edwin and Morkere, had twice followed a similar policy, in 1055 and in 1058, each time with success. Morkere held the earldom that Tostig counted his own, and the thought of using the tactics of the father against the son might well appeal to the exile. It may be that Tostig considered this possibility at length, but eventually he abandoned it, though he would turn to it again when his first ventures failed. One choice remained : to commend himself and his followers to a prince with the ambition and the power to restore him by conquest, and to ride once more through

York, as the viceroy of an alien ruler. Men had been driven from England before and had returned by force: they had come with few or with many supporters, with liege-men or with mercenaries, as sole leaders of their troops or, as Aelfgar, in alliance with a rebel vassal of the English crown. Tostig alone would come as the henchman of a foreign invader, to forfeit his honour for a few feet of the land he betrayed.

*   *   *   *   *

The embassy of the Norman duke reached London and brought their message to the king of the English. Harold was still on Thorney, and he received the ambassadors in the great hall of the West Palace. The words were spoken and the duke's letter was given into the hands of the king. The embassy was dismissed, and the king and his council considered the Norman demands. It seems probable that by now the earls and the bishops had returned to their provinces and their sees, for a fortnight had passed since the crowning of the king, and there was business to be done throughout the land. Stigand, and perhaps Gyrth and Leofwine, may have stayed by Harold, but, other than these, the counsellors who met to advise the king were the chief men of the chancellery and of the court. There were other matters to be attended to, other questions to be answered, other decisions to be taken, all pressing and all of importance, and few hours can have been given in any day to the discussion of Duke William's requirements. The days passed and the Norman ambassadors waited, until at last they were summoned to hear the reply of the English king. The long, first month of the new year was drawing towards its close, and into the early quiet of the reign of Harold Godwinsson disturbances were creeping: there was noise abroad of angry rumour in the courts of Europe, and talk of usurpation and of the seizing of the throne by treachery and violence; men were saying that Harold had been crowned uncanonically and in stealth by Stigand, and even that he had crowned himself; and now report was coming in of outcry in the north and of Northumbrian refusal to recognise the West Saxon king. Many of the whispers touched the honour of Harold himself, and many had their origins in the court of Duke William, and it is little to be wondered at if the king awaited the ambassadors with impatience, and a will to be done with them.

The message of the duke had been brief and explicit. If Harold's reply lacked the brevity of the Norman demands, it was equally explicit. Harold denied that he had broken the treaty or repudiated the compact between William and himself; both treaty and compact were null, for they had been made by Harold as a private individual, presuming an authority which he did not then possess. Again, as the vow which a maiden makes concerning herself, under her father's roof and without her parents' knowledge, is adjudged invalid, so must the oath be to which he had assented, relating to the whole kingdom, when he was himself only a subject under the king's jurisdiction, compelled by the necessity of the moment, and without the knowledge of the nation. At the same time, he could not be required to resign an office to which he had been elected by the common voice of the English people, and from which he could not be dismissed except by that same voice, for his abdication would be neither agreeable to the people nor safe for their military. As to the contract of marriage between himself and Agatha, the daughter of William and Matilda, the consent of the witan was necessary to the marriage of an English king to a foreign woman, and that consent had not been given. A dark humour broke into the constitutional and measured solemnity of Harold's words : his sister, whom he had promised should marry a Norman noble, and whom William now desired he should send to Normandy, was dead; but if the duke wished to have what kind of body she now was, he would indeed send her corpse to Normandy. Accordingly, and for the reasons stated, and except for that one macabre concession, King Harold rejected the duke's demands. The embassy withdrew, and the king returned to his chancellery and the government of England.

* * * * *

Far to the north, a threat to England was receding. In a wooden hall above a Norwegian fiord, Harald Hardraada had learned of the death of Edward and the accession of Harold Godwinsson. After a life devoted to battle, from the Black Sea to the North Atlantic, the king of Norway had languished in peace for two years, and now the realm of England, willed to his pre-

decessor by its last Scandinavian king, had fallen to a ruler whose
father had been raised by Canute, whose grandfather was a rustic
thegn, and whose great-grandfather was unknown. England was
rich, and ripe for plunder, but the expedition would be dangerous, more dangerous even than the war against Denmark
which he had been forced to end with a negotiated peace. Without support among the English themselves, invasion could be
disastrous. Hardraada forgot England and turned his attention
again to his unruly subjects.

*   *   *   *   *

In Flanders, Tostig had come to a decision. Of the four princes
to whom his offer of alliance might seem of value, the closest in
friendship was his sworn brother, Malcolm of Scotland; but
Malcolm's power was small, and would avail little against
Harold. The mightiest was Harald Hardraada of Norway; but
Tostig knew him only by reputation, and of the four realms of
the princes, Norway lay farthest from Flanders and England.
The nearest in distance was Normandy, and William had been
friendly; but the Norman duke was guileful and autocratic, and
under his nephew-by-marriage Tostig might find his position
and his prospects less secure and no more brilliant than he would
have done under his royal brother. The likeliest ally seemed to
be his cousin, Swegen Estrithsson. The Danish king was prudent
and he had built his power from the poverty of exile in Sweden
to the rule of all Denmark, from defeat and flight to what was
effectively victory over Hardraada himself. Tostig decided to
take his suit to Swegen. With a retinue of his English supporters
and Flemish recruits to his cause, he left St. Omer and rode
north, overland, for Friesland and Denmark.

*   *   *   *   *

The month was ending. Harald Hardraada drank in the
smoky twilight of his royal hall and hunted in the tall, pine
forests of Norway. Tostig rode north, through Flanders and
Lorraine, with new purpose, and confident now. Duke William
sat in Rouen and hid his impatience with cold jests, while he
awaited the return of his embassy from England. In England
itself the rumours of insurrection in the north grew and were

confirmed, and King Harold debated with his counsellors how best the kingdom might again be united. When January began, Edward the son of Ethelred had been alive, and western Europe and England had been at peace. War had not yet come, nor even the threat of war, but peace had died with Edward. The clouds were gathering.

FEBRUARY

THE reign of Harold Godwinsson was less than a month old, but already, in the north, his sovereignty was menaced. The last crisis of the reign of Edward seemed about to be renewed. As, in Ocotber, 1065, the men of the north had risen against the dominion of Tostig, so they refused to accept the crowning of his brother. It was not a revolt like the October rising. No Northumbrian army marched south against the king. But the resistance was real, and without the adherence of the north Harold could not hope to preserve his realm. Four months earlier, King Edward had been eager to lead an army against his rebellious subjects. Four years later, the north rose again, and the Norman king laid waste all the land from York to the Tees, burning, pillaging and killing, so that men, women and children dropped dead of starvation, their corpses lying unburied in the empty fields, or turned bandit or sold themselves into slavery. But civil war could afford no solution to Harold.

Northumbrian resentment, carried into active rebellion, could destroy the kingdom, but this formed only one of the problems confronting Harold. The continuation of his rule in the north required the loyal support of the brother-earls of Northumbria and Mercia, and the attitudes of Morkere and Edwin were ambiguous. They had consented to the election of Harold and to his marriage with their sister, yet even a passive northern resistance would be difficult, if not impossible, to maintain without either the tacit connivance or the deliberate inactivity of the earls, and the resistance was real and growing. The latter alternative, of inactivity rather than connivance, is more likely : there is no positive evidence of treason to Harold in the acts of Edwin and Morkere, but something of weakness, and it seems clear that they had inherited from Leofric little more than blood. Their actions, both before and after the coming of the Normans, were those of men of greater wilfulness than will, and their ambitions, their opinions and their loyalties seem to have varied with the circumstances and the company of the moment. At the same time, Harold's freedom of action was much less than that of his subjects in the north. Over his every move, physical and political, brooded the menace of alien intervention. There was no external threat of any significance to the sovereignty of Edward in 1065, or to that of William in 1069, and neither was dependent for the safety of the realm upon the goodwill of individual earls or of the provincial thegnhoods. The fidelity of all the nation was, however, essential to Harold, and, even if he would, he dared not equate the repression of Northumbrian discontent with the harrying of the earldom, as Edward had sought to do, and as William would do.

In 1066, Harold was not more than forty-five years old. Tall, graceful and handsome, and with uncommon strength and immense powers of endurance, *he stood before the people as another Judas Maccabeus.*[1] In war, he was a practised, skilful and vigorous commander, and, although as a soldier he was both courageous and daring, he was also careful, and given neither to rashness nor to empty heroics. The same courage and care informed his activity as a statesman. As a counsellor, he was eloquent and prudent, and no one *was more knowledgeable in the laws of the land.*[2] Despite, or perhaps because of, his unchallengeable position and power in the last years of Edward, he could accept criticism without rancour, and contradiction without retaliation. His dealings with others were directed by a ready understanding and governed by an innate mildness of temperament; and his general policy was one of co-operation and conciliation. He was not afraid to share his plans with those whose loyalty he valued; and, although in battle he could be implacable, in victory he was capable of a generosity to the defeated unusual in any age. It is possible, though unlikely, that he was literate; but his experience was wide and enriched by travel. He had studied the characters and policies of other rulers, and the functioning of their states, not merely through his agents, but at first hand. He had certainly visited Flanders, Normandy and Rome, and he may have journeyed to the Rhine and beyond, to Cologne and Bavaria.

The actions of Harold, like those of any man, were subject to occasional inconsistencies; and, in the more trustworthy contemporary assessments of his character, praise is tempered with criticism. Even when the later diatribes of the Normans are ignored, it is clear that sometimes caution surrendered to recklessness, or to overweening self-assurance. His sense of a justice transcending the personal was misinterpreted: in October, 1065, Tostig accused Earl Harold before King Edward of persuading the Northumbrians to rebel, and it is evident that, at least to Tostig, this was the only credible explanation of his brother's inaction against the insurgents. In his private life, Harold was liberal to the clergy, but not notably conformist. Although, for possibly more than twenty years, he may have been faithful to one woman, Edith Swan-Neck, she was at most his common-law wife, and their union was unrecognised by the Church. Yet there can be little doubt that what happiness Harold knew with women, he knew with her. Edith was probably born in Norfolk, of good family; and it seems likely that her parents, or her mother, had held the friendship of Godwin, and, hence, that their children had known one another for some years before it becomes possible to link the names of the daughter of the Norfolk thegn and the second son of the West Saxon earl. Their relationship may have begun even before Harold entered recorded history as earl of the East Angles, in or about 1045, and it was something much more than the affair of a summer. She may have been with him before the beginning of his public life, and she was with him still, after the end. Harold would marry, with the full rites and sanction of the Church; but, when the king died on a narrow ridge above a sandy stream in Sussex, it was not his queen, Alditha of Mercia, but Edith of the Swan's Neck who came to find the mutilated corpse and to identify her lover by markings known only to herself.

Harold's childhood and adolescence are unchronicled, but, when he was about twenty-three, he was created earl of the East Angles. His earliest military command was naval: in 1048, he almost certainly took part in a vain pursuit of Norse pirates who had harried Essex and the south-east coast of England, and in the following year he captained a royal ship in an expedition led by his father against raiders in the west. In 1046, Swegen, Godwin's eldest son, had seduced the Abbess of Leominster, kept her with him a while and then sent her home. When the story became public, Swegen was outlawed and left the country, his lands were divided between Harold and his cousin, Beorn, and the nunnery of Leominster was suppressed. After an abortive attempt to return, in 1049, Swegen murdered Beorn and his outlawry was confirmed, but he was restored to his earldom less than a year later, only to be driven out again when the struggle between Edward and Godwin came to a head in September, 1051. Harold was exiled with his father and brothers at the same time and fled to Ireland, but when Godwin returned in triumph in September, 1052, his closest supporter was Harold. More than two thousand miles away, barefoot and alone, Swegen was struggling homewards from a pilgrimage of penance to Jerusalem, and less than a month later he died of exposure in the mountainous wilds of Asia Minor. In position, as in character and ability, Harold was heir to the greatness of his father.

Godwin died during the Easter Festival in 1053, and Harold succeeded him as earl of Wessex. This was the most powerful office in England under the king, and the story of the next eleven years is the story of Harold's consolidation of that power, of the gradual strengthening of his authority until it surpassed even that of his father, and the crown itself came within his reach. In 1055, Aelfgar, son of Leofric, and Harold's successor in East Anglia, was banished, allied himself with Gruffydd, king of Wales, and invaded western England, sacking and burning Hereford. Harold marched to his first Welsh campaign, but the invaders retreated before him, and, although he crossed the border into southern Wales, he could not bring them to battle. He retired, disbanded his army, and rebuilt and refortified Hereford. Shortly afterwards, Aelfgar made his peace with Edward, and, in the following year, Gruffydd was reconciled to Edward through the intercession of Bishop Eldred and the earls, Harold and Leofric, and took a new oath of homage to his English overlord. In 1057, Edward 'the Exile', the son of Edmund Ironside, returned to England with his children, but died before he could meet the king. There was now no heir-male to the English throne, who could claim descent from Cerdic and Alfred, other than the child, Edgar Atheling, the son of the dead prince. In the same year Hereford was given into the care of Harold and added to the West Saxon earldom. Three years later,

58

Harold's minster at Waltham was consecrated, and peace seemed to have become a natural condition in England. In 1062, however, Gruffydd renewed his ravages, and Harold mounted a second expedition against him. The Welsh king was at Rhuddlan, on the north-east coast of Wales, and the earl struck suddenly, with a small, mounted force, against the port. Gruffydd escaped by the narrowest of margins, and Harold burned his palace and the ships in the harbour before retiring to Gloucester. It was decided now to destroy Gruffydd's power once and for all; and in May, 1063, Harold and Tostig invaded Wales by sea and by land, from south and north. Experience had taught Harold that the standard English tactics could not succeed in a land such as Wales, and in 1063 he adopted the weapons and methods of the Welsh themselves. The two invading forces met and began to harry the country systematically, and they did so to such effect that within three months the spirit of the enemy was broken. In August, Gruffydd was executed by his own followers, and the Welsh submission was complete.

The Welsh surrender gives the earliest indication of the unique position of Harold in the last years of Edward. The earl of Wessex may not yet have been the designated successor of the English king, but the new princes of Wales swore oaths of fealty and gave hostages to both Edward and Harold, and they promised to obey the orders of both by sea and by land. The possible election of the earl as heir-apparent in 1064 has already been mentioned, and the honours shown, and the titles given to Harold from this time forward are not found among the dignities of even the greatest of his predecessors. He was *duke by the grace of God* as Edward was *king by the grace of God*, and this qualification is given to no other subject. A charter relating to Worcestershire is drawn up *with the consent of Edward, the king, and Harold, the duke*, but Worcestershire was not part of Wessex and lay beyond the jurisdiction of the West Saxon earl. It can be argued that the charters referred to are spurious, but this scarcely weakens their significance : a later forger would have small cause to exaggerate the greatness of the dead 'usurper'.

The last year of Edward's life began and ended, and the duke of the English became king of the English. The first weeks of his reign passed, and the new year moved into February. Only four months before, Harold had faced Northumbrian rebels as the emissary of the old king; now these same malcontents challenged his sovereignty, and his authority as king himself. He had received their earlier demands quietly and with consideration. He did so again now, and his first action was not to muster troops or armies, but to summon from his cloister the most venerated churchman in England, Wulstan, bishop of Worcester.

* * * * *

The Norman embassy reached Rouen, and its leader came, it can be imagined, with reluctance before his master. The message he carried was contemptuous in its dismissal of William's claims; and, however the ambassador censored the phrasing of the English king's reply, he could not hide or moderate the failure of his mission. Yet the duke heard him quietly and without anger. William knew now, if he had not always known, that negotiation was fruitless. In its deeper purpose the embassy had been successful; and William could afford, in later interchanges, to lessen his demands, knowing that Harold, having denied the greater requirements, must also refuse the lesser, or be dishonoured in the eyes of his own people. If William hesitated at all, it must have been now: the war he planned would be waged against an enemy defending a homeland, against a commander of proven greatness, and against an army inspirited by victories won under that commander. There is no evidence of hesitation. It was certain that the power of Normandy alone would not be sufficient to challenge the English succession in England itself; the support of other rulers must be won. Even more importantly, however, William must be sure of the goodwill of his own people: without the free consent of the Norman vassals, the Norman sword might be raised, but it would be edgeless when it fell. He called the most trusted of his counsellors to him; and a second embassy left Rouen for the court of the English king.

The counsellors who came at the duke's bidding were the chief men of the duchy. There were his half-brothers, Robert, count of Mortain, who would in later years build a new Mont-St.-Michel on an island off the Cornish coast, and Odo, bishop of Bayeux, who was to prove himself more a soldier than a churchman, yet would end his life reaching for the papal crown. Other kinsmen came, William's blood-cousins, Richard, count of Evreux, and Robert, count of Eu, and his brother-in-law, Iwun-al-Chapel. The duke's closest vassal was with him, the one courtier who had dared to rally him after the coming of the messenger from England, William fitzOsbern, the seneschal. There were also Roger of Beaumont and Ralph of Toesny, Hugh of Grantmesnil and Roger of Montgomery, Walter Giffard, Hugh of Montfort and William of Warenne, the heads of the great families of Normandy.

Duke William set before the Norman lords the grounds of his claim to the crown of England. Through Emma, daughter of Duke Richard the Fearless and wife of King Ethelred, he was cousin of Ethelred's son. King Edward himself had nominated the duke as his successor, and that nomination had been unjustly put aside. Earl Harold had sworn allegiance to the Norman, and now had usurped the English throne, breaking his solemn oath to William, and the treaty made between them. These were the personal bases of the duke's charge against his rival. Throughout Europe the doctrine of hereditary right was spreading, and it was spreading quickly. Harold could claim no blood-relationship with Edward; the kinship of William might be distant and crossed by a bar sinister, but there was affinity. The concepts of feudalism had grown with the practice of succession through heredity. The crowning of Harold, the election of a king by the will of the people, was to the Continental the survival of a custom outmoded and unnatural, and, by the breaking of the oath, the English earl had become a perjured vassal, his power and possessions, if not his life, forfeit. There were other grounds of claim. Harold was implicated in crimes against the honour of Duke William and of Normandy: he had been the accomplice of his father, thirty years before, in the murder of the Atheling, Alfred, the brother of Edward and the duke's cousin, and, sixteen years later, in the illegal expulsion from England of Norman knights and prelates, the friends and companions of his king, one of them a consecrated archbishop and primate of England. It was conveniently forgotten that Alfred had been an invader, a traitor against the reigning king; that Godwin had twice purged himself of complicity in the 'murder'; that when the prince had been put to death Harold had been at most fifteen years old; that the 'expulsion' had been a panic-stricken flight which began even before Godwin and his sons had landed in England; and that only those Normans who were adjudged guilty of treason by the witan were barred from later return. An element of crusade was also given to the coming invasion : the English Church claimed an autonomy denied by Rome, and it deviated from established doctrines and allowed usages forbidden by the mother Church; William vowed to end these abuses.

The arguments were specious and will not bear close examination; but each contained a germ of truth. William's kinship with Edward was closer than that of Harold; he had been nominated as heir to the English throne; the oath and the treaty had been made and broken. Other men in other times would be accused of murders they could not have committed; and others would die for acts declared criminal after their commission. The arguments were confused, and their validity was debatable; but the man who questioned Duke William's ambitions would have been more foolhardy than brave. The duke turned to his design. There would be no conquest of the island kingdom, but rather a chastisement of rebels. He would bring war against the usurper, not against the English people beguiled into treason. To the power of Normandy would be added the strength of allies, drawn from all Europe by the justice of his cause and the promise of rich rewards. The most potent ally of all would send no armed men, but the invaders would sail under the banner of Christ and with the blessing of Pope Alexander. These things he would promise; but before any might be achieved, before even his envoy left for Rome, the duke must know that the members of his council, the great lords of Normandy, approved of his intent and would stand with him through whatever trials might come.

There was little hesitation in the answer William received, but it was reasoned and forthright, and without either servility or sycophancy. The Norman leaders admitted the justice of the duke's claims, and they approved his purpose. They had no doubt that the venture, once begun, could be accomplished. They pledged their possessions and their powers, their lands and their swords, to the service of their master. But they would pledge only for themselves : the bounds of vassalage were passed in such an undertaking. There were other knights of worth in Normandy, men of proven wisdom, strength and courage, and, though their wealth might be less and their estates more distant, they had the right to hear and to be heard in a debate such as this: *all should be brought into counsel who must share the labour.*[3] William listened, and he accepted the advice given. It was agreed that, when the papal sanction had been obtained, the whole baronage of Normandy should be summoned, and the duke's designs should be laid before them.

The Norman advocate to Rome had been chosen, and he must have left on the weeks-long journey within a few hours, or a day at most, of the ending of the council. His name was Gilbert, and he was archdeacon of the cathedral and diocese of Lisieux.

*   *   *   *   *

The second Norman embassy arrived in England, and the ambassadors were brought before King Harold. The first message of the duke had been arrogant and demanding; the second was lower in tone. It was couched almost in friendship, or in regret for the passing of friendship, rather than in the anger of thwarted ambition. The duke's purpose had been achieved; he could afford a generosity that both Harold and he must know was less real than it might appear, or might be made to appear. Already, while the first ambassadors of the duke were at the English court, rumours of the coming marriage of the king and the sister of the earls must have been noised about, discussed and argued. There was no greater likelihood of success for the later embassy than there had been for the earlier. If Harold would not do those things which he had promised, said the duke, let him at least fulfil the marriage contract with William's daughter. If he would not even do this, then let Harold look to himself; for William would surely come against him, with all the force that he could command. Two years before, when Harold had begun to know that the crown would be his, he had also begun to plan the defence of his kingdom, and alliance by marriage had been the core of his planning. But the two years had passed, and events and circumstances had turned awry those first plans. Another treaty of alliance was now more urgent than the faded contract with Normandy. There was only one answer that Harold could give. The ambassadors returned to their ships with the king's refusal; and it may well be that their company had grown before they sailed.

On his deathbed, Edward had commended to his successor the Norman knights and churchmen who still served the English king. There were many Normans in England; some had risen to the highest offices of the royal court, and one was a bishop of the English church. In the early days of his reign, Harold had made no move against the foreigners, but, when the giving of William's ultimatum changed the possibility of war with the Norman duke into a probability, the time had come when Harold must be sure of those about him. As Edward had urged, an oath of allegiance was required of the alien subjects of the crown, and those who would not give their oath were banished from England. Not all the Normans living in England, nor even the greater part of them, were driven from the country, and at least some of those of high rank remained, if not to serve King Harold, to hold their English estates through the short summer of his reign and into the winter that followed. William, bishop of London, kept his see unchallenged; and Robert fitzWymarc, who had supported King Edward in his last moments, and was himself a relative of Duke William, would be in Sussex at the time of the duke's landing, but not as a traitor to his adopted land, nor to her king. But some were banished, and their complaints were loud enough to whimper down the centuries in the pages of the Norman chroniclers.

Bishop Wulstan reached Thorney within a day or two of the sailing of the Normans, and Harold made ready at once for the long journey north. His rule in the south and west was safe, and, before another month was out, before the beginning of Spring brought the first dangers of invasion by his foreign enemies, he must be secure in Northumbria too. He could not hope that every Englishman would wish him well, but he must make the numbers of those who did as strong as he might. When King William rode north to meet his rebellious subjects, he would ride caparisoned and weaponed at the head of a great army. Harold and Wulstan rode from Thorney with a small retinue of housecarls, armed only against bandits and outcast men. The

West Saxon king was seeking not merely the obedience of his folk in the north, but their goodwill; and the weapons he would use to gain both would be courtesy and reason, not terror and steel.

*   *   *   *   *

The Europe of 1066 bore little resemblance to mid-twentieth century Europe. Christian Spain was confined to the north-west quarter of the peninsula and a narrow, mountainous strip of territory running east from the headwaters of the Ebro to the Mediterranean and south along the coastal plain to Barcelona. In the west, the kingdom of Leon stretched east from the Atlantic some two hundred miles, and south beyond the Douro. East of Leon lay the kingdom of Castille, reaching east to Santander and Burgos, and south to Madrid and the Tagus. Between Castille and the Mediterranean were the kingdoms of Navarre and Aragon and the county of Barcelona, nominally a part of France. South of the Christian states, Spain was broken into independent Moorish emirates, fragments of the once splendid Ommiad caliphate of Cordova. The dominions of the Capetian king of France were, in theory, vast, extending from the Pyrenees and Barcelona north to the Scheldt estuary, and from the Atlantic east to Nîmes in the south, to the upper Rhône and the Meuse centrally, and to Antwerp in the north. In practice, the great duchies and counties of France were autonomous, giving scarcely lip-service to the king of Paris, and the royal rule was maintained only in the Ile de France, the territory about Paris, northwards to Laon and southwards to Orleans, and even there it was not secure. East and north of France lay the Holy Roman Empire, the confederation of German, Burgundian and Italian states that had formed the middle and eastern parts of the empire of Charlemagne, reaching from Hamburg to Rome, from the North Sea and the Baltic to the Ligurian Sea and the Adriatic, and from the Rhône to the Oder. Southern Italy and Sicily formed the Norman principalities of the sons of Tancred of Hauteville. In the far north the Scandinavian kingdoms preserved their uneasy independences. East of the Empire, beyond the Slavic Marches and the dependent kingdom of Bohemia, the Bavarian East March and Carinthia, stretched the Magyar kingdom of Hungary and the

Slavic kingdoms of Poland and Croatia, and, beyond them, Serbia, Byzantium and Russia.

It was through the western marches of the Empire that Tostig rode to seek the aid of his cousin, Swegen Estrithsson, king of Denmark. He went by Lower Lorraine and Friesland, the northern territories of the old Frankish, middle kingdom of Lotharingia, to Bremen and the Elbe, on across North Saxony to the Danish frontier, and into the land where Swegen had finally established his rule only two years before.

Tostig asked the king for Danish support in the winning back of his lost earldom, for Danish ships and the services of veterans of the long wars with Norway. The proposal held little interest for Swegen, and he refused the request, but his own experience had taught him the emptiness of exile. He invited Tostig to stay in Denmark, and offered to bestow on him an earldom large enough to satisfy his need for power. It was not enough. Tostig wanted revenge as well as power, and he extended his offer to the king. If Swegen would press his claim to the English crown as the nearest surviving heir of Canute, and undertake the conquest of England, Tostig would help him with all the force he could command. Swegen would add England to his dominions, and Tostig would be his viceroy. The second offer impressed the Danish king no more than had the first. Canute had been a great man, he said, but he himself was a much smaller man. He had gained, and he held Denmark only with difficulty, and in constant viligance against Norwegian attack. Canute, on the other hand, had inherited the Danish kingdom and won Norway without striking a blow, but he had had to take England by strength of arms, and to risk his life in the taking. Swegen would rather be guided by his own ability, slender as it was, than try to imitate the lucky hits of Canute.

Tostig's reaction to his cousin's honesty was less than gracious. The outcome of his journey, he said, was not what he had looked for, from so gallant a kinsman. Perhaps he would find help where it might be less expected, under a leader less afraid of a great enterprise. The meeting was at an end, and *the king and the earl parted, not just the best of friends.*[4]

THE RULING PRINCES
– 1066 –

England

Potential Allies of England

Normandy

Allies of Normandy.

Norway

Allies or Dependencies of Norway

PAUL & ERLEND EARLS of ORKNEY

HAROLD HARDRAADA KING of NORWAY

MALCOLM KING of SCOTLAND

DERMOT, KING of IRELAND

SWEYN I, KING of DENMARK

HAROLD, KING of ENGLAND

BALDWIN V, COUNT of FLANDERS

EUSTACE, COUNT of BOULOGNE

GUY, COUNT of PONTHIEU

WILLIAM, DUKE of NORMANDY

CONAN, COUNT of BRITTANY

HENRY IV, EMPEROR

PHILIP I, KING of FRANCE

In Normandy, the second embassy had returned to Rouen, and a record of Harold's reply was despatched to Gilbert of Lisieux in Rome. William began to make his approaches to other princes. If Edward had died a few years earlier, or survived a few years longer, the Norman might not have dared attempt an invasion of England. But in 1066, the political situation in western Europe was balanced in William's favour: his father-in-law, the count of Flanders, was regent also of France; the Empire was similarly under a regency; and the buffer states about Normandy were subdued or powerless. The duke's ambassadors rode out to the courts of his neighbours, and with less hope of success to lands as distant as Denmark and Germany.

*   *   *   *   *

They rode north through the winter countryside, the king and the bishop, with their retinue of housecarles. By Ermine Street, or Watling Street and the Fosse Way, they passed the Chilterns, and rode through the Bruneswald and past the Fens to Lincoln, then still north, into the deepening winter, across the Trent and the Humber, to York. They may have turned aside, already in Northumbria, to rest a little at the king's manor of Conisbrough, but the couriers had ridden ahead, and the men of the north knew that King Harold and Bishop Wulstan were coming to York, to meet with them and treat with them.

The king's companion would have been remarkable in any age. Wulstan was born in Warwickshire, *of no mean birth and estate*,[5] and he was schooled at Evesham and Peterborough, under one of the foremost teachers of the Anglo-Saxon period. Nevertheless, he had, when older, no reputation for learning; neither was he famed as an administrator, nor as a diplomatist. Shortly after the appointment of Lanfranc to Canterbury, the Norman primate meditated the deposition of the bishop of Worcester, considering him an ignorant simpleton, unfitted for his office. Yet within a year or so, Lanfranc was his firm supporter; and, when Harold faced the most dangerous, political crisis of his reign, he chose Wulstan, before Eldred or Stigand or any of the noted rhetoricians of the time, to speak for him in the council of the north. The asceticism and religious observance of Wulstan made him celebrated; the quality that made him great was the innate goodness that lit his life and drew to him men of all types and stations. So completely was Harold given to his guidance that, though it might shame Wulstan to command, it never irked Harold to obey. On a journey, the earl would turn thirty miles out of his way to talk with the bishop. William, too, fell under his spell, and *spoke to him as his father*.[6] The miraculous powers attributed to Wulstan may be doubted today, but they were accepted in his own lifetime; and his healing touched not only the bodies of his hearers, but their souls. In his diocese, he acted less as a high dignitary of the church than as an itinerant priest, preaching to his people, ordering their lives, and encouraging the building of churches where these were few.

The witan of Northumbria gathered at York and met their king. That it was a *mycel gemot*, a great meeting, is certain; and it may have lasted several days, through many speeches and declarations. The northern leaders were turbulent; there were grievances to be voiced, debated and answered. They had sworn that the proud north would not surrender to the feeble south, and they were not to be easily subdued. With the king and the bishop sat Earl Morkere, for Harold and Wulstan could not have swayed the purpose of the northerners against the will of their earl, nor even have sat securely among them. Both the king and the earl must have addressed the assembly, pleading the cause, not of Wessex, nor of Northumbria alone, but of England. Harold may have spoken of what he had done and would do, of Tostig and Edward, of William and Hardraada, of his care for the safety of the north, and of his coming marriage with the sister of the Earl Morkere. The words of the king, unarmed and attended by only a few followers, cannot have failed to move his audience, for Harold was an accomplished orator; but they did not quell the stubborn insolence of the Northumbrians. Wulstan rose, and there was an unaccustomed stillness in the gemot. In the north, there was long acquaintance with the bishop of Worcester; and the holiness of the man was venerated in the remotest parts of the earldom.

On the ride from Thorney, Wulstan had cautioned Harold against luxury. In the long peace of Edward's reign, the bishop had said, and in the over-abundance of pleasant things that years of peace bring, the English had developed evil ways. The hard traditions of former times had crumbled; and customs flourished that must weaken the country and leave her, in the end, defenceless to her enemies. He had told Harold, in plain terms, that great trouble would come to him and to England, unless the king set himself to remedy the ills of his kingdom. Wulstan spoke no less plainly now to the unruly Northumbrian subjects of the king. He rebuked their vices, and he threatened them with retribution to come. Their actions against the king were thoughtless and reckless, and he warned them that, if they continued to be rebellious, they would pay for their folly in suffering. The speech of the bishop of Worcester may not have been the last or the longest in the gemot of York, but it was the most telling. Separately, or in one great shout of acclamation, the Northumbrian leaders, *for the reverence they bore the bishop, easily yielded their allegiance* to King Harold.[7]

The gamble had been won, and with it the realm. Harold stood before the witan of the north as the acknowledged sovereign of all England. An allegiance easily gained, might as easily be lost again; but at this moment in history the supremacy of the king was unchallenged in his kingdom. Harold had wagered his authority, his liberty and his life on one bold, swift stroke to capture the imaginations and the hearts of the Northumbrians; and he had triumphed. The tensions died, and the northern lords gave their interest to the ordering of the king's marriage.

*   *   *   *   *

A thousand miles from York, another council was meeting. Gilbert of Lisieux had reached Rome and was preparing to plead the Norman cause before the apostolic court. The man with whom he had primarily to deal, Archdeacon Hildebrand, was, in a very different way, as remarkable a churchman as Bishop Wulstan; the mind that Gilbert must sway to his master's purpose was more farsighted and more subtle than even that of Duke William. Hildebrand became archdeacon during the pontificate of Nicholas II and continued to guide papal policy under Alexander II. He was a small man with a weak voice, but these were no measures of his greatness. Already, in the first years of his archdeaconry, he had been credited with the formalising of the papal alliance with the Norman conquerors of southern Italy, and with the drafting of the electoral decree of 1059, which vested the control of papal elections in the cardinal bishops in conclave. His one aim was the moral and spiritual ascendancy of the Church in Christendom; and his one ambition was to establish that ascendancy. With the support of Hildebrand, Gilbert's mission might fail; against his opposition, it must fail.

Elsewhere in Europe, there was a moment of pause. The Norwegian forests resounded with the cries of the royal hunt, but the longships lay moored on the shores of the fiords. Furiously, and with a bitter heart, Tostig rode back across the low, coastal marches of the Empire to Flanders, his plans and his purposes confused and uncertain. In Normandy, Duke William filled the time of waiting with the sports of the chase, for there was little more he could do before his ambassadors returned from Rome and the courts of the princes. In the streets of York there were bustle and merriment, as the city readied itself for the wedding of King Harold and the Lady Alditha of Mercia.

MARCH

IN 1066, York was the third city of the kingdom, smaller only than London and Winchester. With a population of over eight thousand, more than ten mints, the cathedral-church of the northern archbishop and a market to which came traders from every part of the known world, it was the administrative, ecclesiastical and commercial capital of the north. While the importance of Winchester declined, that of York continued to grow. Now the busy streets were busier still, for the lords of Northumbria, great and small, had thronged with their retinues into the city, to see the face and hear the words of the West Saxon king of all England. They had seen, and they had heard, and they remained in York for the marriage and wedding-feast of King Harold and the Lady Alditha, the marriage that would unite the houses of Godwin and Leofric, and set a seal on the proceedings of the mycel gemot that had ended only days before.

Alditha of Mercia, the sister of the earls Edwin and Morkere, was possibly twenty years younger than Harold; but she had already been married and widowed, and it seems likely that a daughter at least had been born in the short years of her first union. Little is recorded of her life, and less of her character and personality: she moved through great events, and played her sad role against a backcloth of terror and magnificence, pageantry and war; yet she remains a shadow figure, known not for herself, but for the men with whom she was associated. It is written that she was beautiful and proud-spirited, but these may be only the empty compliments of a romantic convention. One fleeting reference, itself scarcely more than a suggestion, gives a touch of the individual to this daughter and granddaughter of earls, twice married and twice widowed within nine years: it avers that, even as she sat enthroned beside the English king, and through the waste of years that witnessed the destruction of both their houses, she rested true in heart to her first love, Gruffydd of Gwynedd, the Welsh prince whose bloody head Earl Harold

71

had sent as a trophy to Edward. Alditha may have had small cause to care for Harold; but her marriage with him was necessary to the king and to her brothers.

The marriage customs of England were older than the English church. They were still the trappings of a secular contract, argued in detail and guaranteed by pledges, rather than the observances of a sacred rite. Betrothal sealed the agreement between the families, and was followed, after a suitable interval, by the giving of the bride to her husband; at neither ceremony was the attendance of a priest required by law. A priestly benediction, however, was becoming customary, and the liturgy for the marriage service of a later age was taking shape. The settlement that preceded the betrothal was necessary: under Anglo-Saxon law a woman could hold property, and the rights of a widow were clearly defined. They were generous and protected; and marriage did not make a wife the chattel of the husband, as she would be in centuries to come. Though the bride's family might gift wealth and estates to the couple, the dower was given by the groom, and land so granted was considered the personal possession of the wife; it might be forfeit to the husband's heirs if she died, or were widowed and remarried, but otherwise her use of it was unrestricted. At sunrise on the day after the wedding, too, the bride could claim of her husband a 'morning-gift', and this was peculiarly her own, as were the presents received during the festivities that accompanied the ceremony.

Marriage feasts among the great were remarkable for their richness, prodigality and intemperance. They continued without interruption until the food and drink ran out, or until they came to a spontaneous closure, and they could last many days. The marriage itself might mark the ending of a feud between the families of the union, and the celebrations demonstrate publicly its passing; in part, the festival at York in 1066 served to proclaim the community of the interests of Northumbria and Wessex. But the happiest circumstances could not ensure a mirthful finish to the merrymaking. The prodigious quantities of alcohol consumed could quicken old resentments and loosen guarded tongues; the local ales and imported wines were heavy and rough, and could aggravate hidden ailments and seek out unsuspected weaknesses. Many wedding parties ended as joyfully as they began; but many terminated in disorder and brawling, in sickness and even in death. From his twentieth year, Alfred the Great was afflicted by a disease that attacked him first on his wedding day; in 1042, Harthacnut *died as he stood at his drink*.[1] at the marriage feast of Tofig the Proud.

No tragedy marred the uniting of Harold and Alditha, and the celebrants crowded the halls and streets of York. This was a royal occassion, royally provided by a king who still must be suitor to his subjects. The Northumbrians, noble and common, drank and danced and revelled and fought, until each drinker, dancer, reveller and fighter fell in a drunken stupor, to sleep and rise and drink again. The day wore away, and the ale flowed. Night came, and the round continued. The first light of dawn thrust aside the early mists, the morning-gift was asked and given, and the empty casks were dragged away and replaced by others. The new day brightened, and still the northerners made merry. The king moved among his people : he had married the sister of the Northumbrian earl, and in the hearts of his subjects he was king of the English.

*   *   *   *   *

Several days had gone by now since the Norman embassy to the court of Pope Alexander had ridden down to the gates of Rome. They had been long days of discussion and debate, friendly, but searching, and the rhetorical skill of Gilbert of Lisieux had been strongly tested. The Roman archdeacon, Hildebrand, undertook the first examination of the Norman cause. The visiting churchman presented and argued the pleas and proposals of his master; Hildebrand listened and considered, construed and advised, and at last he promised his support in the bringing of the appeal. He could not promise its granting : in the hearing before the curia his voice would be one among many. The influence of the cardinal-archdeacon was deep-rooted and far-reaching, and he might persuade where he could not command; but powerful critics would dispute the Norman mission in the sacred college. The deliberations would be lengthy, and the issues would be contested in detail, but the ultimate success or failure of the pleading would hang upon one circumstance : the acceptance or dismissal by the cardinal clergy of the central indictment against the English king.

Conquest formed no part of Duke William's planning. Though he would land in England at the head of an army, and though ordeal by battle would decide the destiny of the island kingdom, the duke meant to rule not as a conqueror, but as the rightful successor of King Edward. The armed overthrow and even the death of his rival could not justify William's claim to the empty throne : the reign of Harold must pass as if it had never been. Without the acquiescence of the English nation, there could be no security for a Norman dynasty in England, and William intended the founding of a dynasty. It would not be enough for the duke to show title to the crown : he must wipe from legal record the dying bequest of Edward, the election of the witan, and the holy anointing of the Englishman he must destroy to reach the throne. It was this need that distorted a vow of knightly service into a swearing of vassalage, and gave urgency to the mission to Rome. Only by proving Harold an usurper could William himself avoid that charge; and one court alone in Europe had an authority sufficient to brand the English king, on untested evidence, an outcast and an enemy before Christendom, a perjurer and a traitor, and a breaker of oaths.

* * * * *

By the beginning of 1064, the possibility that the English succession might fall to Harold Godwinsson had become a probability. The last representatives of the royal house of Cerdic were an aging man and a child. The king was almost sixty years old and his powers were deteriorating, and his marriage with the Lady Edith had been childless for more than eighteen years. As Duke of the English Harold stood already higher than his father had done; and it seemed likely that the old king would die before his great-nephew, Edgar Atheling, reached manhood, or an age where he might formally be designated heir to the English crown. Within the realm Harold's ascendancy was certain; but, beyond the coasts of England, there were dangerous pretenders, and the most immediate lay less than a hundred miles away, across the narrow seas. Only by the prior disarming of Duke William himself might Harold hope to ward off the Norman challenge. William was still young, and he had been married less than eleven years; but there were daughters of the union, and, though thy were no more than children, diplomatically they were marriageable. As grandfather of the English heir, William might be satisfied with an English alliance; and, as son-in-law of the Norman duke, Harold might look for Norman aid against more distant enemies.

In the summer of 1064, the earl of Wessex sought the permission of King Edward to visit the court of Normandy. Gruffydd of Wales had been dead for almost a year; England was at peace, and the marches were quiet. The king's present interests were concerned more with hunting and the building of his new minster on the isle of Thorney than with the strategies and activities of his great lieutenant. The permission was granted. With hawk on wrist and dogs running before him, accompanied by a few retainers and possibly his youngest brother, Wulfnoth, and his nephew, Hakon, the earl rode to Bosham, the manor on Chichester harbour that had been a favourite resort of Godwin. While Harold prayed in the little church which still, in part, survives, and dined in the manor hall, the ship was readied. The travellers boarded the vessel, and the oarsmen rowed her out through the shallow waters of the inlet to the sea. The single sail filled, and a course was set south and east for the estuary of the Seine and Rouen.

Landfall was made without incident, but the coast that rose ahead was not Norman. The currents of the Channel had swept the ship far to the north, and it beached beyond the northernmost provinces of Normandy, in the county of Ponthieu. The mast was unstepped, and the voyagers disembarked; but Harold had been recognised, and the word of his coming had been hurried to Count Guy. The count himself led the hunters, and the English were surprised, seized and carried, closely held, to the fortress of Beaurain, on the River Canches; but one Englishman had escaped, and he made his way safely to Duke William in Rouen. The Norman required little encouragement to intervene: the importance of the prisoners was evident, and Guy of Ponthieu was a vassal of Normandy. Messengers were sent urgently to demand the release of the English earl, and the duke rode north behind them to the border citadel of Eu. Count Guy had experience of the harsh temper of his overlord : he escorted Harold personally to the Norman frontier.

The Norman and the Englishman rode back together to Rouen, and, as they journeyed, the watchful courtesy of the rescuer and the wary gratitude of the rescued gave place to respect and the unstudied comradeship of men, both born to command, and both conscious of their own worth. In the bitter aftermath of the landing it must have seemed to Harold that his planning was frustrated and his purpose defeated; but confidence in himself and in the success of his mission was returning, even as he came with Guy of Ponthieu to the meeting at Eu. At Rouen, in a formal audience, the earl requested the hand in marriage of Agatha, daughter of William and the Duchess Matilda. He asked, as dowry, the duke's friendship; and he offered in return his fealty as a son-in-law, his service in time of need, and his devotion to the duke's interests in England. He did not offer fealty as a vassal, or service as a liegeman; and he in no way guaranteed the English crown to William. This was a prerogative beyond the power of any one man. The heart of the proposal was the alliance by marriage, and this was to be counterpointed by the marrying of a younger sister of the earl to a Norman noble. The contract was agreed and ratified, and the engagement was celebrated; but the wedding ceremony was temporarily postponed, because of the extreme youth of the bride.

The bonds between the earl and the duke were soon tested. In the autumn, Conan, Count of Britanny, rose in revolt and threatened the city of Dol, which was held against him. Britanny had been gifted in perpetuity to Hrolf, the first duke of the Normans; and the seventh duke struck swiftly in defence of his inheritance. Before the harvest was gathered, a Norman force crossed the northern border of the county at the mouth of the River Couesnon, within sight of the abbey-fortress of Mont-Saint-Michel. The crossing was difficult and dangerous, for the river-current was strong and there were quicksands. Harold had ridden with the duke, and at the Couesnon he proved his courage and his strength, dragging to safety soldiers caught in the treacherous sands. The passage of the river was accomplished, and the Norman army pressed on to Dol, surprising the besieging troops of the Breton count and driving them off in confusion. Count Conan fled south to his capital of Rennes, and then north again to Dinan; but the pursuit was close, and at Dinan the rebel vassal was trapped. The Bretons resisted fiercely, but, when the Normans fired the citadel, Conan surrendered. In the short campaign, the growing respect and comradeship between the leaders of the Norman force had ripened; and, on the field of battle before Dinan, William gave to Harold the title and arms of a knight of Normandy. It was an honour the Englishman would have done well to refuse; but a refusal would have been at best discourteous, and Harold's natural caution was stayed by the ready friendship of the duke.

The Normans turned back to the east. The Couesnon was passed, and the army moved homewards through the rich plains of Normandy; and at Bonneville-sur-Touques, on the road to Rouen, or perhaps at Bayeux, the last, fateful act of those summer and autumn months took place. Before the peers of Normandy, Earl Harold swore an oath to the Norman duke in affirmation of the treaty between them, and in recognition of the honour bestowed upon him by William. The terms sworn were the terms of the marriage contract, without addition or extension; but circumstances combined to give the oath a force the contract could not have. In accepting the privileges of knighthood, the earl accepted also obligations, which he may not even have understood; and the swearing took place between reliquaries filled with the bones of saints, which rendered inviolable the vows that were made. It is unnecessary to assume that Harold was tricked or forced into the giving of the oath : to the Englishman, the ceremony was no more than the formal ratification of a treaty he himself desired. To the Normans, it was a promise of servitude, the commendation of a vassal to his lord. Some of the English recognised the significance of the rite, and tried to warn the earl; trusting the chivalry of his host, Harold brushed aside their protests. It was a neglect he would have bitter cause to regret, two years later.

The events of the summer and autumn of 1064 are outlined in the great tapestry that Bishop Odo commissioned for the consecration thirteen years later of his new cathedral at Bayeux. The work was most probably executed by Englishwomen, whose needlework in the eleventh century was famous; and certain spellings and place-names indicate clearly that the chosen designer was also English. As plainly as he dared, the Englishman told the story of those months, clarified by an art at once so simple and so subtle that even today eminent commentators can refer to a scene of major significance as meaningless, and to crucial border-details as purposeless decorations. This is due, at least in part, to the misconception that a work commissioned by a Norman must necesesarily be Norman in outlook. The artist was not a hack, and his sympathies were English: elsewhere in the design he would 'misplace' a scene to emphasise Edward's nomination of the earl of Wessex; in the first sequences he pointed the purpose of the voyage to Normandy and the success of Harold's mission. There is nothing accidental in the placing and shaping of the nude and eager figures that 'decorate' the meeting of Harold and William and the introduction to the daughter of the duke. The imagination of the artist may have been obscene, but it was not senseless. The meaning of the figures is as clear as the upraised finger that later warns Harold against the trap of the oath. They illustrate graphically and precisely the thoughts and intentions of th English earl. Harold's suit before the throne of Normandy forms one of g most expensive portrayals in the tapestry, the wording making the unity of the scene apparent: *Duke William comes with Harold to his palace where a cleric and Aelfgyva*[2] await them. The tapestry is not always accurate: the girl is shown as a grown woman; for the foreign name, Agatha, the designer used a near, Anglo-Saxon homonym. The reading, however, is simplified pictorially. As Harold makes his request of the duke, he points back dramatically to the girl; and the status of Agatha herself is illustrated by one of the oldest of all symbolic usages: as the duke grants her hand to the earl, the cleric lifts the veil of the bride.

The oath of which Gilbert of Lisieux spoke in Rome bore a textual resemblance to the oath of Bonneville; but the terms which Harold had sworn were disordered, and their significance was distorted to suit the purposes of the Norman duke. The indictment against the 'perjured' king centred its emphasis on the abandoned promise of fealty; the broken contract of marriage became no more than a subsidiary charge. The easy comradeship of the Breton campaign was forgotten, and with it the service which Harold had rendered. The urgent ambition of Duke William and the guile of Prior Lanfranc transformed a treaty of alliance into a bond of vassalage.

The Norman churchman was eloquent, and his situation was fortunate: he was advocate for the plaintiff in an action where the defence was unheard. Either directly, or through his vassals and allies, William of Normandy controlled the European seaboard from Cherbourg to the Scheldt. The overall control could have been little more effective than the possible sealing of the English harbours in January, but the roads to Rome were closed to an English ambassador travelling in state. Spies and couriers, merchants and pilgrims might have passed the screen of Norman partisans, *who beset every port;*[3] but the high dignitaries, who alone could have represented the king of England before the curia, would have found all ways through Normandy and France forbidden to them. There is, in any case, no reason to believe that an emissary of Harold attempted the journey. It has been argued that the English king sent no advocate to Rome *because he was proud by nature, or else distrusted his cause.*[4] Harold was proud, but not more so than William. There is no record of the Englishman denying the earthly supremacy of the pope; the Norman was to do exactly that. Far from distrusting his cause, it seems likely that the king trusted it too much, as he trusted the just delivery of a court never noted for simple decisions of right and wrong. The Norman barriers were unneeded. By the time word of the duke's embassy reached the king, it was already too late for Harold to send his representatives to Rome: the suit had been judged, and the official sanction of the Church had been given to the Norman adventure. No summons was sent by the Roman court to the accused monarch; no effort was made to hear witness against his accusers. Yet, even in the papal conclave, there were voices that spoke for England; they were not without power and not without eloquence, but they spoke in vain.

The English king did not allow for the devious influence of Hildebrand. Throughout the long and tempestuous history of his rise and eminence, the great Italian founded his policies upon one cardinal principle: that, in the highest ethic of Christendom, the power that could absolve from sin must be superior to all others. But he did not shrink from the sorriest of political manoeuvrings to achieve his ideal. As archdeacon and later as pope, Hildebrand strove with the vanities of the princes of Europe to maintain the moral authority and the temporal jurisdiction of the papacy. He was not fired by personal ambition, and, when he claimed to speak with the voice of St. Peter, he did so without arrogance. But the instruments he found to accomplish his purpose were frequently both tainted and arrogant; and he was willing to subordinate truth, justice, human dignity and even the preservation of peace to the cause of the aggrandisement of Rome. The Norman accusation rested upon testimony which was tenuous, inconclusive, uncorroborated, and, in part, incoherent; but, if the Church gave its blessing to the Norman cause, and if the English crown fell to the Norman sword, then Duke William swore to hold of God and of St. Peter the kingdom he would win. Fourteen years later, the Norman would repudiate his vow, as firmly as did Harold the oath of two years earlier; in 1080, King William had no pressing need of a support that had seemed essential to Duke William in 1066. But the precedent had been set: that a Christian king would hold his realm as a fief of the Church of Rome.[5]

The debate was lengthy and acrimonious, for there were those among the clergy who did not share the cardinal-archdeacon's vision of glory. In 1080, in a letter written to William a few months before the king's denial of his pledge of fealty, Hildebrand was to complain of the calumny he had suffered on behalf of the Norman: he was accused of advocating a sanction that must lead to the slaughter of many men. The opposition was vigorous, but it was divided; and the lure of the ducal promises was strong. Hildebrand persisted in his argument, and in the end he prevailed. The charge against the English king was found proven; and the pope blessed the Norman cause. A war that was founded on greed and wounded vanity became a Crusade. The victory may not have been so complete as the Norman apologists assert, for, four years after the granting of the sanction, special penances would be imposed on all who took part in the great invasion;[6] but it was, undeniably, a

victory. The couriers rode out from Rome, speeding the word
of success to distant Rouen, and Archdeacon Gilbert followed
in triumph with the gifts of Pope Alexander to Duke William : a
consecrated banner to hallow the Norman arms, and a ring
that held a hair of St. Peter himself.

*   *   *   *   *

The long and angry journey from Denmark was over, and
Tostig was in Flanders and with Judith, in her brother's court
at Bruges, or on the estate near St. Omer that Count Baldwin
had given to his sister and her husband. These spring days which
the earl passed with *his fortunate wife*[7] were restless, and fitful
as the March weather; but they were the last that Judith and
Tostig would spend together before the summer came and
went, and, when the exile rode from Flanders again, scarcely
a fortnight after his coming, husband and wife would meet but
once more. When the third son of Godwin wedded the sister
of the Flemish count, it was a love-match, and so it remained
throughout the fifteen years of their marriage. Tostig had known
other women, and two sons would sail in his company on that
last fatal endeavour in the autumn of 1066;[8] but, from the day
of the wedding-feast until the final reckoning by a Northumbrian
river, this violent, arrogant and unpredictable man lived
chastely and with moderation,[9] content in the wifely care of a
woman who won the admiration and liking of all who knew
her. Now the future was dark, and there was need of a still
centre in Tostig's life. The failure of the mission to his cousin
Swegen had closed the avenue of return to England on which
he had set his first and strongest hopes.

Under the cautious rule of the Danish king, Tostig might
have reached for a viceroyalty in England that would have
assuaged the bitterness of the late months. There was little likelihood of such an authority being given to the Englishman under
William of Normandy, and no certainty that even the lost
earldom would be restored to Tostig by the Norman. The temper
of the duke was harsher than that of Swegen of Denmark; but
with William the return to Northumbria might yet be achieved,
and more readily than with Swegen. When Tostig ruled again
in the north, there would be time to consider the shape of the

future, and to revalue his obligations to his nephew by marriage: now it mattered only that the earldom be regained. Meanwhile, report of the Norman embassy to Rome had reached the Flemish court, and it appeared certain that Duke William would attempt the invasion of England. Each day that passed weakened the Englishman's claim to the duke's attention, as William's involvement in the venture against Harold deepened, and the tempo of Norman planning quickened. It was essential that Tostig share in the duke's counsels; but the exile must come to Rouen as an ally, not as a suitor.

When Tostig left England in the winter of 1065, many of his thegns sailed with him into banishment. In Flanders the immigrants were welcomed and settled; and, as well as supplying the material needs of his brother-in-law, Count Baldwin assigned to Tostig the services of the Flemish knights in the district of St. Omer. The Englishman, therefore, commanded the immediate allegiance of two bodies of trained, proficient soldiery, men whose titles of nobility rested on their prowess in war, and these formed the nucleus of a military force which the earl could bring to the support of Normandy: armed thus, Tostig might purchase the interest of Duke William, if he could not gain it by appeals to justice and affinity. The contingent was small; but there were other soldiers and shipman lacking employment in Flanders, willing to take part in a foreign war, and to wager their lives against foreign plunder. Men were recruited, and the English power in exile grew. The time of waiting passed; and Tostig turned again from Judith and Flanders, south across Ponthieu, to Normandy and Rouen.

* * * * *

The celebrations in York had ended triumphantly. The king's trust in the goodwill and good sense of his northern subjects had won their allegiance; his courtesy had inspired their affection; and his friendship with the Northumbrian earl and marriage with the earl's sister had provoked their acclaim. The witan of Northumbria had accepted Harold, but there were many in the wide lands of the northern earldom who had not seen the king, and, wherever men might be called upon to defend the English crown, Harold willed that they should know its wearer, not as a symbol, nor as a name, but as another man, and one who had walked among them. Accompanied still by Bishop Wulstan, and with the Lady Alditha beside him, King Harold left York to journey again, on a royal and smiling progress through the land that once had trembled before his brother.

*   *   *   *   *

Some thirty miles west of Rouen, among the low, wooded hills north of the Seine estuary, the small, Norman town of Lillebonne lies sheltered in a natural amphitheatre. Enclosed and protected by the hills, except to the south, where the valley looks out to the great river, glistening in the distance, and the higher lands of central Normandy beyond, the site has a history of more than two thousand years. In an earlier period of his reign, on a slight eminence above the town, William the Bastard had raised a fortress, and, although nothing of this survives, a sketch of the great hall, roofless and derelict in its final decay, has been preserved : a range of round-arched doorways opened into a vaulted undercroft, and over this stood the main part of the structure, pillared and arched, and lit by the coupled, narrow windows of the Norman master-builders. It was to the ducal hall at Lillebonne, in the spring of 1066, that Duke William summoned the barons of Normandy, to hear and debate the duke's designs against England. The ambassadors had returned from Denmark and the Empire; Tostig had come from Flanders, offering allegiance and support; the courier had arrived from Rome, bringing word of the upholding of the Norman appeal. It was time that the decision was made. The summonses had already gone out when Gilbert of Lisieux reached Rouen, bearing reverently the gifts blessed by Pope Alexander.

The eve of the great assembly came, and William rode to Lillebonne with his Norman councillors and Tostig. On the following day, the barons gathered, crowding into the hall, and, when the tumult of their meeting had quietened, the duke addressed them. He told them of the claims of Normandy, and of the wrongs done to him by Harold. He described the sending of the embassies to England, and their curt dismissal by the obdurate and unrepentant Englishman. Now William intended, before the year was out, to take by force of arms what was his by right. He was confident of victory, for Rome itself had approved his purpose. But he could achieve nothing alone: without the aid of the Norman knights, his enterprise must founder. He knew the steadfastness and loyalty of the Normans; and he asked only that each man should say what he would do, telling the numbers of the ships and men that he would offer in service to the duke.

The Norman barons were cautious, even with their autocratic lord. They required time to debate the proposal among themselves; and William had no alternative but to submit to their demand. The discussion was lengthy and agitated, and the gathering split into lesser groups, each group conferring anxiously and excitedly. Some of the knights were ready to follow the duke unhesitatingly; others were certain that the venture was hopeless. There were those who would supply ships gladly; and there were those too poor, or too much in debt, even to volunteer their own duties. The difficulties and dangers of the enterprise were apparent: they would be attacking a country richer than Normandy, mustering an army larger than any that the Normans could expect to field, and with a fleet that must outmatch the best that the duchy could produce in the few months allotted by the duke. The rewards to be gained were dubious and uncertain: the pope might bless the duke's arms, but he could not guarantee their victory; and defeat in England would mean not retreat, but at best imprisonment, and more probably slavery or death. The Normans were brave soldiers; but they were not wantonly reckless.

Contention had divided the assembly so completely that it seemed unlikely to reach any conclusion, and once again it was William fitzOsbern, the seneschal of Normandy, who formed the link between the duke and his nobles, as he had done after the encounter in the park at Quevilly. He came among the wrangling groups and drew them together. He appealed to their knightly honour, and reminded them of their feudal obligations. The duke could demand their obedience; it would be unwise to make him beg for it. Let them rather offer more than they could accomplish, to allay the swift anger of their master. William had a jealous temper: if his undertaking should fail through lack of support, they would have cause to regret it.

The barons were hesitant and unconvinced; they feared the sea, and were not obliged to serve beyond it. But they could speak to fitzOsbern more readily than to Duke William, and the seneschal had the ear of the duke. They appointed him to be their spokesman: he knew their minds and could express their will, and they would be bound by his words.

The assembly had chosen the sworn friend and confidant of the duke to speak for them: the result was predictable. Coming to the duke, fitzOsbern spoke first of the great love that his subjects bore William, and of their dedication to his honour. To advance their lord, he said, *they would swim through the sea, or throw themselves into the raging fire.*[10] He spoke of their fidelity, and of the service that the Norman knights gave willingly to the duke, the service that they had given in the past and would continue to give. But, as he spoke of service, the seneschal ceased to be spokesman, in anything but title, of the men who had placed their trust in him. Diffidence turned to pride, and hesitancy to decision. Fear of the sea was forgotten: and fitzOsbern covenanted, in the name of the baronage of Normandy, that when William sailed for England, every knight owing allegiance to the duke would sail with him. Not only would the Normans serve beyond the sea: on their behalf, fitzOsbern boasted that, for every fighting man that the Norman lords owed to the army of the duke, two would be brought. The perfidy of the seneschal stunned his hearers into a disbelieving silence, but the silence was momentary. The speech had scarcely reached its end before the hall was in uproar. The protests clamoured; and the noise became so great that no distinct words could be heard from any speaker.

Duke William now intervened in the debate, for the fracas had become general, all coherence and cohesion had been lost, and the factions had separated into individuals. The duke withdrew from the assembly and sent for each baron in turn. He explained to each his urgent need, and vowed that if the nobles, of their own accord, doubled their due service in the coming war against Harold, their claims upon his gratitude would be remembered. He swore, too, that no custom would be established by such an act, and that no one would be called upon at a later date to render more in duty than his ancestors had rendered. In appeal, the voice of the duke was as persuasive as that of his great enemy : against their wills, the Normans protested their allegiance and their faith in his leadership. In a direct sense, the chicanery of Willam fitzOsbern had failed, but, indirectly it contributed heavily to the success of Duke William's pleas. The violence that followed the seneschal's speech destroyed the possibility of unity among the barons, and left them vulnerable to the personal diplomacy of the duke. One by one, the Normans lords promised their support to William in his enterprise; and, item by item, the numbers of the ships and men pledged by each were recorded by the scribes of the duke.

*   *   *   *   *

The royal progress through Northumbria was nearing its end, and Harold rode back with his small retinue down the long northern valleys to York. The month that was passing had been for the king a time of quiet, an interval of peace between the uncertainties of the first months of his reign and the trials that he knew must come. For a little, Harold could be at rest. In England, his throne was secure; no armadas were building on the sea-coasts of Normandy, and more than a month had passed since last a Norman embassy had challenged his rule; no word came from Norway, and old Hardraada seemed to sleep. The dying month had been also a time of triumph, of many triumphs in many days, as Harold walked among his people, and suspicious, northern hearts warmed to the West Saxon king.

In Normandy too, there had been triumph, and Duke William was unaccustomedly merry on the homeward journey from Lillebonne to Rouen. Tostig rode beside the duke, holding his impatience on an uneasy rein.

APRIL

As the year entered its second quarter, the pattern of events to come was hardening. The sceptre of all England was now firmly in Harold's grasp, and his rule was accepted from the Solent to the Tweed; freed from overt, internal dissension and antagonism, the king could at last direct his fullest energies to the development of the power at his command, and to the securing of his realm against alien inroads. Beyond the Channel, the first Norman opposition to the resolved ambition of Duke William had been muted, if not silenced, by the papal recognition of the duke's cause, and by the subsequent pledging of their support by the assembled barons of Normandy; William's planning was gathering momentum, and the early preparations for the invasion of the island kingdom were already being set under way. The purposes of the main protagonists were firm; that of Tostig faltered.

Some forty years earlier, Gytha, Countess of Wessex, had presented to her husband, Earl Godwin, a third son. Like his elder brothers, Swegen and Harold, and in honour of his mother's kindred, and of the origin of his father's greatness, the new-born was given a Scandinavian name: Tostig. A child when Canute died, Tostig was still adolescent when Harthacnut, the last of the Danish kings of England, followed his father, and Godwin brought to the English throne the half-Norman Atheling, Edward; seven years more passed before the earl's third son was first mentioned in recorded history. The boy grew tall, though not to equal Harold, graceful in movement, and handsome in features. He became strong in body, agile in mind, and ready in tongue. In battle, he proved brave, daring, steadfast, and diligent in the royal service, until events, partly of his own making, turned him first outlaw and then traitor to the land he had served well. He could be stern, and even *over-severe at times in prosecuting evil*,[1] but his generosity to those he favoured was prodigal, and he gave most freely to religious causes. Although neither temperate by nature, nor celibate by inclination, he was capable of both physical and emotional restraint, and in marriage he remained true to the wife he had taken. There was in his character, the same, brooding violence that had warped the life of his eldest brother, Swegen, and which led him to destroy all that his father and he himself had once held dear. Tostig would not live to see the overthrow of the England of Alfred and Athelstan, of Canute and Harold but when the Norman adventurer thrust his banner over the bloody hill-crest of Senlac, he would owe the English crown he won to the vengeful malevolence of the renegade brother of the last Anglo-Saxon king.

Among the surviving records of the England of Edward, there is a character of 1049 which carries the mark of 'Tosti nobilis', together with those of his father and his brothers, Harold and Leofwine. In the same year, when Earl Godwin led a fleet against Danish marauders who were harrying the shores of the west country, the commands of two royal ships which accompanied the West Saxon flotilla were given to Harold and his younger brother. The weather at sea was treacherous and the earl's fleet sailed no farther west than Pevensey where storms drove the ships to shelter. The punitive expedition was abandoned, and Tostig's first captaincy ended without trial of his quality as a warrior. In 1051, the marriage of Tostig and Judith of Flanders took place, and the bridegroom was almost immediately involved in the tortuous, political events of that year. The Norman faction which surrounded the king forced the impeachment of Godwin, and, in September, Edward pronounced the outlawry and banishment of the earl of Wessex and his family. While Harold and Leofwine sped west for Bristol and Ireland, Tostig and his bride rode with Godwin and Gytha, Swegen and Gyrth, to Bosham, where they took ship for Flanders and the friendly court of Count Baldwin. Less than a year passed before the wrongs of 1051 were redressed: in the following autumn, Godwin returned to England in triumph, amid the acclamations of the people. The pro-Norman conspiracy against the power of the West Saxon earl collapsed, the leaders of the faction fled and Tostig stood with his father when the king gave back to the earl the provinces and lands, the honours and dignities of which the family had been stripped. The authority of Godwin had reached its zenith, but the earl was aging. Seven months after the return from Flanders, Tostig helped to carry the dying body of the great counsellor to the king's bed-chamber in the palace at Winchester, when Godwin fell stricken during the Easter Monday feasting of 1053.

Two years later, another of the leading servants of Canute died : Siward, earl of Northumbria. In the eleventh century the number of provincial viceroyalties into which England could profitably be split was limited and the broad territorial divisions of Canute were essentially maintained. Though Tostig may have administered some part of the West Saxon earldom under the tutelage of his father, and must have held the lordships of several rich estates, he could as yet claim no title other than 'noble'. After the passing of Godwin, Harold had succeeded to the seignory of Wessex without opposition, but the East Anglian earldom which he then vacated, was granted to the senior member of the great houses of England still without experience of government, Aelfgar, the son of Leofric of Mercia. In 1055, however, the surviving son of Siward of Northumbria was a child, and the rule of the vast and turbulent northern province and of the detached shires of Northampton and Huntingdon was given to Tostig. There are circumstances which suggest that the recently made earl of the East Angles desired this appointment for himself and that he resented bitterly the increase in power of the Godwinsons which the promotion of Tostig ensured. In that same year, and for a reason now unknown, Aelfgar was named a traitor and outlawed. He was reinstated before the year was out, and his return was due in part at least to Harold; but it is clear that ill-will between the Mercian and Tostig persisted, and was transmitted by Aelfgar to his sons, Edwin and Morkere. In 1057, Leofric died and Aelfgar surrendered East Anglia to become earl of Mercia; but the rivalry between the ruling families of the midland province and Wessex was not appeased. East Anglia and the eastern shires of Wessex provided earldoms for Gyrth and Leofwine, the younger brothers of Harold and Tostig, and three-quarters of England was subject to the direct control of the sons of Godwin.

The early years of Tostig's rule in Northumbria were years of success, and vindication of the king's trust in the favourite he had raised to such a perilous eminence. Even under the harsh dominion of Siward, the northerners had shown little respect for law, and only in parties of twenty or more could travellers hope to journey in safety. The new earl restored order in the north, and he imposed his own strict justice on all, so thoroughly and impartially that the land was freed of robbers, and men could come and go with their goods without dread. The claim is evidently exaggerated; but it states at least a partial truth, and the stern authority of the half-Danish earl was real and un-equivocal to the wayward inheritors of the ancient Danelaw. Tostig effectively deterred also the Scottish raiders who viewed the death of Siward and the coming of an unknown southerner in his place as invitations to plunder. At some time during these years, the earl and Malcolm, King of Scots, met and swore brotherhood; and in 1059 the Scottish king rode with Tostig, Cynesige, archbishop of York, and the bishop of Durham to Edward's court at Gloucester, to pay a belated homage to his nominal overlord.

In 1061, Earl Tostig and his lady made the pilgrimage to Rome, in company with the earl's brother, Gyrth, Archbishop Eldred, the newly appointed successor to Cynesige, and other English magnates. The earl sat in the Easter synod of Pope Nicholas II, which dealt with numerous matters concerning the English church, the business of the council culminating in the papal degradation of Eldred and the denying of the pallium to the Englishman. Tostig can have taken no part in that decision, and he left Rome with Eldred when the deposed archbishop retired in confusion from the Holy See. Some fifteen miles from Rome, however, the party was waylaid and robbed. The English returned to the city, and the angry remonstrances of the now violently aroused earl persuaded the pope towards conciliation : he indemnified the losses of the pilgrims and granted recognition and the pallium to Eldred. The travellers returned to England with the apostolic benediction.

The summer of 1063 carried the fortunes of the house of Godwin to the heights. Between May and August, Harold and Tostig shattered the main fighting strength of the Welsh, and brought an end to the ambitious treasons of Gruffydd, the Cymric son-in-law of Earl Aelfgar of Mercia. The evidence available indicates that Aelfgar himself had died in the preceding year, and probably before Harold's winter raid into north Wales; and it seems likely that, at the time of the final campaign against Gruffydd, Tostig was associated with his brother in the administration of Mercia. This was, at most, a provisional arrangement, made necessary by the youth of Edwin and Morkere, and certainly by 1065 Edwin was in possession of his father's earldom. However justifiable the temporary disposition of Mercia may have been, it cannot have lessened the discord between the sons of Aelfgar and the earl of Northumbria. There is no reason to believe that Tostig as yet considered the resentments of the Mercian earlings of any importance. He was the favourite subject of the king and the dearest brother of the queen. The goverance of one of the greatest provinces of the realm was his; he was a proven military commander and in all England only his brother, Harold, stood higher than him below the king. South, east and north, the reins of power were held by the Godwinssons, and the authority of their house now seemed unassailable. But the seeds of destruction had already been sown, and the soil was fertile.

The king's pleasure required the frequent attendance of Tostig at court. In the earl's absences from Northumbria, the province was administered by his deputy, Copsig, but Tostig forfeited the personal contact with the people of his earldom which might have warned him of the growing antagonism to his rule. To the northerners, the new, possibly West Saxon law which Tostig introduced was no law, and the stern justice with which he at first enforced it turned, with the passing of years of opposition, to tyranny. The weapons of oppression became the instruments of government. When offenders against the earl's will could not be punished by legal process, darker means of retribution took justification from their ends. At Kirkdale in Yorkshire, some twenty miles west of Scarborough, there is a church whose origin dates back to the first days of Christianity in England. On a sundial above the south door is carved the inscription: *Orm Gamalson bought St. Gregory's minster when it was all to-broken and to-fallen and he had it built anew from the ground, to Christ and St. Gregory, in the days of Eadward the king and in the days of Tostig the earl.* It seems probable the Orm named his own son after the boy's grandfather, but the line was to end in treachery and violence. In 1064, Gamel, son of Orm, and Ulf, son of Dolfin, thegns of the northern earldom, were murdered while under the pledged protection of Tostig. At Christmas of the same year, the killing at court of Gospatric, another Northumbrian thegn, was ordered by the queen, at the instigation of her brother.

In the autumn of 1065, while Tostig hunted with the king in the woods of Hampshire, the men of Northumbria rose against their earl. They met in council at York, voted the deposition and outlawry of Tostig, and elected in his place the younger son of Aelfgar of Mercia. The immediacy with which Morkere took command of the Northumbrian forces suggests his early involvement in the fomenting of the revolt, and the erupting malevolence of the long-pent, nurtured enmity of the Mercians towards the deposed earl. The rebels massacred the local adherents of Tostig, though Copsig escaped their fury, and they looted the earl's treasury and marched south to press their demands on the king. At Northampton, Morkere was joined by his brother, Edwin, with the Mercian fyrd, the militia of the midland earldom, and Welsh auxiliaries; the northerners halted and began to treat with Edward through his emissary, Earl Harold, who hurried north to meet them. Tostig was accused of crimes against the church and against the people, of imposing unjust laws and taxes, and of specific felonies such as the murders of Gamel, Ulf and Gospatric. The efforts at reconciliation of the earl of the West Saxons were vain : for the Northumbrians, there could be no settlement that allowed even the possible return of Tostig to the north. Faced with the clear opposition of the witan, and swayed by the legalist counsel of Harold, the king abandoned his first determination to protect the favourite, and accepted the rebel terms. The measures of the York gemot were confirmed, and the banished earl sailed with his wife and children and his supporters for Flanders. More than an earldom had been lost to the sons of Godwin : the unity of the family was broken. The seeming treachery of Harold festered in Tostig's memory, and, in the bitterness of exile, fraternal rivalry changed to an obsessive hatred.

The coming of another spring brought small comfort to

Tostig, and in April, 1066, there was cause for his impatience and unease. Nothing less than the regaining of the lost earldom could satisfy his resentful ambition, and it was becoming evident that alliance with Duke William would not prove as profitable as he had planned. As the duke's strategy developed, there seemed little place in it for the English renegade; and the support which Tostig could offer became reduced in significance as the number of claimants to William's gratitude grew. The sanguine vanity of the exile which buoyed Tostig's dreams of revenge, and the assurance that he could bring to the aid of an invader the friendship and allegiance of *most of the chief men in England*,[2] did not impress the Norman duke as they would the less sophisticated Hardraada, unacquainted with the eloquence of the English earl. When Tostig had come to Normandy less than a month before, the invasion of England had still been scarcely more than a private project of the duke. The Englishman's avowal of aid had been more eager than those of the Norman lords: he had less to lose than William's vassals and his promises were given without the reservations that hedged the undertakings of the magnates of the dukedom. In October, 1065, Tostig had charged Harold before King Edward with connivance in the Northumbrian revolt: in the court of Rouen he accepted readily the accusations of perjury and usurpation against his brother, and he urged vigorously the summoning of the assembly at Lillebonne. But the situation had altered: the duke's venture had been blessed by Pope Alexander; the Norman barons had pledged their service beyond the sea-bounds of the dukedom; and, though no foreign princes had as yet offered their swords in alliance to William, the neutrality at least of Flanders, Denmark and the Empire seemed assured.

It is unlikely that William ever intended a formal confederacy with Tostig. Their meetings in the past had been friendly and intimate, and the kinship of their wives had ensured the Englishman's welcome at the ducal court. But the duke knew well the history and character of his guest: Tostig's attributes must have commended him as a lieutenant in the field but were not qualities which the Norman would seek or salute in an associate in government. At the same time, it could not be to William's advantage to provoke the enmity of a soldier of proven merit, the chosen deputy of the count of Flanders. The regard of Count Baldwin for his brother-in-law had been demonstrated, and the goodwill of the Fleming would be essential to William in the months ahead. Not only did the count command in his own right a military strength little inferior to that of Normandy, but by virtue of his marriage with the French princess, Adela, he was regent of France and guardian of the young king, Philip, to whom William himself owed fealty. Baldwin took little or no part in the direction of French affairs, and his exercise of his powers as regent was casual, but those powers might be decisive for the safety of Normandy in the absence of the duke. William could afford neither to alienate the English exile, nor to indulge him. He avoided the forcing of the issue by postponing the drafting of a covenant between them.

Tostig was ambitious, intemperate and proud, but also keenly intelligent and experienced in the rude diplomacy of the time. His shrewdness was edged with suspicion and he had learned not to place too much trust in the faith or friendship of princes. As the days went by and Norman preparations began to take place without reference to him, the earl came to realise that his dream of alliance with William of Normandy was as empty of hope as his earlier suit to Swegen Estrithsson. He accepted at last the failure of his mission to Rouen, and he determined on a private venture against his brother's realm. His own people had cast him out, and his cousin of Denmark had rejected his offer of allegiance in a new Danish conquest of England : he would not come again to Flanders with empty hands, to live a pensioner of his brother-in-law's bounty. But the forces that Tostig could raise were small and his ships were few. Swallowing his disappointment and the Norman slight he turned to Duke William for aid. It was a proposition that could only be welcomed by William : it freed him of an ally who was likely to prove troublesome, and it offered an opportunity to harass the English defences at little cost, and without risk to the larger strategy of invasion. The raid that Tostig intended could be no more than a diversion, and the damage that it could do to the enemy was marginal; but such diversions can have values far outweighing their immediate effects. The duke gave his permission for the recruiting of troops and the supplying of ships. Tostig summoned from Flanders the forces he had gathered there, the Englishmen who had followed him in exile, and the Flemings whom he had taken into his service, with what ships they could muster, and then he left Rouen for the Cotentin, the great western peninsula of Normandy that looks north across the Channel to the Dorset coast, Hampshire and the Isle of Wight.

* * * * *

England lay quiet under the April skies. The March sowing was past and it was the month of feasting, of celebration and rejoicing. King Edward had rested three months under the flags of the abbey he had given to St. Peter, and the successor he had named was master of a peaceful and united kingdom. The long progress through the farthest shires of the realm had ended, and King Harold was again in York, with his bride and Bishop Wulstan. The defences of the northern earldom had been set in order, and the land seemed secure. But as he sat among the Northumbrian lords, whose loyalties he had ridden north to win, none knew better than Harold how illusory their safety was. The king had faced and countered the most immediate challenge to his authority; but there was at least one other still to be met, and there was as yet no means of estimating its urgency. In the northern capital, danger seemed remote. There was little likelihood that the leadership and battle skill of Earl Morkere would be put to the test, and the men of Northumbria were hard and tried warriors. The alien threat to England was far to the south, and with each day that passed it loomed more darkly. It was in the old kingdoms of the Jutes and the Saxons that the main strength of the English must be made ready. The Easter festival was nearing, and at that time the king would wear his crown in London. There, in the gathering of the southern witan, the measures needed to guard the coasts of Wessex and East Anglia would be decided.

King Harold came from York to Westminster, at the Easter that was after the mid-winter that the king died, and Easter was then on 16 April.[3] In former years, the Easter witenagemot had met in Winchester, the ancient seat of the West Saxon kings but now tradition bowed to necessity and Harold centred the administration of his kingdom on London. Headquarters from which the strategic defence, military and naval, of the southern and eastern earldoms could be directed and coordinated, rapidly and effectively, were essential to his security. Winchester was isolated from the east and north and lay inland. Through the city on the Thames, sprawling beyond its Roman walls, flowed the major part of the commerce of England, and from its gates the Roman roads ran south-east to Dover and north-east to Colchester, north to Lincoln and York and north-west to Chester, south-west to Winchester and Exeter, and south to Chichester and Hastings. The foreign merchants and the trading ships of England brought intelligence as well as goods from Europe; and the old highways, though in poor repair, formed a pattern of communication that would not be improved upon in nine centuries. To London, a hasty summons could bring the support of Wessex, East Anglia, and the nearer shires of Mercia; and from the city and its river-estuary, the king could strike by land or sea, swiftly and with full power, against an invader.

Couriers had ridden from York ahead of the king and his retinue. They sped to London and beyond the Thames to the townships and manors of Kent and Sussex carrying word of Harold's return. As the royal party journeyed southward through the lengthening spring days, other travellers were already hastening towards London: bishops and abbots, the dignitaries of the English church, the king's reeves, crown stewards of the shires and burghs, and the landed nobles, the thegns of less remote demesnes. The palace on Thorney Island and the nearby city bustled with preparations for the reception of the king and the witan; supplies of meat and ale were requisitioned for the feasts to celebrate the ending of Lent; stores of grain were replenished from outlying districts; stocks of candles, tapers and rushes were made good. The royal company passed the Chilterns and the last fringes of the woods that skirted the lower Thames valley, and rode on through the April fields of Middlesex to the marshy Tyburn and Thorney. The lords of England thronged into London, and the council of the realm convened.

The proceedings of the witenagemot of Easter, 1066, are unrecorded, but there is little doubt of their tenor. There was necessary business of the kingdom to be debated and disposed: the sanctioning of the royal marriage would be sought and given; the acts and ordinances of the king and of his representatives were to be assessed and approved. In recent months the abbots of Ely and Abingdon had died and it was almost certainly at this assembly that their preferments were assigned. Stigand had held the former abbacy since the death of the late incumbent and had urged Harold to appoint a successor to the house. But these were lesser affairs; one matter must have hurried all others to impatient conclusions: the main discussion can only have concerned the Norman menace and the means to be taken to combat it.

In the long weeks of the northern progress the threat to the south had not been forgotten. The watch on the Channel coasts had been maintained, spies had been sent into Normandy to report the movements of the enemy, and it seems possible that English emissaries had tried unsuccessfully to reach Rome. By mid-April the king and his advisers must have known of Duke William's suit to the papal court and of its outcome; and they may have known of the council at Lillebonne. There would be small value in further embassies to Pope Alexander but the time of passive observation was past. Against the rising danger, Harold planned to gather *a naval force and also a land force greater than any king in this country ever did before.*[4] The difficulties facing the king were many. Not since the latest days of the struggle against Swegen Forkbeard and Canute, his son, half a century before, had any attempt been made to bring together the national *fyrd*, the full, military power of England. For twenty years there had been general peace, and in the limited campaigns in Wales, few southerners other than the housecarles had tested their skill and courage. Throughout Edward's reign, the ship fyrd had been allowed to degenerate. When the fleet had been called out it had operated mostly as a deterrent. Tranquillity had left the country wealthy but ill-prepared for war. From the king's chancellery, geld-writs went to all the shires of England, listing the payments levied for the hiring and provisioning of the fyrd; *ship-soke* obligations were to be fulfilled by those districts and burghs owing vessels to the crown;[5] the warrior-representatives of the provinces must prepare their weapons and supplies against the issuing of the royal summons.

Harold set his purposes and their reasons before the witan, and the plans for the defence of the nation were agreed.

*　　*　　*　　*　　*

In the Norman forests, trees were felled and drawn to the shores of the broad estuary of the Dives, north-east of Caen, and neighbouring ports where the carpenters and ship-builders waited. Beams and planks were cut and shaped and the low, shallow-draught transports, closer to barges than the longships of the Norman ancestors, began to grow under the axes, hammers and adzes of the builders. At Lillebonne, the careful duke had noted the pledges of his barons and now the pledges were honoured. For the armada that would sail against England, William fitzOsbern had promised sixty ships and his offer had been equalled by Roger of Beaumont, Roger of Montgomery, and Hugh of Avranches. From Hugh of Montfort would come fifty ships, and from two lesser nobles, Fulk the Lame and Gerald the Dapifer, forty each. Walter Giffard had vowed thirty ships, and the list continued, some lords avouching one ship only, others more. The princes of the Norman church also were generous, or politic. Vulgrin, Bishop of Le Mans, offered thirty ships and there were contributions from many of the great religious houses. But outweighing all others were the gifts of the kinsmen of the duke. William's half-brothers, Robert, Count of Mortain, and Odo, Bishop of Bayeux, engaged to supply one hundred and twenty and one hundred ships respectively. William of Evreux promised eighty, and Robert of Eu, sixty ships. The duke's first cousin, Nicholas, Abbot of St. Ouen, would give twenty ships. A single vessel, built for William himself, was the wifely donation of the Duchess Matilda.

Troops also had been pledged. Remigius, Almoner of Fécamp, undertook to provide one ship and with it twenty knights. In Walter Giffard's ships would sail a hundred knights. But the resources of Normandy alone were still insufficient: more men were needed, both soldiers and shipmen. Duke William's efforts to persuade the support of rival powers had failed: the most partisan chroniclers can only gloss the refusals by Flanders, Denmark and the Empire of the Norman offers of alliance. With or without the prompting of the Flemish regent, France was openly hostile. Conan, count of Brittany, wished the duke well in his enterprise, and demanded Normandy for himself. There were lesser princes under the papal banner: Eustace, count of Boulogne; Aimeri, viscount of Thouars in Poitou; Alain Fergant of Britanny, cousin of Conan. They would bring useful auxiliaries to the invading host, but not enough to satisfy William. He sent out a universal invitation to the discontented vassals, masterless knights and mercenaries of Europe, and all whose sins lay heavy on their souls, to win absolution and booty in the holy war against England. The duke determined, too, to appeal in person for the aid of his overlord, the youthful Philip of France.

They met on French soil at the Abbey of St. Germer, a few miles from the Norman border town of Gournay. Baldwin of Flanders was not present, but other councillors of state were with the young king. Duke William spoke again of his claims to the heritage of Edward and of his resolve to take what was his, and tendered to France the prize his ambassador had pawned before in Rome. In return for the help of his liege-lord, the duke swore to hold England as a fief of the French crown and to do vassal service to Philip for the realm he would gain. The matter had already been debated by the French nobles and their advice had been urgent and unequivocal. The ambition of Normandy should be curbed, not advanced. If William were allowed to add the wealth and might of England to the existing power of Normandy, the safety of France would be in jeopardy. Helping the Norman venture would be dangerous and profitless. Only by impoverishing the kingdom could Philip give the assistance which the duke asked and defeat would mean the sacrifice of French lives, goods and prestige. If England should fall to William, the little service he now gave to the king would become less. Philip did not question the counsel of his peers. As king of France he denied the duke's request and as overlord of Normandy he refused his consent to the venture.

With scarcely controlled wrath, William told the king that he would go to England and that he would do the best he could. God willing, he would seek his right. If that right prevailed, France would lack the power to harm him. If the English held against him, he would lose neither heart nor head through

failure. All his affairs would be set in order and he would leave
his dukedom in the capable hands of his wife and of his most
faithful friends. His lands would pass to his children and he
defied Philip to take advantage of them. Whether he lived or
died he feared the threats of no man. Scorning further discussion
the duke quitted the royal presence and rode angrily from
St. Germer and France. From now on William abandoned
all thoughts of a greater coalition against Harold. Though men
of many nations would embark in the transport now building on
the shores of Normandy, they would sail under one captaincy,
and fight under one command. Whatever their tongues, the
orders they obeyed would be Norman, and their will would be
the will of the Norman duke.

* * * * *

Since February there had been in the night sky, if men had
known where to look, an omen of terror which was to burst across
the world on the eve of the festival of the Greater Litany. The
comet of 1066 came to prominence on Monday, 24th April, and
shone each night thereafter for a week, or perhaps for a fortnight, lighting the sky from dusk to dawn. From the earliest
times, the 'hairy star' had been accounted a presage of disaster.
In January, 729, two comets had turned about the sun; and the
Venerable Bede linked them with Saracen ravages in France.
Seventy-one years later, when *fiery dragons were seen flying
in the air*,[6] a great famine followed. Famine again, and
disturbances in the land, were the sequels to the harvest comet of
975. The star of April, 1066, had been first recorded in China,
thirteen centuries before; and later was called after an English
Astronomer-Royal, Edward Halley, giving wonder a formula,
and making a commonplace of awe. But in 1066 the star was
still unnamed, and it hung over Europe like a cross of fire : its
'tail' was riven, and streamed in three, terrible flares southward
against the night. By mid-May, the visitant had passed beyond
recognition; but the baleful sword that had burned in the April
sky burned still in the memory of its witnesses. In Malmesbury, a
monk, Aethelmaer, lamed in youth by attempts at flight, foretold
the tears of mothers, and the overthrow of England. Throughout
Europe, in lands where the events described could have had little

meaning, annalists related the great comet to the coming of the Normans and the fall of the English king.[7]

*   *   *   *   *

The star flamed and died, and the Easter month ended. At a Norman port, in a sheltered harbour of the Cotentin, Tostig's preparations for the harrying of the English coast were completed. The earl's supporters, English and Flemish, had hurried to him from St. Omer in response to his urgent summons. The mercenaries he had been able to hire in Normandy were gathered. In the harbour lay the ships that would carry the ravagers northward, and they were equipped and readied. The force with which Tostig would sail was smaller than he had designed; his closest adherent, Copsig, had not yet come from the far isles of Orkney with the auxiliaries whom he had been sent to enlist. But the exile was in no mood to linger on the territory of the Norman duke. He would find other ships and the crews to man them beyond the Channel. When Copsig did return, the earl and his lieutenant would meet on the shore of Wessex. Impatiently, Tostig awaited a favourable wind.

Across the Channel the Easter gemot was over and the witan had dispersed, leaving London to the merchants, the tradesmen and the craftsmen. No troops marched and no beacons flared on the hills. But in the shipyards of England, in the armouries, and in the halls of the thegns, there was the hasty activity of men who knew that the time was short. New ships were built and the weathered veterans of many sea-days were restored. Axe-heads, swords and the blades of spears were edged and burnished; hilts and shafts were repaired and refitted; helmets, shields and coats of mail were checked. In the palace on Thorney, plans of defence were argued and agreed, and argued again. The fate of England might hang upon the answer to one problem, a question of timing; and that answer could be no more than a guess. If the fyrd were mustered too late, the king might face his enemy before the strength of the kingdom had concentrated, with a power too slight to turn back the Norman tide; if it were mustered too early, the carefully husbanded supplies might melt away before the attack came, the fyrd would disintegrate, and again the protection of the realm would fall upon an army, reduced and weakened. Harold sat with his counsellors in anxious debate, through the last peaceful days of his reign.

At the mouth of the Dives, the forest of masts thickened; and, on the hills that overlooked the estuary, encampments were prepared for the host that would assemble in the months ahead. In Rouen, the dark humour that had shadowed Duke William's return from St. Germer had lightened. In the taking of an Angevin fortress sudden death had come to Conan of Britanny. At the time of the count's most dangerous threat to Normandy, he had ceased to be a threat to anyone. While William himself guarded the dukedom, he had little fear of the Breton leader; but in the absence of the duke the menace of his rebellious vassal would not have been negligible. Now the count was dead and William looked westward only towards friends. The matter might be left at this, but for a singular report. Conan was not the first of William's rivals to die conveniently. Other hindrances to the advancing power of Normandy had been fortuitously removed. Five years before, Herbert, Count of Maine, had willed his fief to the Norman, if he should die without issue. The count died within two years, before his bride, a daughter of the duke, was of marriageable age. Maine did not fall immediately to the Norman, however, and only after a campaign of devastation of the type he directed so well did William succeed against the claim of Walter of Mantes and his wife, Biota, the aunt of Count Herbert. Shortly thereafter, while under the protection of Normandy, both Walter and Biota died. It was, perhaps inevitable that the duke should be charged with accomplishing the deaths of the last, independent rulers of Maine, and the evidence is sufficiently tenuous and suspect almost to be discounted. But William was also accused of inciting the killing of the Count of Britanny and here the evidence would be even more suspect, except for one curious circumstance: the only sources that impute the murder of Conan to the duke are Norman, and one of the three chroniclers who do so is equally one of Duke William's most fervent panegyrists.[8]

MAY

THIS was the month that the Saxons called *Tri-Milchi*, from the now forgotten custom of milking cattle three times daily in the late spring and summer. To the more devout, the first day was *festum apostolorum*, the feast of the apostles Philip and James; but for most Englishmen, Christian and God-fearing, or still, though surreptitiously, worshipping the horned gods of their ancestors,[1] it had an older and more joyous meaning. May-Day was one of the great pagan festivals, celebrating the coming of summer; and pagans and non-pagans alike invoked the blessing of the earth on the sown seed. Only a few were as yet aware of the dangers that threatened the realm; for most, the sky was clear and bright, the crops were planted, and the grain was rising in the rich loam of England.

The pleasures of the great were scarcely more sophisticated than those of their meaner tenants. The English appetite for food and drink was notorious, inbred and unrelated to class: it survived the coming of the Normans, and at length engulfed them. Four meals a day were usual, and the staple diet varied little between high and low. The vine was cultivated, and the grapes of Gloucestershire were famous, but the principal beverage was ale. Then as now, the malt brew was fermented from barley, and several qualities are described in old manuscripts.[2] Flesh meat was abundant, and as a rule less costly than cereals: seasoned with herbs, served commonly with colewort, and supplemented with fish and the perennially popular eel, it formed a large proportion of the regular fare of all sections of the community. The favoured loaf was wheaten but was relatively scarce and expensive, and the customary bread of the Anglo-Saxons was baked of the coarser, darker rye.[3] Wealth allowed diversity: imported wines, rarer fowl and fine, white bread graced the high tables of the richer thegns.

The favourite pastime of the nobles, in England as on the Continent, was the hunt. In the dense forests and on the open parkland, heralded by the blowing of horns and the baying of hounds, the huntsmen on their heavy coursers harried the red deer and the fallow deer, the roe and the wild boar. The kill was not left to the frenzied dogs: the final coup was delivered by the chasers themselves, with spear, lance and net. Lesser creatures did not escape the hunters: with arrow and greyhound, they took the fox, the hare, the wildcat and the game-fowl. More skilful, if less energetic, the practice of falconry was only a little less popular than the wilder exercises of the chase. Gloves were seldom worn, and the birds were generally unhooded, but the sport was well developed. The English flew gerfalcon and peregrine, goshawk and sparrowhawk, lanner and saker, to crane, heron, pheasant and partridge, and the smaller ground animals. Harold himself was a renowned and expert falconer: in the outdoor scenes of peace in the Bayeux Tapestry, the earl is almost invariably shown with hawk on wrist; in the twelfth century, in the earliest extant treatise on falconry in western Europe, Adelard of Bath wrote of the debt he owed to the now lost books of King Harold Godwinsson.

The bonfires of Monday, May 1st, blazed and died. Despite the portent of the wandering star that had lit the late evenings of April, and the dangers that menaced his rule, the English king may well have set apart for a while the cares of state to celebrate with his people, and the Wednesday after May-Day was an anniversary of special significance for Harold. The third day of the month was *inventio sancte crucis*, the commemoration of the finding of the cross of Calvary seven centuries before;[4] and, in 1060, that day had been chosen for the consecration of Harold's minster of the Holy Cross of Waltham. Then, the throne had been distant, the will of the Norman duke had been of small importance, and Tostig had been the nearest brother of the West Saxon earl, and his brotherly rival. In time of peril, or of great decision, as earl and as king, Harold turned for comfort and inspiration to the relic that had become a national symbol. Near Waltham, too, lay the lands that he had cherished most, and the estates of the woman whom he had loved from youth. But the first days of summer passed, and with them the long peace of England. Harold was in London when the messengers rode in from the south, driving lathered horses and shouting for the king. They told of piratic raids and running attacks on Wight and the coasts of Sussex and Kent, and hard on their heels came another courier. The message was brief : Tostig had come with many ships against Sandwich, and he had seized the port and the shipping in the harbour.

*　　*　　*　　*　　*

On a day of early May, the wind for which Tostig had waited blew. It beat northward across the Cotentin to the rock-bound harbour where the exile's fleet lay, sending the white spray scudding, and whipping the pointed pennons at the mastheads of the ships. In the raiding force which Tostig had gathered, there were between a thousand and fifteen hundred mercenaries and retainers of the earl, English, Flemish and Norman. In the fleet, there were perhaps thirty to thirty-five vessels, clinker-built and steep in sheer, with richly carved stems and sternposts, single masts stepped amidships, shuttered row-ports below the gunwales, and steering-oars fixed on the starboard quarters. Some of the vessels were no more than cutters, carrying twenty to thirty men. Others were the successors of the 'longships' that had made the Viking name terrible, and the warfleet commissioned by Alfred to counter the Norse invaders, almost a hundred and fifty feet in length and thirty feet in beam, with benches for up to sixty oarsmen.[5] Now the wind blew, and the ships were ready. The glare of the comet had faded from the night sky, the superstitious dread of the sailors had abated, and the weather promised well. The earl conferred with his captains, and the seamen were called from inns and lodging-houses and mustered aboard. The square, brightly patterned sails were raised, the oars were shipped, the tillers were manned, and the ships rode out into the Channel.

The crossing was unheralded and unopposed, *and soon thereafter came Earl Tostig from beyond the sea into Wight with as many mercenaries as he might gather.*[6] The fleet rounded the south-east tip of the island, where the narrow strand rises to the escarpment of St. Boniface Down, and ran in swiftly towards the long sands of the eastern bay, near the site of the present town of Shanklin.[7] The watchers on the cliffs were given small opportunity to recover from the shock of the arrival. The ships were beached, and Tostig led his men ashore, the raiders moving quickly before any real defence could be organised against their landing, and before any hiding of booty could be effectively achieved. Tostig's most important need was of allies and supporters, but for these he would rely on the southern, mainland shires of Wessex. The military potential of Wight was not in any case great, and the force at the exile's command would soon disintegrate without the plunder promised by his recruiting agents. Before his outlawry, the earl had held several manors on the island, and he was unlikely to be deceived by protests of poverty from the Jute and Saxon heirs of Roman Vectis. Money and provisions were demanded, and they were hastily assembled and brought to the waiting ships by the islanders, only too conscious of their danger, and with the experience of centuries of the mercy that could be expected from alien pirates. The demands were urgent, for Tostig could not afford to linger. He had men enough to overawe the local defenders of the outland estates and ports, but not to meet the full power of England or Wessex, or even of a single shire, aroused, prepared and weaponed. And each day that he waited carried the news of his coming more surely towards London and his royal brother. The loot was taken aboard, the ships were hauled downshore into the rising tide, and a course was set north-east, towards the Sussex coast.

In another summer, fourteen years before, Tostig had sailed in another outlaw fleet eastward along the south coast of England. Then, from all the ports of Sussex and Kent, Englishmen had surged to greet Earl Godwin, shouting eagerly *that they would live and die with him.*[8] From Pevensey, Hastings and Hythe, from Folkestone, Dover and Sandwich, the ships and the supplies had poured, until *the open sea was covered with vessels, the sky glittered with thickly crowding weapons.*[9] In May, 1066, the latest hopes of Tostig hung upon the memory of that distant return with his father. When the English had flocked to the sea-front to welcome Godwin, their acclamation had given the sanction of patriotism to treason, and had changed a piratic raid into a triumphal progress. Now, his offers of alliance rejected by Swegen of Denmark and slighted by William of Normandy, Tostig was wagering his fortune upon a direct appeal in arms

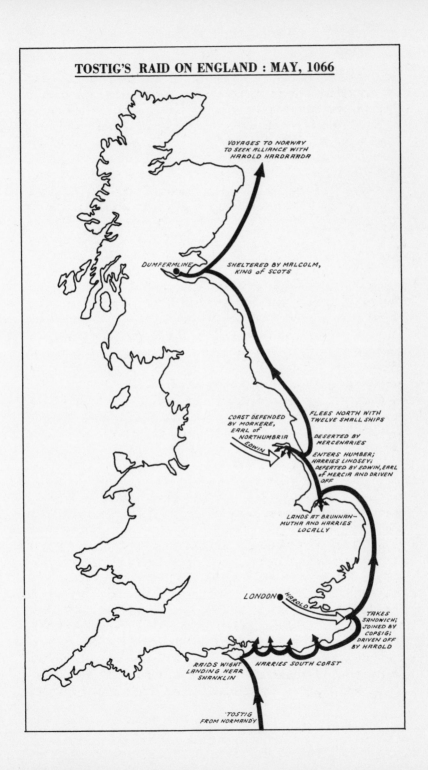

TOSTIG'S RAID ON ENGLAND : MAY, 1066

VOYAGES TO NORWAY
TO SEEK ALLIANCE WITH
HAROLD HARDRADA

DUMFERMLINE

SHELTERED BY MALCOLM,
KING of SCOTS

FLEES NORTH WITH
TWELVE SMALL SHIPS

COAST DEFENDED
BY MORKERE,
EARL of
NORTHUMBRIA

EDWIN

DESERTED BY
MERCENARIES

ENTERS HUMBER;
HARRIES LINDSEY;
DEFEATED BY EDWIN, EARL
of MERCIA AND DRIVEN
OFF

LANDS AT BRUNNAN-
MUTHA AND HARRIES
LOCALLY

LONDON

HAROLD

TAKES
SANDWICH;
JOINED BY
COPSIG;
DRIVEN OFF
BY HAROLD

RAIDS WIGHT
LANDING NEAR
SHANKLIN

HARRIES SOUTH COAST

TOSTIG
FROM NORMANDY

to the people of his native province, upon a testing of the allegiance of the men of Wessex to their chosen ruler. The low, green coast-line of the Chichester rape rose above the horizon, and the time of trial had come.

The first descents on the mainland were made in west Sussex, from Selsey to Shoreham.[10] Again the attacks were sudden, their execution swift and ruthless. Their gay sails billowing before the south-west winds, the landing parties armed and ready on their decks, the ships drove shorewards out of an empty sea. Scantly defended beaches, river-mouths and harbours were seized, local hostages were taken, and the raiders thrust inland, spreading to pillage the estates and small towns between the coast and the downs, and retiring to their guarded ships before resistance could be concerted. The southern demesnes were wealthy, and the plunder was good; but the tribute was not given willingly, and the men whom the intruders hurried before them to the shore came not as volunteers to Tostig's service, but sullenly as prisoners. At first, the earl must have restrained his supporters, for he needed above all the goodwill of the southern English. But it rapidly became apparent that, in Wessex at least, there was no disaffection from the West Saxon king; and there was no echo of 1052 in the greeting received by the king's lost brother and his foreign mercenaries. Tostig's mood changed : while his men feasted and caroused, drunk with growing riches and success, their leader saw once again the failure of his planning. With a bitter wrath that seared more deeply at each unhailed approach and each cursed departure, the exile pressed on to the east, to Brighton and Rottingdean, to the tidal lagoons of Pevensey and Bulverhythe, and to Hastings, huddled in a cleft of the Fairlight cliffs.

The tempo and tenor of the attacks changed. The booty won in Sussex had been rich, but in the Kentish ports beyond the Hastings peninsula and the marshy estuaries of the Brede and the Rother[11] there were prizes yet more valuable. With the rising certainty of defeat, Tostig gave free rein to the greed of his followers and to the cruelty that lurked within his own nature. The *butsecarls*[12] harried, looted, burned and slew, the black smoke rose above ruined homesteads, and where the invaders had passed, a wasteland was left. Men and women died, and their murderers wrenched from the bodies the petty trinkets that had provoked their killing. The piles of booty mounted on the open decks of the ships, and the zeal of the marauders mounted with them. But still no recruits came eagerly to live and die with Earl Tostig. Vengefully the renegade sped on, north-east to Folkestone and Dover, and then north round the South Foreland; *and he did harm everywhere along the sea-coast where he might, until he came to Sandwich.*[13]

Ten centuries before, when Britain had fallen to the legions of Rome, between the Isle of Thanet and the mainland of Kent there had lain the broad waters of the drowned valley of the Wantsum. Sheltered north and east by the rising chalk of Thanet,[14] and capable of carrying the largest of the imperial trading galleys, the sea-way had run north-west from Richborough to Reculver, ports throughout the occupation and, in the last years, key fortresses in the defence of the province against the growing insolence of the Saxons and Jutes. By the eleventh century, however, though light vessels could still penetrate the Wantsum, the days were gone when war-fleets and heavily laden merchantmen could pass in safety through the strait from southern waters to the estuary of the Thames.[15] Southward from Reculver, dwindled now to a village of small importance, the channel was silting up, and vast drifts of sand were building new coasts where open sea had rolled before, south and east of Thanet and the choked and deserted harbour of Richborough. The origin of the drifts is uncertain : the most likely source was the great bank of the Goodwin Sands, and legend tells of a stronghold of Earl Godwin and Swegen, his son, on the lost island of Lomea, which had stood where the Goodwins lie to-day, and which had been overwhelmed by the sea in the reign of Edward the Simple. Above the spreading sand-flats, on the south side of a wide anchorage two miles from the ruins of Richborough, the new town of Sandwich had risen, to become the main south-eastern port of late Anglo-Saxon England. In time, the sands would leave Sandwich too behind; but for several centuries yet it thrived as a primary centre for the wool-trade and the herring-fishers, a secure haven against the Channel storms, and a gathering-place for the English fleet from the days of Ethelred.

The taking of Sandwich gave Tostig both his best and his last chance of accomplishing the true object of the raid on England. Again the surprise was total, and the principal base of English naval defence in eastern Wessex fell after what appears to have been little more than a token resistance. The port was entered, the harbour and the shipping that lay there seized, the town occupied, against a weakness of opposition that to first thought seems incredible. But the failure of the defenders, like the success of the raiders, was only local and temporary; and there were several factors that operated strongly in Tostig's favour. The era of sudden Viking descents had ended, and large-scale piracy had declined. The return of the exile, unsupported by powerful allies, was neither foreseeable nor expected; military intelligence was as yet rudimentary, and the information that was available indicated that an attack from Normandy could not be looked for before midsummer. The English preparations to meet the Norman threat were only now beginning; and the raiding force was sufficient to subdue the regional militia that could be rallied, in a time of apparent safety, immediately to the protection of an outlying and restricted area, however important. Most significantly, in an age when land highways, other than to and from London, were practically non-existent, and while the sea-lanes from the south-west were closed by the barricade of the enemy fleet, the lack of communication between even the closest neighbours was such as to stultify the most carefully planned, defensive co-ordination against a determined and unheralded assault. Whatever the causes, scope and limitations of his conquest, Tostig held the gateway to south-eastern England, and his main effort to win adherents was now to be made.

* * * * *

Although the English preparations to meet invasion were still at an early stage, there can be little doubt that the overall planning had been completed in the weeks since Easter. General measures agreed in the London gathering of the witan were translated now into specific assessments of the needs and obligations of the earldoms, shires and hundreds, the territorial and administrative divisions of England. Throughout the land, the king's representatives knew the dangers that threatened the

realm and the efforts that would be demanded of them in the
months ahead. Meanwhile, arms and armour were being made
ready, and the rebuilding of the war-fleet disbanded in the reign
of Edward was under way. But events moved as yet without
apparent urgency. In those first days of May, there seemed to be
no imminent likelihood of an attack from Normandy, and Scandinavia remained quiet. Within the kingdom, the political difficulties which had confronted King Harold on his accession had
been overcome. The loyalty of the south was assured; and the
provisional allegiance at least of the temperamental northerners
had been won in the March gemot at York, and it had been
cemented by the king's marriage and the royal bridal progress
through Northumbria. The immediate problems facing Harold
and his councillors were the deployment of the huge forces
available, the supply of the army and, above all, the timing of
the royal summons to the fighting-men of England.

Among the Germanic peoples, universal service in war was
traditional; and in a land where, in times of need, every freeman
might be required to bear arms against the enemies of the king,
the potential might of the English army was incalculable. Traditions change their value, however, with changing circumstances
and customs that operate effectively among small, nomadic
tribes are unlikely to remain effective when the nomads settle as
farmers and townsmen, the tribe becomes a nation, and the homeland extends over many millions of acres. At a time when communications are still inadequate, the rise of new and separate
communities with particular ties and interests gives origin to
provincial chauvinisms, to narrowly regional adherences and
antagonisms. Partly as a result of these developments, and partly
with mere increase of numbers, the national army also loses
shape and unity, and grows to be unmanageable in direction,
unwieldy in manoeuvre, and undependable in action. The un-
disciplined bravery and the reckless bravado that had made the
first, savage assaults of the old tribesmen irresistible become in
later ages tactical liabilities. In England, although a spirit of a
wider patriotism had been fostered by the West Saxon and
Danish kings, the great *fyrd*[16] had seldom been called out since
the unification of the kingdom, and no attempt had been made
to mobilise *all the people of England*[17] since the last, desperate

months of the struggle against Canute, half a century before. The modified fyrd of later years was smaller, but functionally more effective.

In 1066, three elements made up the English army : house-carls, territorial musters, and mass levies. Of these, the levies in mass of unlanded men, small peasants and townsmen formed possibly the most numerous, but certainly the least significant element, in any military sense. Poorly armed and largely untrained, the levies were now usually regional and defensive in purpose, giving weight to the local operations of the fyrd. Their service was commonly restricted by law to their home areas, and it was also necessarily restricted in duration, by the rudimentary logistics of the period, and by the simple economic needs of peasant husbandry and the fishing seasons. As it had done in the past, the main fighting body of the fyrd consisted of the select musters, from the earldoms, or in graver emergencies from the country as a whole, of the richer land-holders, thegns and ceorls,[18] men who owed war-service as a duty to the crown. The service entailed was determined generally by the extent of the holding. The fundamental unit of land-tenure in Anglo-Saxon England was the *hide*, a measure which varied from forty to one hundred and twenty acres, and five hides constituted the customary estate of a thegn, while a ceorl who gained possession of such an acreage might himself aspire to the higher social status.[19] The obligations of thegnhood included attendance upon the sovereign; and it had become an accepted practice that, when the king went to war, one well equipped and fully trained soldier, with subsistence and wages for two months, should be provided for the army by every five hides throughout the English dominion, as required. This rule applied whether the five hides were held by one man or several, and it supplied the basis for an army sufficiently strong in numbers and proficient in arms to meet and counter the attacks of most assailants.

The army of the territorial musters and mass levies had been characteristic of Anglo-Saxon England up till the death in 1016 of Edmund Ironside, the eldest son of Ethelred, and the last princely opponent of the Danish conquest. With a history of varying fortune, the old fyrd had been capable of great courage, hardihood and endurance; but it had depended for morale almost wholly upon the spirit of its chiefs, and it had lacked above all a centre of strength, the rallying centre given by professionalism to any organisation, and in particular to an army. This central lack had been remedied under the Danish kings. Still largely amateur, in the most English sense of the term, the fyrd had been stiffened by the introduction of the housecarls, the *hiredmen* of the Danish and the later English leaders, and the finest professional soldiers in Europe. Mercenaries had fought in England before, and five-hide liability could be commuted to the payment of a mercenary's fee; but such warriors had served as individuals, selling only a temporary allegiance, and commutation had been the exception rather than the rule. The housecarls, on the other hand, were recruited as the permanent household brigades of the king and the earls; they were accustomed to living, training and acting together, as segments of a greater unit, and they formed a guild of mercenaries whose fighting qualities were matched by an unswerving devotion to their lords, and by the observance of a code of honour as rigid as that of the *samurai* of mediaeval Japan. Superbly weaponed and skilled, the heavily armoured housecarls were both guards and shock troops, the defensive core of the army, and its striking head in attack.

The reserves at the royal command were potent, and they were adaptable to most circumstances of war; but the restrictions upon the length of service which could be demanded of all excepting the housecarls limited severely the latitude of the English king's response to a known threat, the timing of which was unknown. Between the summoning and the assembly of the fyrd, some delay was unavoidable; and delay could be fatal if the summons to the fyrd were issued only after an enemy landing, particularly in Wessex. Yet, once mobilised, the main body of the army could be held together at best through little more than two months, waiting in uneasy tension for an attack which might not materialise, and ultimately and inevitably disintegrating. Hence, strategically, the advantage lay with William of Normandy. Against an England armed and keyed to readiness, the duke's venture stood small chance of success; but the decision of where and when to strike was his, and a sudden and unheralded assault upon an unmanned coast with an undefended hinterland beyond could succeed. In other ways the duke's advantage was also immense. In the south of England were the most certain allies of the House of Godwin, and the principal sources of its strength. If the challenge to the throne had come from Hardraada of Norway, there might well be time enough to gather the fyrd of the southern earldoms, and to overthrow even an established invasion of the north. Norman beach-heads, however, would lie less than a hundred miles from London; they would menace the richest provinces of the realm, and hamper the grouping of the main defensive forces, while a resolutely pressed attack might drive the king from his centres of power, and decisively prevent the concerting of an effective English resistance.

The coming of Tostig crystallised the dilemma of the English leaders. While it appeared probable that the Normans could not mount a full invasion before late July, little reliance could be placed on casual reports from Normandy; and spies infiltrated into the dukedom were unlikely to have penetrated the higher councils of the enemy, or to have learned more as yet than less official observers might record. Yet the raid on the south coast might be no more than it seemed: the vengeful action of an embittered and vindictive exile. The reports of Norman unpreparedness could be accurate, in which case an immediate calling out of the whole power of England would be premature. On the other hand, it was certain that many ships were being built in the harbours about the estuary of the Dives, that arrangements for the reception of an army were being made, and that the maintenance of that army, once assembled, would be costly. William the Bastard was given neither to procrastination, nor to extravagance. The duke might have determined in favour of an early attack; and the raid could mask a reconnaissance in force, or be a feint to draw the English defences and to distract attention from the launching of a major Norman offensive. In this event, rapid mobilisation was essential. Whatever the significance of Tostig's manoeuvre, Harold could not leave Sandwich in enemy hands. Although the decision now made might cost him both throne and life, the king did not hesitate. The royal summons went out to all parts of England; the ships of the war-fleet already sea-worthy were ordered to Sandwich; and Harold himself moved with all haste against his brother.

*   *   *   *   *

While the raiders lay in anchorage at Sandwich, Tostig was rejoined by his former deputy, Copsig, returned from the Orkneys in command of seventeen ships and their crews, enlisted in the islands on the exile's behalf. The Norsemen were sea-warriors of a quality Tostig could not hope to find in the ports of Flanders and Normandy, and they were intended to serve the double purpose of increasing both the earl's actual power and his tactical power in negotiations with the princes of Europe. Copsig had been sent to the northern isles at some time during the winter months of waiting, at the latest soon after Tostig's bitter ride from Denmark; but the voyage or the recruitment had proved more difficult than the Northumbrian and his master had estimated. The delay may have been due only to adverse winds, or it may have been owed to a need to persuade the sea-wolves to sail without the warrant of their overlord. Shortly before, Orkney had fallen to Norway,[20] and the consent of Harald Hardraada was, in legal theory at least, necessary to the hiring of shipmen in his dominions. In temperament and history, the Vikings were a turbulent and unruly race; but the most reckless were unlikely, for less than the richest rewards, to offer deliberate provocation to a king notoriously 'hard in counsel' and not prone to forgiveness of insult. Yet Copsig's mission was urgent, and he could have had little opportunity to obtain royal authority for his bargaining with the distant subjects of the Norse king. With or without Hardraada's permission, the earl's lieutenant gathered a force of some eight hundred mercenaries, and set out at last with his seventeen ships on the seven hundred mile voyage to the south. Copsig can scarcely have known or predicted the later movements of Tostig after his own departure, and it seems probable that the small fleet first sailed directly to Flanders, arriving when reports of the harrying of Wessex were already reaching the Flemish court. The time for waiting and negotiation had passed; and a day's sailing brought the thegn to the meeting at Sandwich.

The coming of the Norse auxiliaries swelled the raiding force

by almost half its original number, and yet more considerably
in fighting ability; but the power at Tostig's command was still
too slight to stay the attack which now threatened. Scouts, agents
and well-wishers along the great highway that ran north-west
through Canterbury and Rochester[21] hastened word to the earl
that his brother had left London; and, *when Tostig learned that
King Harold was towards Sandwich, then he went from Sandwich, and took some of the butsecarls of there with him, some
willingly, some unwillingly.*[22] After the seizure of the port, forced
parleys had begun between the invaders and the men of Kent,
but they had been fruitless; the primary aim of the attack had
now failed utterly, and the richness of the booty that the pillagers
had taken could not disguise the failure. Among the mercenary
seamen who thronged the cots and lodging-houses of Sandwich,
not enough volunteers could be found to man the ships captured
in the harbour, and Tostig had, perforce, to make up the prize
crews with pressed men. The actions of the exile were hurried
now : none knew better the swiftness and vehemence with which
Harold could strike at an enemy. Discussion ended, supplies and
arms were commandeered, and, with a fleet grown to sixty ships,
the renegade ran before the advancing storm, beating eastwards
against the wind along the south coast of Thanet, out and away
from the shores of Wessex.

When the marauders reached the open waters of the Channel,
Tostig's initial intention may have been to return to Rouen; but
the south winds were blowing strongly again, and the ships were
driven northwards, unable to regain either Normandy or
Flanders.[23] Passing the wide estuary of the Thames without incident, the fleet swept round the east and north coasts of Norfolk,
almost to the Wash, and put in to the harbour of Brunnan-
mutha,[24] a then prosperous port at the mouth of the Burnham,
a small river of the Fens. The pattern of the south-coast attacks
was repeated. Manors and townships in the surrounding countryside were devastated, and the pirates retreated to their ships
before an effective retaliation could be organised. By this time,
Tostig had abandoned any thought of withdrawing to Normandy : his chosen route now lay to the north. Weather and the
rapacity of his followers may have contributed to the choice,
but still dominating his actions was the vision of revenge that

had directed him first to Swegen and then to William. Southward, the future offered only the tedium of exile, or subordination to the wilful duke of the Normans; northward, the sea-way led to Scotland, the ever rebellious vassal of the English king, and beyond to the empire of Hardraada, the last and most powerful claimant to the heritage of Canute. Leaving Norfolk behind, Tostig skirted the long curve of Lincolnshire and entered the Humber. Landing was made on the south bank of the river, and the raiders spread inland to ravage the nearer districts of Lindsey. The days of scarcely hindered pillage were over, however: the brother-earls, Edwin and Morkere, stood ready to defend their provinces. Word of the earlier inroads had been brought to the midlands and the north, and the course of the fleet had been marked by watchers on the eastern shores. Even as the ships beached on the river-flats of the Humber, Edwin of Mercia was hurrying to oppose his sworn enemy with the fyrd of his earldom and the levies of Lindsey.[25]

Much damage had already been done when Earl Edwin came up with the traitor whom he had helped to banish six months before. Towns had been burned, and many men had been killed; but their avenging was swift. Guided and spurred by the wake of destruction left by the pirates, the Mercians fell upon an enemy scattered and unprepared for attack. Easy victory had left the raiders over-confident; what scouting arrangements had been made were ineffectual. The counter-thrust was conclusive. Tostig's supporters were routed and thrown back on their ships; and when they fled the Humber and rounded the long promontory of Spurn Head, they found the Yorkshire coast held against them by Earl Morkere and the eager axes of the Northumbrian fyrd. Now northern England was alerted and strongly guarded. The seamen who had hired their services to the renegade for quick reward saw their profits endangered, and the danger was not balanced by any chance of later increase. English, Flemish, Norman and Norse, they demanded that Tostig turn back, to coasts where raiding was lucrative; and when the hatred that drove him deafened the earl to their protests, they deserted him. Seizing the larger ships and what loot they could carry, the surviving mercenaries left their erstwhile commander with the leadership of only his most devoted servants, exiles who had as little to lose and as much to gain as Tostig himself in the greater strategy of the rebel. It was the end of the private venture against England. The force which had put out from Sandwich with sixty ships and more than two thousand men disintegrated. The earl surrendered the shredded dream of a revolt that would sweep away his brother and place himself upon the English throne. With a fleet reduced to twelve small vessels,[26] and accompanied by only his personal retainers, Tostig set sail for Scotland and the sheltering court of his blood-sworn ally, Malcolm, King of Scots.

* * * * *

The king rode into Sandwich with the housecarls of Wessex and East Anglia and the mounted contingents gathered during the hasty journey through Kent. Thegns and burgesses hurried to meet the horsemen; but the invader was gone, and there was no possibility of pursuit. The vessels abandoned by the fleeing adversary were hulks and small coasters, and the ships sent on from London had not yet arrived. There was nothing to do now, but wait. Harold had left the central government of the kingdom under the capable regency of his brothers, Gyrth and Leofwine. Warning of Tostig's attack had been despatched by swift messengers to the king's representatives throughout the realm, and the chancery had issued the summonses to the fyrd. The royal household and the warriors who had ridden with the king were settled in Sandwich, and on the manors and in the villages of the hinterland. Stores and supplies were requisitioned. Damage to the port was repaired; camps for the troops who would assemble were laid out; fortifications were restored. Across the Channel, the mercenaries of Europe were moving along the roads to Normandy, the encampments were spreading on the hills above the Dives, and the squat transports were rising on the Norman shores. As May was ending, the remnants of Tostig's armada limped towards a Scottish port; and in Norway, Harald Hardraada still caroused and slept. England waited, Wessex waited, Harold waited; and in the uneasy quiet, from north, west and south, ships and men came with all speed to serve their king at Sandwich.

JUNE

I N quieter times, the early days of the new month would have
been given over to the summer festival of the Christian year,
the feast of Pentecost.[1] Edward had customarily worn his crown
in London at Whitsun but in the one summer of his reign
Harold lay at Sandwich and there was neither the occasion nor
the opportunity for ceremony. The English fleet and the first
contingents of the fyrd were gathering at the south-eastern port,
and Harold's concerns were the provisioning and deployment of
his forces. The king's attention was now concentrated upon the
Channel coast. North and west, the realm seemed secure. The
southern earldoms throbbed with activity under the viceroyalty
of Gyrth and Leofwine. The resolute and swift response of
Mercia and Northumbria to the harryings of Tostig had proven
the readiness of the northern earls in their own protection. Beyond Offa's dyke, Wales was subdued: after the defeat and
death of Gruffydd, key territories of the marches had been
ceded to England,[2] and the Welsh underkings appointed by
Harold, Bleddyn and Rhiwallon, were occupied in a running
civil war with the sons of Gruffydd. Malcolm, King of Scots,
was in no position to challenge directly the authority of his
English overlord, recognised or not. The nearer provinces of
Ireland were friendly: Leinster and Dublin were still ruled by
Dermot Mac Mael-na-mbo, who had given shelter to Harold
himself in exile in 1051, and who would show like grace to the
king's sons in their later adversities.

No Norman fleet followed Tostig's raiders, and messages from
Edwin and Morkere told of the continued northward flight of the
renegade. The danger of invasion lessened and it must soon have
become apparent that the mobilisation order had been premature. But Harold was now committed. While the fleet
assembled, the king and his advisers made preparations for a
lengthy defence. There were one hundred and fifty miles of
coastline to be guarded, and it was obviously essential that

Harold be free to take personal control at any threatened point;
it was therefore equally essential that the special burdens of
the separate divisions of the English power be delegated to lesser
commanders. At the same time, the organisation of the commissariat presented urgent problems, and further delegation of
the royal authority was necessary. The notables of Wessex and
East Anglia were, however, well known to the king, and the
assignments in themselves must have been made with little difficulty. Defensive strongpoints, such as Hastings and Pevensey,
along the coast were selected, and units of the land-fyrd were
distributed among these, with their chosen leaders. The administrative care of the navy was entrusted to a churchman, Aelf-
wold, abbot of the Benedictine house of St. Benet of Hulme in
Norfolk,[3] while tactical command was deputed to a Norfolk
thegn, Eadric, who had been *rector navis* in the time of Edward,
and who would pay for his service with outlawry after the
coming of William.[4] As the preparations continued, Harold remained at Sandwich, for he intended, initially at least, to sail
with the fleet; and it can be assumed that, when the details of
the coastal defence were decided, couriers were sent from the
naval base to intercept the converging musters of the fyrd and
to direct them to their allotted posts. The ships came in, the
soldiers left, and the king waited.

*   *   *   *   *

The twelve small ships rounded the northern shores of
Lothian and turned westward, into the firth of Forth, to pass
Inchkeith and anchor in what is today Inverkeithing Bay. Tostig
landed on the farther bank of the firth and rode the few miles
north-west to the palace of the Scottish king at Dunfermline.
Malcolm Canmore welcomed his blood-brother, and supplied
the needs of the earl's remaining adherents; but the help he
could offer was limited. Military operations against England,
other than sporadic raids into the northern districts of Northumbria, were beyond the power of a ruler whose authority was
restricted even within his own realm. The careful logic of
Tostig's earlier years was distorted now by hatred, and his suit
to the king of Scots was unavailing. Malcolm would protect the
exile but he could not give support to ventures that were both

rash and hopeless and which could lead to the ruin of his own kingdom. Though the reception of the English visitors was friendly, however, even their presence at the Scottish court might ultimately have proved dangerous; and it may have been Malcolm who suggested politicly that one man alone in Europe could bring to Tostig the revenge he craved, Harald Hardraada, King of Norway.

At the age of fifty-one, Harald Hardraada was the most renowned soldier of the age.[5] A giant in stature, powerful of muscle and harsh of mind, he was, as the name given to him indicates, hard in counsel, despotic in rule. Driven into exile in his youth, he had fought in most parts of the known world, and wherever he had fought he was remembered, usually with terror. Even in the past two years, while Norway had rested in uneasy peace with its neighbour-states, the king's energies had been expended in constant punitive actions against his own recalcitrant subjects. Such petty squabbles were scarcely enough to try his strength. Warfare was for Hardraada a natural condition, with military victory its expected outcome; but for two decades victory in war had eluded him. The inconclusive ending of the struggle with Swegen of Denmark had left the Norwegian king both frustrated and without occupation. When word of the death of Edward had reached Norway, the king had considered the revival of the old Norse claim to the dominions of Canute. Hardraada had rejected it but he was ready for a new adventure, at the head of an army tempered by long years of battle, and growing refractory in idleness.

Harald, son of Sigurd and half-brother of Saint Olaf, was born in 1015. The years of his childhood were years of struggle in the north, and Harald was still a youth when, in 1030, his half-brother was overthrown and killed on the field of Stikkelstad, in the battle which gave Norway to Canute. Wounded, and deserted by his retainers, the young prince escaped from the defeat with one companion; in the winter that followed, he recovered his strength under the care of a peasant who did not even suspect the rank of his fugitive guest. There was no safety in Norway, and, in the spring of 1031, Harald left his birthland and passed through Sweden to Russia, where he made his way to the court of King Jaroslav at Novgorod. The next several years were spent in Russia, where the exile rose rapidly in the favour of his host; but, though he prospered enough to win the heart of Jaroslav's daughter, Harald became at last restless in indolence. He sought the permission of the king to leave, made his avowals and his farewells to the Princess Elizabeth, and, with a few companions, set out on the long journey south to the legendary city of Byzantium, which the saga-tellers called Mickelgard. When Harald arrived in the Byzantine capital, an expedition against the Saracens of Sicily was in preparation, and its general was to be the ambitious and skilful George Maniakes. The Norwegian prince was given command under Maniakes of the Warangian Guard, the body-guard of the emperor, composed almost wholly of Scandinavian adventurers, and the counterpart in Byzantium of the housecarls of Canute.

During the years 1038 to 1040, Harald waged war against the Saracens, both in Sicily and in Africa. He took part in eight pitched battles and in the capture of many of the castles and towns which Maniakes won back for the empire. The Sicilian campaign was one of the last of the major successes of Byzantine arms; and, though the African campaign can have been little more than a punitive raid against the principal supply bases of the Sicilian Saracens, that it could be made demonstrates the extent of Maniakes' success. With the ending of the campaign in Sicily, Harald and the Warangian Guard returned to Asia Minor; and, either during the journey or immediately thereafter, he and his followers were dispatched to the Piraeus to quell disturbances in Athens. This they did effectively, and *Harald the tall* caused an account of their deeds to be inscribed in runes upon the stone figure of a lion, which was to be taken from Athens centuries later by the Venetians, and which is still preserved in Venice.[6] At some time during the next four years, when Harald remained in the service of the empire, the exile made a pilgrimage to Jerusalem, possibly as a representative of the emperor; but soon after his return his ties with the Byzantine court were broken violently and irrevocably. He came back from the Holy Land to find himself out of favour, scandal suggesting that he had refused the advances of the aging Empress Zoë, and he left Byzantium hurriedly. Seizing as hostage an imperial princess, a niece of the empress, Harald took to his ship. He burst the chain that guarded the Bosphorus, landed his hostage, and sailed north.

It was in 1044 that Harald appeared again in the north. He came first to Novgorod, where his marriage to Elizabeth set the seal upon his friendship with her father. Harald hurried on with his bride, and passed over with her into Sweden. There he met and made an alliance with Swegen Estrithsson, defeated and driven out of Denmark by the conquests of Magnus, King of Norway. Harald had set his mind upon a return to the country of his fathers, but not as a mere subject of his conquering nephew. The invasion of the two princes took Magnus by surprise, and for a time their ventures met with varying success; but the Norwegian king was a statesman of some skill as well as a soldier. He sent embassies to his marauding uncle, offering a share in the government of Norway in exchange for aid against the Dane and part of the treasure which Harald had won in the south. The bribe was too close to his desire for the exile to refuse. He deserted Swegen and joined Magnus, and the allied kings reversed the victories which Harald himself had won with Swegen in the preceding three years, driving the Danish king out of Jutland and all the Danish isles.

Swegen had now almost abandoned hope, but within a few months of his defeat the position was suddenly and dramatically changed. In late 1047, Magnus died after a riding accident, and on his death-bed he bequeathed the crown of Norway to Harald and that of Denmark to Swegen. Harald did not accept the latter part of his nephew's will, but by the time he had established his rule in Norway, Swegen had retaken possession of Denmark. The history of the following sixteen years is that of ceaseless struggle between the Norwegian and Danish kings, of Swegen's efforts to hold, and Harald's attempts to despoil the heritage of Magnus south of the Skagerrak. But, though Harald won many battles, he could not duplicate the conquest that seemed to have come so easily to Magnus. In some part, throughout the years of warfare, Swegen maintained his government in Denmark, and at last, in 1064, Harald accepted the loss of the southern kingdom. He acknowledged the title of the Danish king, and, in the treaty that brought peace to the Baltic, the two rulers agreed to an ending of all disputes between them, and to the prevention of further attacks on either side of the Scandinavian straits.

The fire burned again in Tostig's brain. Swegen, William and Malcolm had failed him, and his own purpose had faltered before the steady enmity of his brother's subjects; but one hope still remained. The fame of the warrior-king of Norway was without equal in the west, and his claim to the English throne was strong. If Tostig could bring with him the might of Norway and alliance with Hardraada, he might yet return in triumph to the land that had rejected him. With the help of the Scottish king, the renegade's few ships were refitted and provisioned; and on a long summer day, Tostig set sail for the east and the realm of Harald Hardraada.

* * * * *

It was a month of ships: the war-cruisers that hastened to King Harold at Sandwich; the twelve skiffs that brought Tostig to Scotland, and on to his meeting with Harald Hardraada; the fighting galleys, the longships that lay unused in the Norwegian fjords; the ungainly transports that were to carry Duke William on the course that would either make him the first prince in Europe, or destroy him. At the mouth of the Dives, and along the neighbouring shores, the Norman fleet was nearing completion now. Most of the ships were little more than sea-going barges, but among the thousand-odd vessels there was one of special note. It was a large ship and richly decorated; christened the *Mora*, it was the special gift to her husband of the Duchess Matilda. The *Mora* was to be flagship of the invaders, and it would bear the duke himself. The timbers were ornamented, the sails were chequered, and at either prow or stern there was the golden figure of a boy, pointing forward and blowing an ivory horn.[7] At the masthead there hung a great lantern that would light the way of the host on their voyage towards England.

The foreign adventurers who would shore up the Norman forces were beginning to arrive; and certainly the farthest travellers must already have set out, from Burgundy, Germany and the remote Norman colonies in Apulia and Calabria in southern Italy.[8] Several of the leaders were probably already with William, nobles of Britanny, Poitou, Ponthieu and Flanders; and among the earliest to join the duke must have been the haughty and vengeful count of Boulogne, Eustace, who had been brother-in-law to King Edward. Count Eustace, by his own standards, had wrongs to redress against the people of England, and more particularly against the supporters and family of Godwin. Fifteen years before, the great earl had scorned to chastise his Kentishmen for insults and injuries offered to the king's brother-in-law, when Eustace of Boulogne had demonstrated his courage and chivalry in a running fight with the burghers of Dover, the Frenchmen doing most of the running. The count's revenge was still to come : he would prove those qualities on the hill of Senlac, hacking from horseback at the already fallen body of the dying English king. But, while preparations for the invasion continued and the foreign soldiery hurried along the roads to Rouen, the Norman duke had other business with which to deal. The council of regency which administered the dukedom in William's absence had not yet been established, and there were matters of church and state that required the duke's attention.

A church council under the auspices of the duke was convened in mid-June at Bonneville, where, two years before, Harold had pledged his oath of service to William as betrothed husband of the duke's daughter. Two appointments were to be made, to the abbacies of St. Evroul and St. Stephen. The abbey of St. Evroul was a relatively ancient foundation; the abbot had died, and at Bonneville his successor was given the pastoral staff. The second appointment was of greater significance. When, in 1059, the six-year-old marriage of William and Matilda was at last recognised by the papal council, one of the conditions of penance required that a new monastery be raised and endowed by each of the erring spouses. Both houses were destined to be built at Caen, where work on Matilda's abbey of the Holy Trinity began soon after the return of Lanfranc with the marriage dispensation. It was several years later, however, that the first stones of the duke's abbey of St. Stephen were laid, and the main edifice of the *Abbaye aux Hommes* was not consecrated until 1077. Nevertheless, by the summer of 1066, the endowment was sufficiently advanced for the formal organisation of the brotherhood of St. Stephen under an abbot. The staff of office was thrust by William upon the most renowned churchman in Normandy, the self-denying prior of Bec, Lanfranc of Pavia. The Italian minister of the Norman duke's ambitions took a further step upon the upward path which he so assiduously decried and so consistently followed.

The abbey of the Holy Trinity, the *Abbaye aux Dames*, was now nearing completion, and from Bonneville the duke and duchess and their court travelled directly to Caen. Once an island, a defensive centre of the Vikings and fortified by them, but later in decline, this city had taken on a new importance when a castle was built there by William. The journey to Caen was swift. Three days after the council at Bonneville, Matilda's still unfinished minster was hallowed, and in the service of consecration the duke and his wife made another costly avowal of their penitence : their eldest daughter, Cecily, was dedicated to the Church. The girl was still a child, and it was not indeed until nine years more had passed that she took the veil, to become in time abbess of her mother's foundation; but it might be debated whose was the sacrifice. The Church however was satisfied; and the holiness of William's intentions was made patent. With cleaned hands and purified heart, the duke returned to Rouen and the important business of the preparation for war.

* * * * *

Along the southern coast of England, the garrison musters were taking up their posts. In the small ports of Hampshire, Sussex and Kent, in forts, the crumbling walls of which still bore witness to the skill of their Roman builders, behind hastily thrown-up stockades in earth entrenchments, some older even than the Roman forts, the men of the fyrds of Wessex and East Anglia stood to their weapons. Soldiers had marched there before, and when the battles had been fought the armies had disbanded. These came, but they did not fight, and they did not disband; and the lumbering wagons, drawn by the heavy shire-horses of England, rolled along the trackways of the south, laden with the supplies requisitioned for the defenders. Such a campaign had not been attempted in the English past. There had been times of lengthy war, in the age of Alfred and his successors, and later in the disastrous years of Ethelred; but then there had been at least the excitement of battle and the lure of booty to encourage morale. This was a campaign without booty, to hinder battle, and to discourage the enemy from war. It is no little measure of Harold's greatness, as a strategist and as a leader of men, that he could envisage, plan and maintain a course of action so contrary as this to the traditions of his people, while the days grew into weeks, and the weeks into months, and still the watch was kept upon the West Saxon shore.

The ships came to Sandwich, and it was with a fleet of about seven hundred vessels that the king sailed at last from his south-eastern base. The navy's purpose was, in effect, identical to that of the land-force: to prevent the landing of the invaders. But greater mobility meant a more active duty for the sailors. The general design of the Norman transports must by now have been known to the English, and the confidence of the Saxon commanders in their ability to challenge the enemy at sea could only have been high. However, the direction in which the attack would come was still unknown. The tactics of sea-war were still primitive; victory at sea depended ultimately upon ship-to-ship grappling and hand-to-hand overthrow of the opposing crew. This rendered too hazardous any attempt to 'singe the Duke of Normandy's beard', in the shape of a direct assault on the Norman transports in their home anchorage; reinforcements could be brought rapidly from the shore to the threatened vessels, and the idea of the fire-ship was as yet un-developed. Accordingly, the role of the fleet in the period of wait-ing must be to maintain an alert in the Channel, cruising at large and with widely dispersed scouts between the possible limits of the invasion course. This was the strategy determined, and the first tack westward carried the king to the Isle of Wight, where the royal headquarters were established.

*   *   *   *   *

The voyage to Norway was made without incident, and Tostig passed northward through the Skagerrak to Viken, the south-eastern province of the kingdom. There he came at last to the hall of the king and his final hope of revenge upon the nation that had driven him into exile. The angry disillusion that had

followed the successive ruin of his earlier manoeuvres had lightened to swift optimism with each fresh scheme of alliance. To
Denmark and Normandy, to Wessex and Scotland, Tostig had
come with high confidence which rose anew in the ice-dark
waters of the fjords. The claims and promises the renegade had made to Swegen and William, he would make again
to Harald Hardraada. But after Harald there could be no more
claims or promises: there would be none to hear them. It
would seem that, as he entered under the smoke-darkened
beams of Hardraada's palace, Tostig must have known that he
must persuade the Norwegian, or surrender for ever the dream
of an armed return to his forfeit power.

Hardraada's greeting was courteous, but cautious. The purpose of Tostig's visit was evident, and the Norwegian king had
no wish for war with England. The earl spoke of the wrongs
that had been done to him, of the treachery of his brother and
the theft of his patrimony. He sought no more than was his own;
he asked first in Norway, as he had asked in Denmark, only for
help to regain what he had lost. The king answered without
enthusiasm. The Norsemen had long experience of the ways of
the English: they were not to be trusted. He could not expect
his warriors to fight for such a cause; they would not serve
under an English commander. Harald himself had no liking for
the venture. Even if successful there would be little profit in it;
failure would leave the king far from home, his army depleted,
his land at the mercy of Swegen of Denmark. England was
strong. When Edward had usurped the English crown from
the heirs of Canute, he had defied Magnus of Norway, and
Harald's nephew had bowed before the defiance. Yet Magnus
had been a great king: he had added Denmark to the Norse
empire, and he had held it until his death. Even Harald had
been unable to win back the southern kingdom; and the power
of Swegen was less than that of Harold Godwinsson.

It was an answer for which Tostig was prepared. If the profit
seemed slight, he could remedy that. Let them help each other.
His brother, Harold, was a tyrant, hated and feared. If the
Norwegian host came merely to restore the exile, the English
would dread the later vengeance of their king and be afraid
to speak out against him. If Hardraada came, however, to claim

for himself the heritage of Magnus, the nation that had venerated Canute would welcome him joyfully. Together let them end
the tyranny of his brother and when all England lay under
Harald's hand, Tostig would rule one half of the realm in
Harald's name. As under-king, he would take the Norseman
as his liege-lord and serve him faithfully while he lived.

Hardraada was still dubious, and Tostig turned to the other
objections raised by the king. The invasion could not fail : it
would resemble Magnus' conquest of Denmark, not the dead
conqueror's vain expedition against Edward's England, nor
Harald's own long and friutless campaigns against the Danes.
England was indeed strong, but its rulers were divided. Magnus
had succeeded, because the Danish lords had supported him;
the common men who might have resisted him had been left
without leaders, and Swegen had been unable to rally them.
When Hardraada had moved against Denmark, the whole
nation had opposed his coming; Swegen had won their allegiance, and Harald could not overcome them. So too Magnus'
challenge to Edward had been doomed to failure, for the witan
of all England had taken Edward as their sovereign. But Harold
had seized the English crown by treachery. The people were
disunited and disaffected. The country was ripe for conquest.
Tostig was the equal of his brother in all but title, and even
in absence his influence in England was greater than Harold's.
He would give his allegiance to the Norwegian king, and would
undertake to bring to their side all the chief men of the invaded
realm. Hardraada was the first soldier of the day; his army was
trained and battle-hardened. Against their combined forces
Harold of England would be helpless.

Tostig's skill in debate had not deserted him and as he spoke,
the doubts that had oppressed Hardraada melted into indecision
and changed finally to acceptance. The words carried conviction,
and they accorded with the deepest wishes of their hearer. The
venture that had seemed fanciful and hopeless became more
than possible. It would give new purpose to the aging warrior
and occupation to his restive subjects. It seemed to the king that
he had only to reach out to grasp success, and with success a
glory and a power that the north had not known since the death
of Canute had signalled the break-up of his empire. Hardraada

gave Tostig his hand and their alliance was agreed. There was much still to be discussed, but, for better or for worse the long pursuit was over and Tostig's purpose was achieved.

*   *   *   *   *

Before Tostig left Norway, plans had been agreed, and Harald Hardraada's summons had gone out to his subjects and satellites, throughout Norway and to the distant isles of Shetland and Orkney, to Iceland and the Faroes, to the western isles of the Hebrides and beyond to Ireland and to Man.[9] The exile himself hurried with the tidings to St. Omer and the wife and family he had scarcely seen in three months.

Far to the south, Duke William set about the organisation of the duchy in his absence. His presence would soon be needed at the growing camp above the Dives and before then the administration of Normandy must be placed in capable hands. He was moving steadily now towards the completion of his purpose, unaware of the gift of fortune that the winds of May had brought to him. Across the Channel, Harold waited in impatient idleness as the summer days passed and still no word came of the invading armada. In the fortresses and camps along the English coast, the soldiers ate and slept and practised their arms, grumbling at the worktime lost to no seeming purpose. On the grey waters themselves, the fleet kept their unending vigil on the empty southern seas. The uneasy quiet persisted, and the first inroads were made on the carefully husbanded supplies.

JULY

THE royal message-token had gone out to all the *thing-lands*[1] of Norway, and King Harald had summoned to him a levy of half the Norsemen able to bear arms. In the preparation for war, the difficulties faced by the Norwegian ruler were fewer than those met by his rivals in England and Normandy. Harald Hardraada lacked neither warriors, weapons, nor ships. The great era of the Vikings might be past, the rich and bloody era of ceaseless marauding along all the sea-coasts of the west; but the sea-wolf traditions were strong, and the lure of distant plunder was still compelling. The men who followed Hardraada were used to fighting, and enough would come. The leaders of the people, too, the *jarls* and *lendermen*,[2] were battle-tried and discontented in their lately enforced domesticity. The Norse fleet had not been weakened by a frugal and complacent disbanding, such as King Edward had brought about in England, or by a slow disintegration of old skills, such as had taken place among the landward-looking Normans. The ships and men were ordered to gather within one month at the Solund Isles, at the mouth of the Sognefjord, on the west coast north of Bergen.

The surname Hardraada, 'hard-counsel', was well chosen for Harald Sigurdsson. Although the king was, in general, *of a worthy and considerate manner of living*,[3] he was also *most greedy of power, and of all distinction and honour*. Harald *avenged cruelly all opposition*, and it is evident that his rule in Norway was despotic. In England, matters of high policy were, to a certain extent at least, subject to the decision of the witan. The strongest kings weighed carefully the advice of their counsellors; the weakest surrendered to them. In feudal Normandy, rule was more authoritarian; few voices could influence the designs of William the Bastard. Nevertheless, the duke had submitted his project of war against England to the debate of the Norman nobles in council. No saga suggests that Harald Hardraada either sought advice, or encouraged debate. The

Norwegian expedition was decided upon arbitrarily by the king. The *things*, the regional parliaments of the Norse realm, were not consulted and it seems likely that Harald did not sound the opinions of even his greatest vassals. But, while the will of the king might demand obedience, it could not silence all discussion among a people little accustomed to discipline. The Norsemen were noted neither for meekness, for brotherly love, nor for unprotesting parades to the chopping-block.

Many of Hardraada's subjects were confident of success: King Harald's achievements had been great; in battle, he was both courageous and fortunate, and *bravery is half victory*. If any leader could accomplish such a conquest, it was Harald Sigurdsson. Others feared the enemy they would meet: England was difficult to attack and very full of people; and the English thegns were so resolute in their defence that any one might overcome two of Norway's best men. There were differences in the highest places. Thorir of Steig, who had given the title of king to Harald, could foresee only disaster and the purposeless sacrifice of many good soldiers; he refused the support of himself or of his followers to a venture that must lead to ruin and death. For the king, Ulv Ospaksson, the royal marshal, was incensed by the insults levelled by the dissidents at the Norse warriors: he was still ready to win gold, but he would give up his office when two Norwegians must fly from one Englishman; in his youth the reverse had been true. But Thorir had risen under Magnus, while Ulv was one of Haralds' oldest companions; their allegiances were divided in beginnings. At the last, neither Thorir nor the marshal sailed with their lord. Shortly after the coming of Tostig, Ulv died, and Harald appointed another in his place.[4]

The merchant town of Oslo had been founded in Viken by King Harald, at the head of the great southern fiord then called the Folden.[5] The surrounding countryside was extensively cultivated and the town formed both a well-supplied and pleasant place of residence and a convenient base, offensive and defensive, in the war against the Danes. Hardraada spent much time in Oslo and it was there that he had entertained Tostig. In those days, however, the principal town of Norway was Trondheim, more commonly known by its ancient name of Nidaros. In

Nidaros stood the greatest churches of the realm, and the chief houses of the kings. Harald's predecessors, St. Olaf, his half-brother, and Magnus, Olaf's son, had each built a palace there; and Harald himself was raising a stone hall, still unfinished at his death, beside his nephew's house. The size of these buildings can be gauged from a description of King Olaf's household in Trondheim : his palace, Skulegarth, consisted of a huge, central hall with other rooms set about it, and with many outhouses beyond the main structure; to maintain his state in Nidaros, the king employed sixty court-men, thirty pursuivants, and thirty house-servants, and he had as well many slaves.

When Tostig had left on the return voyage to Flanders, King Harald travelled north from Oslo to Nidaros with his train. Accompanying him, presumably, were his wives, the Russian Princess Elizabeth and Thora, a Norwegian noblewoman, their children, and his close vassals. Without putting aside his first wife, and without apparent opposition from court or church, Hardraada had married Thora, daughter of a Norse magnate, Thorberg Arnisson, in the winter of 1048, soon after his accession as sole king in Norway; his sons, Magnus and Olaf, were the offspring of this second union. It seems likely that the love of his youth kept its hold upon Harald's affections throughout his life, but the children of Elizabeth of Novgorod were girls, Maria and Ingigerd. The marriage with Thorberg's daughter may have been contracted with the aim of producing a male heir, and in this purpose it had succeeded. Yet, though dynastic necessity may have demanded a son, when the king set forth on his last journey, Elizabeth sailed with him, while Thora remained in Norway; and the dearest to Harald of his children was the eldest, Maria, and it was said of father and daughter that they *had but one man's life between them.*[6]

The king came to Nidaros. Among the Norwegian leaders now with Hardraada were Styrkar, the marshal, the successor of Ulv Ospaksson, and Eystein Orre, called 'the gorcock'. A son of Thorberg Arnisson, Eystein was the king's brother-in-law and the most able of the lendermen; he was the best beloved of Harald's companions and the affianced husband of Maria. Another son of Thorberg joined Harald in Nidaros; this was Nicholas, who held at that time the stewardship of the near-lying province of Helgeland. Far to the south, the fleet was assembling on the Sognefjord; and on the open waters of the river Nid, spreading to form the Trondheimfjord, rode the ships of the king and those who would sail southward with him. But in the palace that Harald had built, down by the river, there was work to be done before the wind could be taken. Hardraada was a realist : in the battles that lay ahead, the strongest warrior might fail; the realm could not be left without a ruler. When the king left Nidaros, his heir must be chosen and proclaimed to a people always ready to support a venturesome pretender.

* * * * *

Similar business occupied the late days of Duke William in Rouen. When he went to take command of the growing encampment by the Dives, he would leave behind all routine matters of state; but, in his absence, the government of Normandy had to be held in strong hands. However, the duchy was united and the Norman barons were loyal. The succession was clear and the sons of William and Matilda were healthy. Though Philip of France was unlikely to be saddened by the fall of his nominal vassal, and though he did everything he could to disturb the duke's preparations, his power was insufficient to threaten seriously the Norman fief. The convenient death of Conan of Britanny had removed the one remaining possible menace. William appointed a council of regency. He entrusted the supreme authority to Matilda, but behind the duchess were councillors of proven merit, led by an aged, but famous soldier and cousin to the duke, Roger of Beaumont.[7] The duke made his farewells[8] and hastened westward.

William's captains numbered among them the most illustrious names in Normandy. His own sons were still too young to take any part in their father's campaigns. The eldest, Robert, the 'sleepy duke' of later chronicles, was little more than ten years old. Of the Norman leader's companions, the closest in blood were his half-brothers, Count Robert of Mortain and Bishop Odo of Bayeux; but another of the duke's more devoted followers would be his step-son, Gerbod of Flanders, who was the son of Matilda by her first marriage to a Flemish dignitary. This early marriage may have had much to do with the trials which beset that of Matilda and William in its beginning: their union was adjudged uncanonical by the church; all Normandy was laid under a papal interdict for the matrimonial sin of the duke; and not until after the birth of at least two children did Lanfranc obtain for his master the dispensation of Rome for a match that had been consummated six years before. But time had soothed away any resentment that William might have felt; the marriage was canonised and successful, and the legitimacy of his children was accepted. Gerbod sailed with his step-father against the English 'usurper', and was to be rewarded by the victor with the rich earldom of Chester.[9]

The presence of the duke was urgently required at the Dives. On the low hills above the winding river, the tented city spread. The ordered companies who came, the followers of particular lords, were interspersed with motley groups of masterless men, the followers only of fortune and the pickings of war, and among the country people, the fear of pillagers grew. Great events might be afoot; but herds must be grazed and crops must be ripened. The stern discipline which Duke William had yoked upon the Normans was extended over the men of many races who crowded into the camp. Already there were murmurs against the wisdom of the venture. Some who had pledged their loyalty in the Spring, when the prospect of battle was still distant, became faint-hearted when the trumpets began to sound, when on the estuary below stood the ships that would carry them towards the terrors of the unknown, to possible ship-wreck and beyond, to the arms of an adversary whose power loomed larger as the challenging time neared. The courage and resolution of one leader, one face towards which men could look, was needed to restore the doubters, to inspire the waverers, and to weld the jostling fragments of the host into the single instrument of his will.

Despite the careful guard which the Normans and their allies had maintained along the Channel coasts, King Harold of England had managed to send agents into Europe. Some of these spies had made their way to the Dives, and one of them was arrested by the duke's officers and brought before their commander. William questioned the Englishman personally. Although the practice of espionage was still rudimentary, the principles at least were understood; the spy had been given what would later be called a 'cover story', and he had been carefully instructed in its recitation. The explanation of his presence was not accepted by the Normans, but the duke was in a magnanimous mood. *'What need,'* he asked, *'has Harold to hire for sums of gold and silver the devotion and industry of you and your like who come to spy on us? What surer proof of our intentions and preparations could he wish to have than myself in person to inform him?'*[10] If these words had seemed bantering, the menace in those which followed was unveiled and unmistakable. *'Take this message to him from me,'* William said, *'he will have nothing to fear, and will be able to live in peace to the end of his days, if, by the time this year is out, he has not seen me in that place where he thought himself most secure.'* The duke then ordered the release of the prisoner, and instructed his officers to set the spy on a ship for England.

Several of the Normans who had witnessed the interrogation were startled by the duke's defiance. They feared over-confidence in the leadership of the invasion. King Harold's strength was great; he was extremely rich and could hire many powerful mercenaries; his fleet was vast and his crews were expert, hardened by frequent exposure to danger. In all aspects, the might of England surpassed that of Normandy. Even if William's arms met with initial success in his personal struggle with Harold, such a prosperous land could not be reduced in less than six months. The forces of a Roman emperor would scarcely have been enough. The nobles who stood about the duke voiced their scruples, possibly hesitantly, but frankly. It was not cowardice which spoke, but caution.[11]

The duke listened with patience and then he spoke again. *'We know,'* he said, *'the wisdom of Harold: it arouses fear in us, but strengthens our hope. In vain does he spend his wealth; he is wasting his gold without ensuring thereby his crown.'* That Harold planned no retaliatory invasion of Normandy, William construed as weakness. The English king offered his followers only English gold in payment for their services; no such restrictions hedged the promises of William. When the victory was won, he would distribute among his supporters not only the riches of his own purse, but the wealth of England as well. *'The* man who has the audacity,' the duke continued, 'to dispose of those goods which are in his enemy's possession just as if they were his own will without doubt triumph over that enemy.' The military information which the English agents could bring to the king mattered little. 'Let them know,' William concluded, 'what with good luck we shall be in a position to demonstrate: that it is the valour of soldiers rather than their number which wins battles. Besides, it is in order to secure his ill-gotten gains that he will be fighting, whereas we are demanding what we have received as a gift and acquired by our own kind services. It is this basic certainty of our cause which, brushing aside all peril, will secure us victory, honour and glory.'

The appeal to their courage, acquisitiveness, national pride and sense of justice swayed the duke's audience back from doubt. Yet the sincerity of the speaker is scarcely to be doubted. The slight which Harold had put upon his erstwhile host and prospective father-in-law had rankled deeply in William's mind; and the swift anger of the Norman had festered to a hatred of the English king which would not rest until every memory of Harold Godwinsson had been debased. Flimsy in essence as his claims and arguments might be, Duke William never faltered in his belief in the rightness of his cause and in the holiness of his mission. But England was not yet won and the duke turned his attention to the making of an army.

* * * * *

Beyond the horizon scanned by the Norman sentinels, the English fleet patrolled the northern waters of the Channel and the soldiers of the English king kept their watch on the Wessex coast. In Flanders, the bells of St. Omer rang to greet the return of Tostig, jubilant and eager for the coming weeks to pass. Knights and men-at-arms, in solitary haste, or journeying merrily in troops, still sped down the long roads to Normandy; they were fewer now than those who had travelled the highways of the duchy in the first weeks of summer, but the same lure drew them. West and north of the threatened realm, in Man and in Ireland, in the Scottish isles and in the sea-islands reaching out to the farthest dependencies of the Norse king, to the Faroes and Iceland, men were preparing for the rendezvous of the northern alliance in Orkney. On the mainland of Orkney itself, the earls Paul and Erlend saw to the supplies to be collected against the coming of their overlord, while the ships of the Orkneyingers and their vassals gathered in Scapa Flow.

* * * * *

A slowly spreading shadow overcast the last days in Nidaros before the departure of the king. The mood of Hardraada and his followers darkened and many omens and dreams were told that presaged disaster. Harald himself dreamed that he spoke with his martyred half-brother, King Olaf, thirty-six years dead. The ghost foretold the passing of the king: soon Harald's corpse would feed the crow, the *'witch-wife's steed'*.[12] Pagan beliefs were still strong in Scandinavia, and they would keep their hold through ages yet to come. The later kings, Olaf, Magnus and Harald, had all built churches in Norway and the greatest of these were in Nidaros; but the instinct that took Hardraada to St. Clement's church before he left Trondheim may have been older than Christianity in the north. By the comamnd of King Magnus, the body of his father, St. Olaf, had been laid in a shrine in St. Clement's minster. The sepulchre had become a place of miracles. The shrine was mounted with gold and silver, and studded with gems; within it was a sheltered area, arched, with closely plaited hangings behind and padlocked gratings in front. King Harald went to the shrine and unfastened the padlocks. Under the jewelled coffin of his brother, the king clipped his hair and nails; then he came out, relocking the shrine and taking the keys with him. These he later threw into the depths of the Trondheimfjord. By the sacrifice within the shrine, Hardraada sought to propitiate the spirit of Olaf, on the eve of his most stern trial; the removal of the keys sealed the shrine lest any illwisher gain access to reverse the spell and compass the destruction of its maker.

Word was brought to the king that the fleet was assembled in the Sognefjord. Harald had learned from Tostig of the designs of Duke William and it seemed evident to the Norwegian that swift action would be necessary to circumvent these designs. The exile had sworn to Hardraada that the English would rise to his coming, but needless delay might mean arriving in England to find the country already held by an alien conqueror. The preparations for departure were hurriedly completed. By the will of King Harald, his heir, Magnus, was proclaimed joint-king with his father; the youth was at the same time appointed to rule over Norway in the absence of Hardraada. The king's second son, Olaf, would sail with the invasion fleet; so would the queen, Elizabeth, and the princesses, her daughters, Maria and Ingigerd. Thora would remain in the north with her elder son. The king and his family, with the Norwegian leaders and men who had joined Hardraada in Nidaros, boarded the waiting ships. The anchors were drawn in, the sails were raised, and a course was set for the south and the Solund Isles.

* * * * *

As the Norse king sailed to meet his people, his ally in Flanders was hastily mustering fresh forces to bring to his support. In Normandy, all was ready for the great venture; and the duke and his officers began to watch wind and weather. At the summer headquarters on the Isle of Wight, King Harold Godwinsson still looked south, unaware that danger now threatened on two fronts. As the second month of the long vigil ended the guard held on the Saxon shore; but the grumblings grew, while the enemy whom Harold had dismissed hurried southward on the first stage of the journey that would bring him, with sudden violence, against the thinly defended, north-eastern flank of England.

AUGUST

THE achievements of both the Norman and the English leaders in the summer of 1066 were remarkable. Large and motley armies were assembled and maintained with a resolution that would have been unthinkable to lesser men. When July ended, the English garrisons had manned the defences of the southern coast through two long months of high summer. With a reward of little more than the knowledge of duty done, and stiffened by merely a scatter of professionals, the amateur soldiery of England had already held their position longer than would the Norman levies and the mercenaries of half Europe, lured with promises of the richest plunder in the western world. Lodged closely in their city of tents, and overseen by the premier barons of Normandy, the servitors of the duke were restrained from violence and pillage only by the stern presence and merciless justice of their commander-in-chief.[1] Throughout the summer, the English king lay with his reserves on the Isle of Wight; and during those months, the dispersed chain of posts that reached from the Solent to the Wantsum guarded the realm without recorded disturbance, under the discipline of the thegns of the southern shires and the housecarls of Harold and his brothers. June and July were gone, and six weeks more would pass before the carefully husbanded supplies of the English commissariat gave out and the king gave his reluctant permission for the disbanding of the fyrd. The same six weeks would drain the resources of the Norman provisioners and drive the invaders from the camp above the Dives into precipitant action.

Massive as the English achievement was, it contained the seeds of possible disaster. As August began, the weather was still warm and dry; Duke William had but recently come to the Dives; the fyrd and the fleet kept their watch on the West Saxon shores; King Harold was still at the headquarters which he had established on Wight in June. By now, however, Harold must have accepted that the gamble he had taken in May had failed. The raids of Tostig had not presaged the main effort of the Normans. The mustering of the fyrd had been premature and soon the bulk of the stores garnered by the royal agents would be exhausted. The king's rebel brother had vanished into the north,[2] the seas were free of enemy shipping, and an illusory peace had settled again over the realm. But the illusion was incomplete: troops of armed men moved in the land; from Mount's Bay to the Wash there were homes missing fathers, husbands and brothers: as the harvest drew near, there were fewer hands to work the fields than there had been in living memory. Though the guard on the Channel remained intact and unchallenged, England had suffered, in effect, a major strategic defeat. Unless the Normans attacked within the next few weeks, the first line of the defence of the south must break. When the food-stocks were done, no more than token forces could be left along the coast, forces that might hinder an enemy landing, but could not prevent it. However bravely the defenders might resist, a beach-head would be won, and might be firmly established before the fyrd could be regrouped in sufficient strength to oppose the invaders in direct conflict. Harold had personal experience of his rival's courage and tenacity, and of William's quality as a leader of men. Given a foothold in England under the ducal gonfanon, the Normans would fight well, and their expulsion would be difficult.

Few sources describe in any detail the reign of the last Anglo-Saxon king, and most of these are hostile, the works of pane-gyrists of the king's enemies. But it can be assumed that in the third month of his sojourn on Wight, when still the Channel lay quiet under the searching eyes of the English navy, the king's thoughts became heavy. Tostig had come and gone, but the Norman attack had not followed. Returning spies warned of Duke William's preparedness, but the army of invasion rested on the coast of Normandy. England faced a defeat, attributable not to the acts of the enemy, but to the hasty decision of Harold himself. The circumstance which the king had laboured to avoid now threatened remorselessly. Harold knew the character of the Norman invasion: the deliberate rapine and burning with which William was used to harry the territory of an opponent. If want thrust the English leaders back upon London, the southern shires of Wessex, so long the special care of Godwin and his second son, must be abandoned to the intruder. South of the downs and the great forest of the Andredsweald, England would be exposed to the brutality of the Norman duke. Men of Sussex and Kent would die and their families would be made homeless for the error in judgment of their king and his councillors.

In the month now beginning, William of Normandy would pray for a calm sea and a south-east wind no more fervently than the king who awaited his coming. Only haste could redeem haste. If, driven by over-confidence and the demands of his followers, the Norman invaded within these next weeks, there was little doubt that he would be destroyed; and there was equally little doubt that, once ready, William would be held back only by the weather. Harold had campaigned with the duke; as a soldier among soldiers, he must have studied the nature of his host. The duke was bold and shrewd; but his boldness was flawed by impatience and his shrewdness was not proof against vanity. This combination was to bring him to death in the end, when, king of England for more than twenty years, he would rise from a sick-bed in Rouen at the taunts of the French king, and ride unsteadily to one last holocaust in the burning streets of Mantes.[3] But now Harold reigned in England, and the fates of two armies and two nations hung upon the impatient will of the Norman. William had sworn to attempt the crown of Edward and, *by the splendour of God*,[4] he would redeem his oath with the least possible delay. In William's character lay Harold's best hope; the sea and the wind would arbitrate between them.

Many messages must have passed between the Isle of Wight and London, but there is no evidence that Harold left his summer headquarters between the arrival in June and the final departure in early September.[5] It is unlikely that members of the royal family accompanied the king on his march to Sandwich, or on the voyage to Wight; the presence of Gyrth at least was needed in London, and women, other than camp-followers, have seldom been welcome on campaigns. To the frustration of inaction and the mounting anxiety over supplies were added isolation and the emotional hunger which separation must entail. In London, the king's brothers gleaned the remnants of the old year's stocks for the threatened army; with Gyrth and Leofwine were almost certainly Gytha, their mother, and the queen, Alditha of Mercia. Edith Swan-Neck may have joined her lover in the south but it is more probable that she too was left behind on one of her estates north-east of the city, with their children. In 1066, three sons of Harold were growing to manhood: Godwin, Edmund and Magnus. In the years that followed their father's fall, they were to trouble the western shores of his lost kingdom, but at the time of his crowning they were still youths. Two daughters had also been born to Earl Harold: Gunhild and Gytha. This younger Gytha later fled the England of William, finding refuge at first at the court of Swegen of Denmark, and finally in marriage with Vladimir, Prince of Novgorod; through her, the blood of Harold Godwinsson would be preserved in the royal lines of Russia and the kingdoms of the north. These were, in all likelihood, the children of Edith. But there was new cause for pain in the king's absence in the summer of 1066. The claims of Godwin Haroldsson and his brothers to the English throne could never be more than tenuous. While Harold lay on Wight, his queen prepared for the birth of an atheling, an heir-apparent to the king who waited to fight for the preservation of his heritage.

* * * * *

Beyond the North Sea, the threat which Harold of England had dismissed developed quickly. While Northumbria slept under the complaisant government of its Mercian earl, and the English king gave his energies wholly to the defence of the south, Harald Hardraada came to the Solund Isles and the waiting Norwegian fleet. Later centuries have degraded Hardraada to little more than a braggart swashbuckler, not to be compared as a captain or a leader with William the Bastard; but in the mid-eleventh century, few outside the frontiers of Normandy would have agreed. Already legendary, the Norwegian king stood in reputation with the greatest of the Viking adventurers; and the soldiers he commanded were drawn from the most warlike race in Europe, with a history of battle and fighting prowess rivalling those of Macedon and Rome. There were over two hundred ships of war collected in the Sognefjord, with many provision-transports and small vessels as well; some fifteen thousand Norsemen had answered the summons and there would be others. Auxiliaries would join the fleet at Shetland and at Orkney, off the Scottish coast and in the mouth of the Tyne. The force which Harald Sigurdsson would lead against England would be one of the greatest ever assembled under *the banner which was called the Land-ravager*[6] and its members were the sons of the warriors who gave the word *berserk* to the English tongue.

Within a few days of the king's arrival, the ships and men were ready. The rapidity with which a Viking host was gathered and set in motion, the ease with which the Norsemen could turn from peace to war, have confounded the thinking of chroniclers and even of later historians, accustomed to the slow and elaborate preparations of the more sophisticated south. The same qualities which lent near-invincibility to the 'nations on horseback', the Turks and the Mongols, were possessed in their days of glory by the Scandinavian peoples, to whom the sea and a swift ship were the steppes and horse of the Asiatic nomads. Inevitably, strategic flexibility influenced also the approach to tactics. The suddenness, speed and ferocity of the Norse attacks were traditional. Just as, two centuries later, the European knights in their formalised pavane were helpless against the heirs of Genghis Khan, so had more sedentary races collapsed before the Viking marauders who came out of an empty sea, plundered and slew, and vanished again while terror still paralysed their victims. The summons of the Norwegian king had been answered, but Harald Hardraada intended no mere orgy of looting. This was to be a campaign of conquest, such as Magnus had directed against Denmark and Swegen Forkbeard had led in the England of Ethelred. With the king went the closest members of his family, except for the son who must remain behind as under-king of Norway, and the boy's mother; and to purchase at need the service of his allies and of his future subjects, Harald carried with him a large part of the royal treasure, including an ingot of solid gold, so heavy that twelve strong youths could scarcely lift it.

Despite the massiveness of the armament and Hardraada's confidence in his mission men dreaded the outcome of the months ahead. While the ships still lay off the Solund Isles, superstition conjured omens and visions of despair from the forebodings of the voyagers and disquiet grew in the fleet. In the sagas, the sense of doom which attended the sailing of the Norse armada is crystallised in dreams which echo the warning given to the king himself in Nidaros. The ghost of King Olaf had foretold death to Harald. On board the king's ship in the Sognefjord, a man called Gyrd dreamt of a great loss. It seemed that he saw ravens and ernes settled on every stern, choosing their prey, while on the neighbouring island a witch-wife sang of the disaster to which she lured the Norwegian host. On a near-by ship, another dreamer, Tord, saw the fleet come to England and a great battle begin, with banners waving bravely. But it was a battle without hope for the invaders. In front of the English, a witch-wife rode upon a werewolf, and in the wolf's mouth there was the body of a Norseman. Blood dripped from the jaws, and when the carcass was eaten the witch-wife threw another into the greedy jowls, and all the others, one by one, until Hardraada's army was consumed. It was not a time for delay. Once at sea, the superstitious fears which had bred in idleness would give way to excitement and lust at the prospect of action and of the rewards of victory. *When King Harald was clear for sea, and the wind became favourable, he sailed out into the ocean.*[7] The course was set south-west for Shetland.

* * * * *

The debris of centuries would turn the open water to marsh, and the marsh at last to firm earth; but in the time of William the Bastard, the lower valley of the Dives formed a vast, shallow lake invaded by the tides and overflowing in periods of flood.[8] It was an excellent anchorage and in the first days of August the wide estuary was crowded with shipping. There were more than a thousand vessels in the now ready Norman fleet.[9] The ships varied greatly in size and intention; in general, however, the principles and pattern of construction were constant. Open boats with single masts, flat-bottomed, broad of beam, and shallow of draught, the Norman transports were built neither for ocean voyaging, nor for battle, but as sea-going ferries and barges. They were poor craft in comparison with the 'great ships' of the English navy, or with the 'dragons' of the Norse kingdoms; but they were capable of the crossing to England. There were none too many. The lading was to be heavy and cumbersome, as unwieldy as the vessels themselves. Not only soldiers were to be carried, with their arms and equipment, but the horses of the knights, victuals for the entire force and war-machines, including three portable castles of a structure which a later age would term 'pre-fabricated'. It seems likely that the largest of the Norman ships would bear no more than sixty men, and that there were few of these. The smallest were little better than dinghies. The most common type could probably accommodate about forty passengers and crew and the average capacity throughout the fleet appears to have been approximately twenty-five to thirty men, or their equivalent in material of war.[10]

The army in the hill encampment now totalled between fourteen and fifteen thousand men, of whom possibly one third were to be classified as non-combatants. Many rolls of many names exist today, listing the 'companions of the conqueror'; in fact, fewer than fifty of those who sailed with Duke William can be detailed with any certainty.[11] Within a hundred years of the event it had become fashionable for the founder of a Norman family's fortune in England to have taken part in the great expedition; benefactors of church establishments and patrons of individual chroniclers could purchase a dubious immortality from their grateful clients.[12] Records compiled even in the twelfth century are therefore of limited reliability, showing frequent, demonstrable departures from known truths. Inevitably, most of the voyagers to whom names can be given with assurance were noblemen, churchmen, or gentlemen: lords of the Normans and their allies and known retainers of these lords. Among the barons of Normandy who did not accompany the duke were some who would set their marks on the later history of England, either personally, or through their descendants. With old Roger of Beaumont, in the council of regency, William had associated Roger of Montgomery and Hugh of Avranches. The latter, son of the powerful viscount of the Avranchin was in after years to be rewarded for his services with the earldom of Chester in succession to Gerbod of Flanders; the former, viscount of the Hiemois and future earl of Shrewsbury, was to plant the title of his Norman seignory indelibly on the geography of the usurped realm of his master. Another who remained behind was William of Percy, whose heirs were to establish a virtually independent monarchy in the eastern marches of the Scottish border, to vex not only the lands to the north, but the English kings as well.

Nearest to the duke in his councils were his half-brothers, Robert, count of Mortain, and Odo, bishop of Bayeux. Robert 'the Magnificent', also called 'the Devil', sixth duke of the Normans, had never legitimised his union with Herleva, the tanner's daughter of Falaise and mother of the bastard heir to the duchy. Some time after the birth of William, however, the duke had married off his mistress, in the traditional manner of satisfied princes. The chosen husband had been Herluin, viscount of Conteville; and Robert and Odo were the sons of this match. The presence of the duke's half-brothers in the invading army is beyond question, and, after the crowning of William, both were to hold great possessions in England. Manors given to the count of Mortain would be reported by the Domesday commissioners in nearly every shire from Sussex to Yorkshire and, in 1076, the overlordship of the Celtic south-west was to be given over to Count Robert, together with the tenancy and land-revenues of most of the Cornish peninsula. The allegiance of Odo of Bayeux would be similarly recompensed. Though the bishop would in time aspire even to the papacy, he was not noted either for piety, or for unworldliness. In an age of trumpeted reform in the church, he is known to have fathered at least one child,[13] while his rapacity and cruelty were to be included in the quoted causes of his ultimate downfall.[14] But, in 1066, Bishop Odo was one of the strongest, most loyal and most favoured supporters of Duke William; and there were notable precedents in the Norman episcopacy for the combining of secular and ecclesiastical powers. Within a year, Odo would be made earl of Kent, and, in the absence of his royal brother, the bishop-earl would act as joint-viceroy of England.

The other magnates to whom William would entrust his newly won kingdom in the spring of 1067 were also already in attendance on their master. These were Hugh, lord of Montfort-sur-Risle, his namesake, lord of Grandmesnil, and William fitzOsbern, lord of Breteuil, the duke's seneschal and his oldest friend. The influence of each in England was to be pervasive and enduring. Hugh of Montfort would end his days as a monk at the abbey of Le Bec; but, before religious devotion claimed him, his devotion to William was to be richly blessed with the expropriated lands of Englishmen. Lavish too were to be the endowments of Hugh of Grandmesnil; he would later be accused of deserting the king by returning to Normandy at the importunities of a frustrated wife, but he was to settle eventually in England, the possessor of vast estates and sheriff of Leicester. William fitzOsbern was related to the ducal family through both father and mother; before and after the invasion, he would be the most trusted of William's advisers. In the months to come, he would conquer the Isle of Wight for the duke[15] and receive many English lordships. One of the earliest and most important of the Norman castles, at Norwich, would rise under his guardianship, and the marcher earldom of Hereford would be assigned to him. Earldoms were to be awarded to two more of the known company at the Dives. Robert of Beaumont, eldest son of Roger and heir to one of the most noble titles in Normandy was to be created earl of Leicester; and the representative of a family only recently come to prominence, William of Warenne, would become earl of Surrey, and cement his alliance with the Norman king by marriage to Gundrada, sister of Gerbod of Flanders, and daughter of the queen.

Odo of Bayeux was not the only Norman prelate to win temporal greatness in England in arms with the duke. Geoffrey of Montbrai, bishop of Coutances, was to sail with William and to add to his already considerable wealth the income from more than two hundred and fifty English manors; he may also have held, for a brief period, the earldom of Northumberland. Other names are attested among the nobles now gathered at the Dives. Two were heirs to Norman counties: Geoffrey of Mortagne, son of Rotrou, count of Perche; and William of Evreux, afterwards count of Evreux, grandson of an archbishop of Rouen and a distant cousin of the duke.[16] A closer relative, though of a lesser status, was Gulbert of Auffay, a great-grandson of Duke Richard III and one of the very few Normans who would refuse to profit from the service they accounted duty. Walter Giffard, lord of

Longueville-sur-Scie, was probably the eldest of the duke's supporters and certainly a cause of confusion to chroniclers, who have tended to confound him with his son; this may have been Giffard's second expedition against England, for he may have taken part in Edward's abortive venture in 1035, following the death of Canute. Ralph of Toesni, lord of Conche, was brother-in-law to the seneschal, fitzOsbern, and head of a powerful family. Humphrey of Tilleul was brother-in-law to another of the deputies chosen by William in 1067, Hugh of Grandmesnil, and was to be accused with him in 1068, or 1069, of desertion at the pleading of his wife. William Malet, lord of Graville-Sainte-Honorine, the Norman son of an English mother, tenant of Alkborough in Lincolnshire in the time of Edward, had a role yet to play in the drama that linked his destiny with that of his mother's country.

Little can be said about the remaining Normans who definitely accompanied the duke. Turstin 'the White', son of Rolf, Rollo, or Rou, was to hold estates in the west country of England and possibly in the Welsh marches. The descendants of Engenulf of Laigle would be lords of Pevensey. Robert of Vitot was to die soon after the founding of the Norman kingdom. Five names are known principally from the registers of their transactions with the church in the days prior to the invasion. A moiety-redemption payment of six pounds to Erchembald, son of Erchembald the viscount, is recorded in the cartulary of the abbey of the Holy Trinity at Rouen. The gifts of Gerelm of Panilleuse to the same abbey were to be confirmed by his brother, Oger of Panilleuse. Those of Roger, son of Turold, would be avouched by one of his knights. Osmund of Bodes, a knight, gave a similar donation to the Holy Trinity. A successor of Robert fitzErneis, a kinsman of the Tessons, a great house of central Normandy, would certify his grant to the abbey of Fontenay. Wadard and Vital are two of the few individuals named in the Bayeux tapesty, and Domesday references indicate that they were followers of Bishop Odo. Taillefer, 'Cleaver of Iron', was a juggler or minstrel, called by that nickname and noted for his skill and the quality of his singing.

Foreign allies and mercenaries had arrived in large numbers to swell the Norman host. They had travelled from Britanny and

Flanders, the French provinces and more distant lands. Only two of the allied commanders however, can be identified unquestionably. The more prominent in the near-sighted regard of the Norman chroniclers was Eustace, count of Boulogne, drawn now by the lure of gain. The other had made less noise in the world but was to stand high in the war councils of Duke William : he was Aimeri, viscount of Thouars, who had ridden with his retainers from Poitou. The comital house of Ponthieu, the north-eastern neighbour and satellite of Normandy, was represented by an unnamed knight, a *noble heir of Ponthieu*;[17] this may have been Count Guy himself, the gaoler of Earl Harold in 1064, but the description scarcely fits the ruling lord of the county and it seems more likely that the noble heir was an otherwise unremarked son of Guy, Ivo of Ponthieu.

There were others among the men of Normandy, Britanny and Flanders whose presence in the invading army was historically probable.[18] Of the Normans, two were highly placed and kinsmen of the duke : Robert, count of Eu, was to receive as his guerdon vast estates in Sussex; Richard fitzGilbert would be the ancester of the Clares, earls of Hertford and of Pembroke. Walter Giffard the younger, the son of the lord of Longueville, would be a substantial landowner in England at the time of the Domesday inquest. Geoffrey of Manneville was to become sheriff of Middlesex and to found the family of the Mandevilles. William Patry of La Launde had once welcomed Harold Godwinsson as his guest. Not all the Normans in this secondary listing were nobles. Remigius, almoner of the abbey of Fécamp and afterwards bishop of Lincoln, led the knights sent by his abbot. William Faber, once a smith, a forger of arrow-heads, but now a monk of the house of Marmoutiers, would be entrusted by King William with the first building of the great abbey of Battle. Huon Margot, a monk of Fécamp, may already have been in England, on one of the granges gifted by King Edward to the monastery. Stephen, son of Airadri, was a seaman, the pilot and steersman of the duke's own ship, the *Mora*.

A leader of the Bretons who came to fight for William the Bastard was almost certainly Count Alan the Red, of a family whose possessions stretched through northern and eastern Britanny; the English estates of Alan the Red would centre on the huge 'honour of Richmond' in Yorkshire, and in some later year he was, for reasons now unknown, to conspire with his brother to win the hand of Gunhild, the daughter of King Harold and then a nun at Wilton. Another lord of Britanny who probably served the Norman duke was Ralph of Gael, or of Wader; the son of a Breton mother and an English father, a thegn of Norfolk who had been 'staller'[19] to King Edward, Ralph of Gael would be the only proven English traitor in the Norman host, and he was rewarded for his treason with the earldom of Norfolk, the shire where he may have been born. There were several Flemings whose presence at the Dives was likely. Gerbod of Flanders began the journey towards his brief tenure of an English earldom. Gilbert of Ghent, the son of a Flemish count, would hold broad lands in England, and share with William Malet the guardianship of the first Norman castle at York. From Flanders came also Walter Bec and, in the retinue of Eustace of Boulogne, the brothers Arnold and Geoffrey of Ardres. From the French county of Blois and Chartres, giving away all that he owned, Geoffrey of Chaumont journeyed to win a new fortune by the strength of his arm.

More names might be added : Normans, such as Hugh of Ivry, butler to the duke, Roger Bigot, later sheriff of Norfolk, and the brothers of Ralph of Toesni, Nigel and Robert; the Breton, Count Brian, elder brother of Alan the Red; and the Flemings, Roger Muschamp and his son, Robert, seneschal to Gilbert of Ghent, Drogo of Bevrere, and Adelolf of Marq, who may have come in the train of Arnold of Ardres. But, known and unknown, the thousands who had gathered at the bidding of the duke now rested in the great encampment under the watchful eye of William himself. They waited for a southerly wind, the wind that would give them sea-way for England. While the wind that carried Harald Hardraada towards his western dependencies blew down from the north and east, they waited as the English had waited in the summer months past. Now William of Normandy had to attempt to match the achievement of his rival. His task was both heavier and lighter : heavier, because the army which he led was in the first weeks at least, a rabble of small cliques and regional groups; lighter, because there was not for the Normans the tension of uncertainty, of wondering if and when and where the blow would be delivered, and because eventually the wind must change, and the waiting must end. William had not contemplated more than a short delay, once his army had been brought to a sufficient strength, so he had not allowed for a campaign of inaction. In the storms and incessant rains of August, his arrangements were to be tested to the breaking point.

The froth of words blown about William by his panegyrists obscure the man and his deeds, but it is clear that in August the duke succeeded at least in his primary aims. The many troops became an army. Scarcely to be compared with other captains as a strategist or a tactician in the field, William the Bastard founded his greatness upon two qualities: tenacity in the pursuit of an objective and the ability to inspire in men an almost blind faith in his leadership. His strength of purpose and power of personality operated successfully in minor endeavours as well; and this was to be demonstrated in the month now passing. While the contrary winds detained them, the duke fed the entire army at his own expense and forbade pillaging, forcibly and effectively. *He displayed moderation and wisdom, providing generously to meet the expenses of his own knights and his guests, and allowing no one to take anything by force. People living in that part of the country were able to graze their flocks of sheep and herds of oxen in absolute safety in cultivated fields and tracts of wasteland alike. Harvests stood intact awaiting the scythe without being trampled by arrogant cavalcades of horsemen, or suffering from the surreptitious inroads of foragers. Every man, even the weak and unarmed, could roam the country at will and hum a merry tune from his saddle as he rode along, without having any cause for alarm at the sight of squadrons of knights.*[20] But the days went by without an end to the easterly gales, and the supplies accumulated at the Dives were limited. As he stood on the hills above the crowded river-basin and looked out over the rain-swept sea, Duke William's patience shortened.

*   *   *   *   *

It was about the end of the first week in August when the Norwegian fleet reached Shetland. The ships that brought the Norse king and his followers to the islands resembled the ungainly transports of the Normans only in general layout. They were single-masted and square-sailed, open-waisted, but with raised decks fore and aft. When trouble was not expected, the side-rails of the middle part were hung in decoration with the shields of the crew and at night, while some of the seamen were housed under the forecastle, most were sheltered by a large awning which was drawn over the undecked waist. There were transports, *byrdinger* or 'ships of burden', in the Norwegian invasion force too; the bulk of the fleet, however, consisted of the longships, the warcraft of the Northmen. Long and narrow, the Viking warships lay low in the water compared with some of the huge trading vessels of the Mediterranean nations; they were less seaworthy than the *byrdings*, but they made up in speed and manoeuvrability. As well as the square mainsail they carried a jib or foresail and between the gangways in the waist there were thwarts for the oarsmen who pulled the craft in a dead sea and into action. Even in the lesser ships the Norse crews were not small, and one hundred and twenty men was no unusual complement for a longship. When Earl Thorfinn withdrew from a battle in the Pentland Firth in 1046, there had been on board his 'dragon' seventy corpses and many more men seriously wounded, but still a sufficient crew to equip the vessel for sea. Besides the rowers there were crewmen to relieve at the oars and others to man the fighting decks while the attacking ships closed on their opponents.

Hardraada was ready, if necessary, to fight a battle at sea. The reputation of the English navy was high and if the southern waters had already been cleared of the Norman threat by the time the Norwegians neared Northumbria, the Norse king might well find his way barred by the whole strength of the defending fleet. But there was as yet no danger of an English attack and the most reckless pirate was unlikely to challenge the king and his escort squadron on the short voyage to Orkney. After a stay in Shetland of two or three days at most, Harald embarked again. The ships cleared the mainland and set out across the waste of water that lies between the northern islands and Orkney, the sea-passage that the Northmen called *Dynraust*, the 'thundering, roaring race'.

*　　*　　*　　*　　*

In St. Omer, Tostig awaited the summons of the king to whom he had pledged allegiance. Ships and men waited too, the ships that the earl had managed to gather in the weeks since his return, his remaining English followers and fresh recruits hired in Flanders. The rebel's force did not compare with the fleet which had sailed from Sandwich in May. Many of the Northumbrian exiles had fallen before the onslaught of the Mercian fyrd. Flemings enough had been lost in Lindsey to make the men of Flanders chary of answering too eagerly the new overtures of the English earl, despite the evident favour of their count. But the size of the force was of minor importance; it could be at most a token auxiliary to the huge armament of the Norwegian king. Tostig's presence was his main contribution to the allied effort. Not all the surviving English adherents of the renegade could have been in St. Omer in August. Some had almost certainly been left in Norway, to serve as liaison between earl and king, or surrendered as hostages. Others must have been detached to take word to Scotland of the happenings in the north, and to persuade Malcolm 'Big-nose' of his obligations to his sworn brother. Among those who waited with Tostig were perhaps Copsig and the earl's sons, Skule and Ketel. Copsig, however, known in both Orkney and Flanders, and the most trusted lieutenant of the exile, was the most likely intermediary between Tostig and Hardraada; and the later friendship between Olaf Haraldsson and the sons of Tostig may well have been the fruit of a Norwegian summer. If Skule and Ketel were children of Judith, neither could have been more than fifteen years old in 1066, and Olaf was at most a year or two older. But all three were of a sufficient age to take part in the campaigns of their fathers, and the giving of hostages was a common feature of eleventh-century pledges of alliance.

He was a tall man and a strong, scowling-browed, a great man for words, and the most warlike of men; he had not many friends.[21] Arrogance and self-pride isolated Tostig from the general admiration and liking that came so freely to Harold yet the few who were close to the man loved him fiercely. His marriage with Judith of Flanders was happy and lasting; his sister, as queen, had procured murder on his behalf; King Edward had been ready to wage civil war to protect his favourite; and in the final hours of the exile's life, the brother whom Tostig had betrayed would offer forgiveness for the wrongs done to himself and to England. But there was no room for reconciliation or compromise in the rebel's nature. Tostig fitted into no standard mould. It has been simpler to ignore Tostig, or at least to reduce the role he played in 1066, than to attempt to explain him. The third son of Godwin was a traitor who sold his sword to a foreign adventurer and died in a vain attempt to conquer his native land : to most commentators he has been little else. Yet the vanity, the ambition, the subtlety, the force, and the ability to delude even himself with words and visions of this wayward and scarcely known individual turned awry the course of history; and the legacy of his activities would hinder the growth of English culture and civilisation for one hundred, two hundred, or even five hundred years, the period depending upon the standpoint and interests of the observer. Anglo-Saxon England had become the art-treasury of the western world; under the Normans this heritage was largely lost. Though the witan would continue to forgather in the reign of William, its voice would be hushed; two centuries would elapse before the most rudimentary parliament could meet and speak purposefully again in England. Lanfranc and his successors were to wield ruthlessly and efficiently the power given to them; not until the sixteenth century would the despotism of an alien orthodoxy be lifted from the English spirit. In the late months of 1066, England was to be given over to barbarism, and Tostig would be the main architect of the disaster.

The Northumbrian revolt of 1065 took the north of England from the hands of one of the best soldiers in the nation and gave it into others possibly willing, but certainly inexperienced. Dangerously as this affected the vulnerability of the north-eastern coasts it was the least of the consequences of the revolt. The gemot that exiled Tostig reduced by about a third the power of the Godwinssons and ended their watch on all the most exposed shores of England. It broke the unity of the family and turned Harold's most able collaborator into his most implacable opponent. The pursuit of an alliance against his brother became Tostig's sole purpose. Yet the ride to Denmark brought only rage and disappointment. In Normandy, the chosen ally again failed the impatient earl. The raid on England finished in ruin and near despair. Scotland offered little more than shelter. But the refusal of Swegen of Denmark gave an edge to Tostig's determination. Before disillusion hurried him from Rouen, the renegade spoke powerfully on the Norman duke's behalf. The attacks on Wessex and the eastern shires weakened the English defences and drew the English king into a premature and wasting mobilisation. The voyage to Norway awoke an old dream in the Norse heart and called out against England an enemy that Harold Godwinsson had already discounted.

The influence of Tostig on European and English affairs in 1066 was thus pervasive. But it was more than merely extensive : it was critical. The exile became a catalyst in the deliberations of the other principals. He was the agent whose movements could not be localised, whose intentions were not patent, and whose effective power at any instant was not assessable. Guided not by reason, but by obsession, his activities were the unpredictable factor in the development of events. The very hopelessness of his ventures and his determination persuaded others of a hidden significance beyond their understanding, and this gave his actions importance. In Normandy, Tostig's supporting of Duke William's claims can at most have hastened the compliance of the barons. In England, however, the renegade's attacks on Wessex forced an early strategic decision which might otherwise have been postponed till much later in the summer; hence, if the expedition had not been launched in May, a major autumn invasion of the south coast would probably have been met by an English army well supplied and not staled by months of waiting. Tostig's meeting with Harald Hardraada was similarly critical in timing as well as in effect : there could be little doubt of the outcome if William of Normandy's powerful, but heterogeneous, musters were to encounter the full strength of the English fyrd in Wessex; that they would not do so, would be owed to the exile whose aid the duke had dismissed, and who now awaited the courier of his last and greatest ally.

*   *   *   *   *

Some eighty miles of sea separate Sumburgh Head from Hrossey, the 'island of horses', the mainland of Orkney. The voyage from Shetland took about two days and it was in mid-August that the escort ships of the Norwegian king rounded the south-eastern headland of Hrossey and turned north-west to rejoin the waiting fleet in Scapa Flow. Then as now, this was the principal anchorage in the islands, a vast basin open by many channels to the outer seas, but sheltered on the north and east by the mainland itself, from the Atlantic by Hoy, the 'high island', and southward by the smaller southern islands of the group. Greeted by the earls Paul and Erlend, Hardraada and his company disembarked on the shelving foreshore of the Hamnavoe in the south bight of Hrossey, and made their way to Birsay, in the north-western region of the mainland. Off the coast, but linked to the mainland at low tide, lies the islet of the Brock of Birsay, where Earl Thorfinn had built a church and a castle, the chief residence and stronghold of the great earl and his successors; here Harald's queen and their daughters were to remain until word should come that England had fallen to the king.

Among the first tasks of the royal council must have been to send messengers to Flanders and the Scottish court. The present waiting might be necessary, but it was not in Hardraada's nature to brook delay easily; and there could be small advantage in hesitating once the expedition was under way, with the fleet lying ready in Scapa Flow. The sooner the attack could be made, the more effective would be the surprise and terror of its coming. The longer the confederates held back, the more probable it would be that the English king would learn of his namesake's purpose. Yet, until King Harald had reached Orkney, no certain date could have been fixed for the rendezvous with Tostig off the Northumbrian coast, and much depended upon the earl's collaboration. By the middle of August, the decision must have been taken to leave the islands, weather permitting, in the first days of September. Within hours of the decision, a ship must have sailed, carrying to St. Omer the summons that would bring Tostig to Tynemouth as the first week of September ended. The embassy to Malcolm, king of Scots, was less urgent, but it was likely also to have sailed shortly after the Norse schedule of operations had been agreed. The earls of Orkney held territories in Scotland as fiefs of the Scottish crown and Ingebjorg, Earl Thorfinn's widow, had recently become the wife of King Malcolm. Temporarily

at least relations between the islands and Scotland were friendly;
Earl Paul and his brother were to take part in the approaching
campaign; and though he owed his throne to English arms,[22]
Malcolm had never been a willing vassal of Saxon England.
There were ties of interest between Scotland and Norway and
the invitation of King Harald Sigurdsson to war in the south
must have reinforced the demands of Tostig on his sworn
associate.

The days passed, and the number who sat in the earl's hall on
the Brock of Birsay grew. Tributaries, allies and would-be allies
of the Norwegian king came from all over the north-western
sea-dominion of the Northmen. Like the army of Duke William,
the Norse host was a fusion of men of many lands. In August,
1066, it might have seemed that all the ancient enemies were
poised at once to strike at England. The bonds that linked the
Norse settlements were strong: even stronger was the lure of a
campaign of conquest under the leadership of the most famed
soldier in the north. With the Norwegians, the men of Shetland
and Orkney, and the remaining emissaries of Tostig, there were
captains and fighting men from Iceland and the Faroes, northern
Scotland, the Scottish isles and Ireland. Few, however, can be
identified. From Ireland came a king, the *Ri* of one of the
hundred or more *tuatha*, the petty princedoms into which
the island was divided; he may well have been of Scandinavian origin, but his name is unremembered in the sagas, or
in the Irish chronicles. From distant Iceland, to join the half-
dozen named Norsemen who sailed from Orkney with King
Harald, came Godred Crouan, the son of an Icelandic chief.

*　　*　　*　　*　　*

The armies waited and the tension grew, as the days of August
ran out. In the south, the wind still blew from the east and
storms whipped the Channel, hampering the watch of the
English fleet and holding back any Norman attempt to leave
the estuary of the Dives. Beyond the Dover straits the storms
died out and the seas were calmer. There are no hints in the
sagas of hindrance by weather to the sailing of the ships of the
Norse alliance. North of the straits, too, there was activity to
distract the whole attention of the waiting soldiers from the

fears and boredoms of idleness. In Flanders and Orkney, the final preparations were nearing completion. Almost immediately after the arrival in St. Omer of the messenger from Hardraada, Tostig must have moved to the Flemish port where his ships were lying. There and on Hrossey and in the firth of Forth the last supplies were being embarked. It was a time of apprehension for Judith of Flanders and Elizabeth of Novgorod and the other wives who would be left behind when the allied fleets sailed.

In England and Normandy, it was a time of gathering despair. On either side of the Channel, there were provisions now for days, rather than weeks; with the food-stocks, tempers were shortening and morale was falling away. Murmurs grew against the long delays and there were defections from both armies. In the Dives encampment, Duke William was unshaken in his purpose, he may have feared that before the winds which thwarted him had blown out, another conqueror might have seized the realm he had striven to win. By now word may have come from Flanders of the movement in the north. The shape of the future was hidden, and the duke could not foresee the fate of the great expedition which menaced both Harold of England and himself. William could not have realised how powerfully nature worked on his behalf; how surely the odds that had been so strongly against him were pulling back; how each day forfeited to the evil weather brought success more nearly within the Norman grasp. Across the Channel a different fear was rising. All records suggest that there was in England no awareness of the impending Norwegian attack, and in the English chronicles the excursions of Tostig are lost after the flight to Scotland. But August was ending, and England faced another danger : the harvest was late, and prospects of replenishing the exhausted stores of the nation were threatened. And still the invaders did not come.

SEPTEMBER

B Y the first or second day of September, the vassals summoned by Hardraada had at last assembled in Orkney, the supplies for the voyage were on board, and the fleet was ready. The weather held fair, and a northerly wind blew. The time for leave-taking had come : the captains made their farewells and boarded their ships. Across the broad waters of Scapa Flow, anchors were raised, oars were shipped, and tillers were manned. On the royal 'dragon' the trumpeters blew a long blast, the rowers of the fleet bent to the oars, and the longships and transports moved slowly away from the watchers on Hrossey and Hoy. As the leading vessels slipped through the southern and eastern outlets of the anchorage, Harald Sigurdsson may have looked back towards the low rises that hid Birsay and the castle of the Orkney earls. There, behind the strong walls of the broch, the queen and princesses of Norway waited in safety : the wife whom Harald had first loved when he came as a landless exile to her father's court at Novgorod and the daughters of their union, one of them perhaps closer to the king even than her mother.

The course of the Norse armada ran south-east in its first stage, leaving far to the west the island of Stroma, where the fabled mill of Frotti lay sunk in a whirlpool, churning salt for the world's seas, and, nearer, the Pentland Skerries and northern Caithness. Making about forty nautical miles a day,[1] the fleet drew away from the northern Scottish mainland, to cross the Moray Firth and make landfall again at Rattray Head and Buchan Ness. The shoulder of Buchan must have been turned during the second day out, and the Norsemen then veered west of south, to follow the Scottish coast-line to the Firth of Forth. Such a fleet had seldom been seen in these waters since the days of Canute. By the time Fife Ness was reached, riders from Buchan and the more southerly coasts must have been hurrying news of

the approach of the Vikings to the Scottish court at Dunfermline. On the fifth day of the month at the latest, the Norsemen
entered the Forth estuary, and Hardraada may have pushed up
the firth to anchor that night in the shelter of the bays off
Inverkeithing. It was now that the Scots who were to serve in
the expedition joined the invaders; and it was now too, if ever,
that Harald of Norway met Malcolm, King of Scots. The
coming of the Norse king can scarcely have pleased Malcolm.
Like Swegen of Denmark, Malcolm Canmore sat on a precarious throne, his freedom as an autonomous ruler depending
upon a balance of power among the more powerful states that
surrounded him. Again like Swegen, the Scot was noted for
prudence in all his dealings. There could be no profit for the
Scottish king in a Norwegian conquest of England. His realm
would then be encircled by the Norse dominion, at least during
the lifetime of Harald Sigurdsson, and its independence would
hang upon the whim of the Viking emperor. Yet even now
Malcolm could not afford to offend Hardraada, and, as the
sworn brother of Tostig, he had promised aid to the allies. That
aid he gave in ships and men. If the invasion prospered, this
would be remembered in Scotland's favour; if it failed, the loss
could be borne, and he could repudiate those Scots who fell as
private adventurers. But Malcolm himself would not take part
in the venture. If the Norsemen were victorious, the presence of
the Scottish king would add little to the conquerors' debt to the
Scots; if they were defeated, it could cost his life and bring about
the ruin of his kingdom.

No more than a day can have been spent in the anchorage in
the Forth. Hardraada was impatient, while Malcolm Canmore
had no wish to hinder the Norseman's going. By dawn on the
sixth of September, the uneasy meeting had come to an end. The
Scottish king rode back to his capital, and the Viking fleet moved
eastwards past the coast of Lothian, heading for the open sea
and the two day run south-east to the rendezvous in Tynemouth.

*   *   *   *   *

Another parting had taken place some days before, in a
Flemish port. As the last preparations were being made in
Orkney, seamen in Flanders were readying their ships. The sail-

ing tide came to flood, and again Judith, the once-fortunate wife
of Earl Tostig, favourite of a king and ruler of a quarter of
England, said farewell to the husband whose exile she had
shared, and whose great loss her brother's bounty had helped to
make bearable in the ten months since their banishment. They
had spent little time together in these months. While Tostig had
thrashed about Europe seeking allies against Harold of England,
Judith had remained in Flanders, at Count Baldwin's court, or
in the vice-regal household that had been established for her in
St. Omer. The spring and summer of 1066 were for the countess
a time of suspense and fear, as each rebuff drove her lord further
beyond reason in his quest for vengeance on the brother who
had abandoned him to his enemies. Tostig's return from Norway
must have brought with it an almost unhoped-for relief to the
woman who waited. The countess would wait again, but in the
decision of battle there would be an end to waiting. And the ally
Tostig had found was, in reputation at least, the most powerful
in western Europe. The final goodbyes were made, the earl
passed on board with his sons, Skule and Ketel, and Judith
returned to the long days among her women and the longer
nights alone.

In the Channel the wind was changing now, sweeping up from
the south-west round the cliffs of Kent to the northern sea.
Tostig's ships ran northwards before it, and then beat west
against rising storms towards England. The coast of Northumbria
was sighted, and the little fleet turned north, past the still unsuspecting and undefended shores of the earldoms of Morkere
and Oswulf.[2] On the seventh or eighth day of the month they
came to the narrow estuary of the Tyne and the meeting with
Hardraada.

*   *   *   *   *

In the garrisoned strongpoints along the coasts of Hampshire,
Sussex and Kent, the carefully husbanded supplies had finally
run out. Through the four months of summer, King Harold had
held together the great fyrd of southern England, waiting for an
enemy who did not arrive. The king's commissioners had stripped
Wessex of grain and livestock to meet the needs of the army, and
now the exhausted countryside could give no more. However

questionable the royal authority might be in the northern earldoms, in the lands his father had administered before him the
influence of Harold Godwinsson won him a devotion such as
few leaders had commanded. In May the men of Wessex came
gladly to serve their king. But now necessity outweighed loyalty.
The new harvest was almost ready for gathering, but without
the reapers it would fall and rot in the untended fields. *When
the Nativity of St. Mary came, the men's provisions were
finished, and no one could keep them there any longer.*[3] On or
about the eighth of September, when already far to the north
the first of his enemies were launching the attack on England,
King Harold gave orders for the fyrd to be disbanded, and for
the fleet to return to the Thames.

The king himself rode back to London. It seems possible that
his route may not have been direct, but that he may have followed the south coast as far as Hastings, if not beyond, before
turning north through the forest tracks of the Andredsweald.
This is suggested by scattered allusions in the chronicles of these
months, both English and Norman. The close guard on the
Channel was ended; but, after the efforts of the summer months,
it is unlikely that in early September such a captain as Harold
Godwinsson would abandon Sussex and Kent to fate. The winds
were changing, and there were storms in the southern sea, but
the weather alone could not promise security. Although the great
mass of the fyrd was gone, the housecarls remained under
Harold's immediate command. If they could not prevent a
Norman landing, strategically positioned they could at least
hinder it, and, more significantly, they might succeed in channel-
ling the direction of its thrust.

Some details of the defence of the south after the disbanding
of the fyrd are certified by the records of the time. The Isle of
Wight and southern Hampshire, covering the approaches to
Winchester and the heart-land of Wessex, were still protected.[4]
Along the coast of Sussex, particularly eastwards from Beachy
Head to the wide, marshy bay where the flats of Dungeness now
lie,[5] the defensive troops were withdrawn, and the castles and
forts on which they had been based destroyed, or rendered useless
as refuges for an invading army.[6] East of the bay of the Rother
and the Brede, however, from Romney to Dover and beyond,

the chain of guard was maintained,[7] principally by the men of the ports themselves, though at first perhaps with a stiffening of housecarls.

Duke William was unlikely to follow the example of Tostig and strike first against the Isle of Wight. It lay too far to the west, when even a moderate sea might bring disaster upon the invaders, injuring their horses sufficiently to cripple the later movements of the army. To that extent the west could be considered secure. East of Romney, however, a successful landing would be dangerous. The country was more or less open, and the duke, once ashore, would have a clear run north-west through northern Kent to the Thames and London. Such a freedom of manoeuvre on the part of the invader had to be prevented at all cost, until the fyrd could be regrouped and Harold could face William in the field. Hence, the main English power must be concentrated in Kent, and, since a Norman invasion could no longer be warded off at all points, the king's best hope lay in directing the enemy attack into a region where its initial impetus would be blunted and, if possible, contained, more by the physical nature of the terrain than by the expenditure of troops. The required conditions were offered by East Sussex, in the hinterland of the deceptively attractive base-ports of Pevensey and Hastings.

Between Beachy Head and the Fairlight Cliffs that marked the south-eastern limit of the Hastings peninsula, lay the tidal lagoons of Pevensey and Bulverhythe and the harbour of Hastings itself. For some ten miles inland from the coast the countryside was gently undulating, green, and only lightly wooded. But it was a siren's welcome that this land gave to the invader. To the west, his way was blocked by the Sussex marshes, curving up through the rape of Chichester to the South Downs and the western reaches of the Andredsweald, the forest of Andred. To the north the great forest continued, stretching through the present counties of Hampshire, Surrey, Sussex and Kent, almost from Winchester to Canterbury, thrusting southwards within a mile of the coast north-east of Hastings. There were paths through the forest, but they were not paths that could be taken by an army, particularly a mounted army, in a strange land and in constant danger of ambush and attack. The region was a trap for the unwary and the ill-informed. Still more perilous was the only defensible position the country afforded: the Hastings peninsula.

Today the Sussex coast curves with scarcely a break north-east from Beachy Head to Rye Bay, but most of that coastline and much of the land behind has been won from the sea over the past nine centuries.[8] The tidal lagoon of Bulverhythe and the great bay that covered the present promontory of Dungeness and reached inland from Fairlight and Romney to Appledore and Tenterden have already been mentioned. These helped to form the peninsula on which eleventh-century Hastings stood. On a modern map the boundaries of the peninsula may still be traced: north, the river Brede; east, the lost bay north from Fairlight; south, the sea; west, Bulverhythe and the streams which fed it. The Brede was then much broader than it is now, and it was tidal as far as Sedlescombe, six miles north of Hastings town. The river flowed into the eastern bay near the site of present-day Winchelsea. Bulverhythe lagoon ran north from the sea almost to Crowhurst, a manor some two miles north-west of Hastings. Between Fairlight and Bulverhythe the sea-coast followed more or less the line it does now. The peninsula covered approximately fifty square miles, and consisted mainly of the ridge that runs north-west from Fairlight Cliffs to Ash-down in the Weald and the slopes on either side of the ridge. The isthmus was about four miles in width at high tide between Sedlescombe and Crowhurst. Its effective width, however, was considerably less, for much of the land about the Brede and the Bulverhythe streams was marshy, and the drops into the marsh-land were steep. The exit from the peninsula was at its narrowest before Battle Hill, where the northern and western waters diverge, and Fairlight Ridge is broken and falls away from Tetham Hill into the 'sand-lake' that gave a local name to the battle soon to be fought there.

Among the apocrypha that have encrusted the story of the last Saxon king is the legend that Harold, on his journey to London in early September, 1066, paused on Battle Hill and told those who rode with him that here he would meet William of Normandy. With its trappings of hindsight, the tale is both untrustworthy and unsatisfactory, but it accords with the known character of the English leader that he should supervise in person the devolvement of the summer defensive chain, and set the pattern of the later defence on its own ground. He can scarcely have hoped to drive the Normans into the Hastings trap, but Duke William *might* land in that area. Crowhurst was one of Harold's own manors and he must have known the country about Hastings well. If the king must offer battle to the invader, it was obviously preferable to do so on a position of his own choosing. The Roman castle of Anderida still existed at Pevensey, but the small peninsula on which it stood was practically inaccessible except by sea. Unless the Norman commander were to choose a wholly defensive role, Pevensey was useless to his purpose. If the adversary could be brought to East Sussex, either by his own folly, or by the actions of the king, it would not be at Anderida that he would establish his camp, but at Hastings. Once within the trap, he could be held helpless by an English army strongly stationed on Battle Hill, while the English fleet came from the east to cut his only avenue of escape. That Harold lured his enemy first to Pevensey, and thence to Hastings and Senlac, cannot be asserted. That William of Normandy came there cannot be denied.

*   *   *   *   *

The combined Norse and allied fleets now numbered more than three hundred ships, under the unified command of Harald Sigurdsson and Tostig. The commanders did not linger in Tynemouth. Nothing was to be gained by delay, and already messengers might be on their way to Durham and York with news of the coming of the Northmen. The invaders sailed swiftly south, past the still undefended shores of Oswulf's earldom to the estuary of the Tees, and made their first landings in Cleveland, the north-easterly region of Morkere's earldom, between the Tees and the Esk. The hinterland was ravaged, and the whole district was brought to submission with little, if any, opposition. The next landing, however, encountered more than a token defence. At Scarborough, *the weather fell calm and they lay there the night over*.[9] But when King Harald demanded the surrender of the port, it was refused, and the Northumbrians met the invaders in arms. The resistance was brave and initially successful, but, against such a force as Hardraada led, it was hopeless. The old town of Scarborough was dominated by a high cliff. Whether the Northumbrian leaders did not recognise the importance of the position, or could not spare the men to defend it, cannot be stated, but the Norwegian king seized the opportunity the defenders had allowed him. When the early onslaught was beaten off, Hardraada sent part of the army to take the height. On its crest the Norsemen raised a huge pyre and set fire to it. *And when the pile was in clear flame, his men took large forks and pitched the burning wood down into the town, so that one house caught fire after the other.*[10] The resistance faltered and failed, and Scarborough surrendered. The submission came too late. King Harald gave the town to his men, to kill and plunder as they willed.

The country about Scarborough now hurried to submit to the allies, but the warning had gone out to the more southerly reaches of the Northumbrian coast and westward to York and Earl Morkere. The ultimate destination of the invasion cannot yet have been clear, but in Holderness the local levies were gathering. When word came to York of the Norse ravages and of the huge size of the enemy fleet, Morkere sent immediately for aid to his brother Edwin in Mercia, and within hours too couriers were speeding south to King Harold in London. They would not reach Westminster for several days; meanwhile Hardraada was moving south again. After the sacking of Scarborough the Norse king did not return to his ships, but continued by land with the bulk of the army, presumably holding to the coast, his route paralleled by the fleet. He passed the eastern slopes of the low hills of the East Riding, along Filey Bay and by Flamborough Head into the broad coastal plain of Holderness, and there he found his way barred by the fyrd of the East Riding. Against the allied army the local troops could hope to fight no more than a delaying action, and the invaders crushed them with little effort. The small battle was enough, however, to cancel any intentions Hardraada and Tostig may have had of marching directly against York, and after the defeat of the levies the army was embarked again. The southward voyage continued, until about the middle of the month when the armada rounded Ravenspur to enter the broad estuary of the Humber.

* * * * *

As the four-month vigil along the English coast drew to its close, William's situation in the encampment above the Dives was worsening rapidly. After less than two months, supplies to the Norman camp were already becoming short,[11] and if they failed, even Duke William would be unable to restrain the mercenaries at least from pillage. As it was, the long idleness, broken only by drilling, was producing disaffection among the followers of the duke. *This prince, whom neither the delay caused by contrary winds, nor the terror of shipwreck, nor the cowardly defection of several of those who had sworn loyalty, had succeeded in shaking from his purpose,*[12] might remain true to his ambition. William might also count on the unswerving devotion of the Norman barons, whose fortunes were bound inextricably with his own. But his less dedicated supporters would not await indefinitely the fulfilment of his promises to them. And now, within weeks, the equinoctial gales might come to end all thoughts of the campaign against England until the passing of winter. The time had come when even defeat would be more bearable than continued inaction.

The sign for which the duke had waited came at last. Early in September the weather changed. It was in the second week of September, on or about the twelfth day of the month, that the trumpets sounded in the Norman camp. The supplies, machines of war, and horses were hurried aboard the waiting transports; and, urged on by their officers, the men who had waited so long for this moment followed. The devout duke made his last devotions and hastened to the *Mora*. There was good cause for prayer and better for haste. The weather had not settled fair, and they must sail while the wind lasted. The army was on board, and on the *Mora* the trumpets sounded again. The sails were unfurled and the ships stood out from the shelter of the estuary towards the open sea.

As he waited impatiently off the Dives for the fleet to regroup, Duke William did not know, and could not have known, that only a day or two before the English naval forces too had received their sailing orders. These were simple : to return to London, and there to refit. They must also have been galling : after four months of cruising the Channel, conscious of their supremacy at sea and eager to engage the expected enemy, the English captains were required to return tamely to base. The nature of the orders was clear; their interpretation, however, rested with the commanders. It is probable that such men would make of their last sweep of those summer months a defiant demonstration of power, at once a threat and a challenge to the would-be conquerors of England. King Harold had gone back to his capital, and the great fyrd had melted away, but a gesture could still be made by the fleet swinging south-eastwards from Wight in a wide and belligerent sortie through the central waters of the Channel before the ships turned northwards for Thanet and the Thames.

The Norman armada pushed north-east into the narrow sea; and somewhere between Cap d'Antifer and Beachy Head the two fleets met. The date, the time and the location of the battle that took place are lost; but the engagement appears to have been brought to an end by the sudden rising of a storm. It could not have come too soon for the Normans. Losses on both sides were heavy, but the quality of the ships involved made it inevitable that the invaders' losses should be greater. Among the English ships, several were damaged, and a thegn of Essex who took part in the action, Aethelric of Kelvedon, died, from the effects of a wound, soon after the fleet reached London.[13] Another of the Englishmen was to suffer less directly. Neither as duke nor as king was William the Bastard noted for a forgiving nature, and those wanton enough actually to raise arms against him remained his foes even when their power to menace was destroyed. The Norfolk thegn, Eadric, who had commanded under Edward and presumably retained his authority under Harold, fled, an outlaw, to Denmark on William's accession.[14] It seems likely that he led the fleet in the Channel skirmish. The Norman losses are undetailed, but that they were considerable will appear later; and it may have been in this action that the first to die of the duke's named companions met his fate : Roger, son of Turold.[15] The storm rose, the English commander broke off the engagement, and the Norman fleet ran south-east past

Upper Normandy to the haven of St. Valery on the broad estuary of the Somme in Ponthieu.

* * * * *

King Harold came back to London, the city which had grown, almost within the short course of his reign, to be the centre of England. The city still bustled with the business of peace, as yet unaware that two enemies had launched massive assaults upon the kingdom. Nor could the king know that, while the seemingly more immediate challenger had been beaten off, the less expected was striking, almost unopposed, against the heart of his most northerly province. After the long neglect of the summer months, there were urgent matters of civil administration to be seen to; and there were revised strategies of defence and retaliation to be studied. These last days of false peace were not made easier by a severe illness, possibly gout, which had come suddenly upon the king.[16]

It was still before the middle of the month when the battered English fleet reached London, to anchor below London bridge, off Southwark. Magnified by the boasting of the seamen, the news spread within hours through the markets and ale-houses of the city: the navy had intercepted Duke William's armada, and the power of Normandy was destroyed. From Westminster, King Harold himself hurried to the ships to welcome the victors. What followed is conjecture; but it offers an explanation of what are otherwise the least explicable happenings of the year: the actions of Harold in the first weeks of October, 1066. The report of the fleet commanders was necessarily more sober than the rumour of the streets. But only in part: modesty has never been a notable characteristic of military leaders. The enemy had not been destroyed, but he had been badly mauled. The Norman loss in ships and men had been considerable; and when the storm arose, the survivors had fled westward before the wind, away not only from the English, but even from Normandy itself. If Duke William were able to attack again before the winter gales put an end to his hopes for this year, it would be with a force so reduced that he must be crushed.

The king was still with the fleet when the couriers from the north arrived. *Then King Harold, to the south, was told when he came from the ships that King Harald of Norway and Earl Tostig had come up near York.*[17] The brief triumph was over; but it was with a renewed confidence that Harold set about the preparations to meet the northern threat. He threw off the sickness that had almost crippled him, so rapidly that those about him accounted the cure miraculous; and some attributed it to divine intervention, with the ghost of King Edward interceding on his successor's behalf. The housecarls were recalled from the south, and the fyrd of Wessex and the southern midlands was mustered again. For the time being, it seemed that the south was safe; but in the north, half of Northumbria was already under the invader's hand, and the Norsemen pillaged at will. The preparations were more rapid than even those who had known earlier service with Harold Godwinsson could remember. Before the third week of the month ended, the English king marched with his army to meet the challenge of Hardraada and his own brother.

* * * * *

The abbey of Leucone had been founded early in the seventh century by St. Walaric, who brought the gospel to much of northern Gaul. On his death, the body of the evangelist had been enshrined in the abbey minster, and in time the original name of the house gave way to one commemorating the canonised founder. The abbey stood on a low cliff above the estuary of the river Somme, and below it grew a small town which likewise became known by the title of the establishment which dominated it : St. Valery-sur-Somme. By the middle of the eleventh century the influence and wealth of the abbey of St. Valery were great; the advocate of the monastery was a distant kinsman of Duke William himself, and Gulbert of Auffay, who sailed with the duke, was of the same family. The house lay within the domain of the counts of Ponthieu, but Count Guy, who had once been imprisoned by William, and who had later been the gaoler of Earl Harold, was now a faithful adherent of the Norman duke.

On the twelfth of September the Norman fleet entered the mouth of the Somme and anchored below St. Valery. As the English captains had reported, the invaders had been mauled, and it was a dispirited army that went ashore from the storm-wracked ships. But the English commanders had exaggerated their victory: the invasion fleet was damaged, but not crippled. The losses in men and supplies had been high, but not critical. Perhaps two thousand had died, or had fled in the aftermath of the disaster; but some of these could be replaced, and the power still under Duke William's hand was not as negligible as the English shipmen had allowed their king to believe. More significantly, the duke's confidence may have been bruised, but his belief in his destiny and his determination were unshaken. With the energy and tenacity which were his most constant characteristics, he set about restoring the morale of his supporters and replenishing the stores on which their continued service immediately depended. *Warding off adverisity by prudence, he kept secret as far as possible the deaths of those whom the waves had engulfed and had them buried in secret. Accumulating supplies from day to day, he put an end to scarcity. By various encouragements he rallied those who were yielding to fear and restored heart to the faint-hearted.*[18] Meanwhile, new followers were coming to swell the army. A monk of Fontanelle, an abbey near Rouen, arrived at St. Valery with a gift from the abbot, and, gaining access to William, *placed at the service of his expedition twelve chosen youths, mounted and armed with a hundred marks for the expenses.*[19]

The duke was soon ready to try again. The weather, however, remained obdurate: *it was cold and wet, and the sky was dark with clouds and rain.*[20] From day to day, the weather-cock on the abbey tower decided William's emotion: if the south wind blew, he came back joyfully from the church; if the north wind suddenly rebuffed the south, his tears flowed down and his face was wet with grief. The pious duke did not neglect the help that Heaven could give. There were more and more prayers and ceremonies. The duke *struggled with the sacred arms of prayer even to the point of having the body of St. Valery, a confessor well pleasing to God, carried processionally out of the basilica in order to obtain that a contrary wind should give place to a favourable one.*[21] The shrine was placed on a carpet on the plain, and the whole army knelt before it. A little celestial bribery was tried to speed the intercession of the saint. The offerings of the worshippers were so liberal that the relics were buried beneath them. But the days passed, the prayers and offerings were not acknowledged, and still the north wind blew.

* * * * *

The Norse fleet pushed up the broad waters of the Humber, past the northern flats and the foothills of the Wolds, and on into the narrow, twisting channel of the Ouse. Under the guidance presumably of Tostig their objectives were now clear : to attack York, and cut the lines of communication between Northumbria and the south. The first landing in this phase of the campaign appears to have been made on the right bank of the river, near the site of the later Norman foundation of Selby, where there was a church dedicated to St. Wilfrid. However, the area was then heavily forested and offered no secure base for operations against York; on the following day the invaders took to the ships again. The further voyage was short, and the Norsemen anchored finally on the left bank of the river, close to the village of Riccall. The country here was more open, and the allies were now only some ten miles from York itself by road. The anchorage served a subsidiary purpose : to guard against surprise by a Northumbrian fleet. The advance had met no opposition since the victory in Holderness, but there were probably warships at the disposal of Earl Morkere. Too weak to challenge the enemy, the Northumbrian naval force could do no more than retire watchfully before them into the Ouse, and then into the tributary stream of the Wharfe and to Tadcaster, where they were to lie throughout the campaign.[22]

The Norse anchorage lay a mile or so below the junction of the Wharfe and the Ouse, effectively barring any nuisance tactics by the Northumbrian ships. Hardraada and Tostig at once began their preparations for the assault on York. But the easy progress was ended. About a week had passed since word was brought to Earl Morkere of the coming of the invaders. The torpor that seems to have possessed the earl since the visit of King Harold to the north and the marriage in York of the king and Alditha gave place suddenly to a frenzy of activity. The carelessness of half a year was to be redeemed. From all of central and western Northumbria the fyrd was summoned; and before the Norsemen were ready for their march on the northern city, Morkere's brother Edwin had arrived in York with large contingents of the Mercian fyrd. In the army that waited to defend the Northumbrian capital there were the people of six counties, many thousands of men, among them priests as well as laymen. When the report reached the city of the landing at Riccall, the earls chose their site of battle. They would meet the invaders beyond the walls, south-east of York, at Gate Fulford.

At the present time, two roads lead from Riccall to York, and both probably follow the ancient trackways of the eleventh century. One of these closely parallels the river Ouse, through the villages of Stillingfleet and Naburn, while the other runs more directly northwards through Escrick. Both routes would be used by a large army moving on York along the left bank of the Ouse. A little more than two miles south of the city, however, the roads converge before Gate Fulford and, in 1066, a single way then continued north on a low ridge or causeway sloping down to the river on the west and to a watery ditch and marshland on the east. This was a good defensive position, provided the defenders' line could be held. Attack would be restricted to a fairly narrow front; and the numbers of the invading army, compressed by the convergence of the roads, might prove more an encumbrance than an advantage. But both Edwin and Morkere lacked experience of war, and there is small indication that they intended a defensive battle. The impetuosity of the Northumbrians was proverbial; and if, in the excitement of a partial success, the brother earls allowed a weakening of their general line, courage would avail the English little against tacticians as skilful as Hardraada and Tostig.

On the morning of the vigil of St. Matthew, Wednesday, the twentieth of September, King Harald of Norway and Earl Tostig set out from Riccall with the main bulk of their army. It was still early in the day when the Norsemen reached Gate Fulford, to find the forces of the two earls advancing towards them. With a readier eye for terrain than his opponents could hope to boast, the king ordered an immediate halt, seizing the advantage of the ground, and drew up his men in battle order. Apart from the absence of cavalry, this was Macedonian in structure. The banner of the Land-Ravager was raised beside the river, and the greater mass of the Norwegians was arrayed about it. There Hardraada commanded in person, and with him stood Eystein Orre, his prospective son-in-law, and possibly Olaf, his young son and heir. The centre and right wing of the army stretched thinly across the rising ground and down to the ditch and the bog, under the leadership of Tostig. The Northumbrians may have halted briefly when the enemy was first sighted, but they were soon moving forward again, slowly, with all their troops in line. The earls were committed to attack. Edwin of Mercia apparently led the English right against King Harald, his younger brother commanding on the left.

The initial shock was delivered by Earl Morkere against the allied right. The fighting was hard and the resistance was stubborn but this was the least protected part of the Norse front and here the English advantage was greater. As the Northumbrians pressed forward, the enemy gradually gave way before them; *and the Englishmen followed, thinking the Northmen would fly. The banner of Earl Morkere advanced them bravely.*[23] But Tostig's withdrawal was not a rout, and although here and there small groups of the attackers penetrated the defensive screen, the Northmen did not fly. In the dust and confusion, clamorously jubilant and confident, the raw English levies thrust on. Towering over the men about him Hardraada watched the struggle beside the ditch, until the moment for which he had waited came at last. The Northumbrian left was now firmly within the trap. The king ordered the charge to be sounded, and struck with his main strength against Edwin and the weakened centre of the defenders' line. For a time the Englishmen resisted bravely, but their situation was hopeless. The centre broke, King Harald turned to destroy the right wing, and Eystein Orre attacked the rear of Morkere's division. Clustered about their leaders, the Northumbrians continued to defend themselves, but the issue was decided. While Hardraada was driving the remnants of Earl Edwin's troops into the river, Eystein and Tostig made such slaughter among the English left wing that the ditch was *so filled with dead that the Norsemen could go dry-foot over the fen.*[24] Soon the rout became general, and the Northumbrian survivors fled before their conquerors to York.

The battle at Gate Fulford destroyed the power of the north of England to resist the invaders. When the dust settled, and the Norsemen rested on their swords and axes, Harald Sigurdsson had lost many men, but the fyrd of the Northumbrians and Mercians had ceased to exist. Among the dead were the bodies of a hundred priests. The day's work was not yet done: Harald was too experienced a general not to consolidate a victory so dearly won. Sending part of the army back to the ships under the brothers Eystein and Nicholas Thorbergsson, presumably with the wounded, Hardraada and Tostig continued their interrupted journey, *and entered York with as great a force as seemed to them necessary*.[25] There was no will to oppose them among the last defenders. Harald's terms were not harsh: he demanded provisions and hostages, and offered the Northumbrians a lasting peace in return for their allegiance in his campaign against the southern earldoms and King Harold Godwinsson. The city was not sacked, and the lives even of those who had fled from Gate Fulford were not threatened. It was a wise policy: if the war lasted into the winter, Hardraada would need the city as a base of operations, and the compliance of the people among whom his army would be billeted.

The citizens of York had no option but to accept the terms given. It must have appeared now that Tostig's promise to King Harald was redeemed; but few of the English leaders, who heard the requirements of the Norwegian king before their city, could have welcomed the scowling earl who stood at the king's right hand. The wording of the chronicles[26] suggests that Edwin of Mercia may have been taken captive after Fulford, but that Morkere escaped the slaughter by the ditch. If the earl had been present at York, it is unlikely that even Hardraada's protection would have saved him from the vengeance of Tostig. While Earl Morkere remained at large, the surrender of York could not guarantee the subservience of all Northumbria to the allies. Further clauses were added to the armistice conditions. On the morning of Monday, the twenty-fifth of September, King Harald would meet the Northumbrian representatives again. On that day, hostages would be brought to the Norsemen from the whole province, officers would be appointed to rule in Harald

Sigurdsson's name, and the king would allot fiefs to his supporters. This gemot was arranged to take place at the crossing
of the river Derwent known as Stamford Bridge.

The supplies provided by the city were carried to the conquerors, by a hundred and fifty hostages. These were chosen
by the king's ally from *the children of the most considerable
persons; for Earl Tostig was well acquainted with all the people
of that town.*[27] Hardraada had accomplished his primary aim,
and he retired to Riccall and the security of the ships. The king
was very merry: on the coming Monday, the subjection of
Northumbria would be concluded, and Harald need not look
for further warfare in the north. In the weeks of Autumn, the
Norse army could recuperate and refit, readying themselves for
the long march south and the final struggle with King Harold
of England.

*   *   *   *   *

The northward march of Harold Godwinsson in September,
1066, ranks with the greatest military movements of history; in
distance, speed and number of troops involved, it was without
parallel or precedent in its own time. Only part of the army was
mounted. Saddle-horses were standard equipment of the housecarls and the thegns of the select fyrd; but the lowlier followers
of the king, archers and spearsmen, seldom possessed armour,
harness, or horses. Travelling day and night, the fyrd of Wessex
thrust north along the ancient Roman highway to York, gathering as they went reinforcements from the earldoms of Leofwine,
Gyrth and Waltheof and the southern shires of Mercia. It is
probable that Leofwine himself was left in command in the
south, while Gyrth rode with his royal brother. Among the
other leaders of the army were possibly Earl Waltheof and
Bondig the Staller. The main strength of central and southern
England was marching with the king, and to swell the levies
came volunteers from parts as distant as Worcestershire. Before
the host reached the borders of Northumbria, it was joined by
men hurrying south: survivors of the disaster at Gate Fulford,
and those who would not submit to the Norse conquerors.

The news of the defeat of the northern earls could only spur
King Harold to greater urgency. The tempo of the march quick-

ened. Arrayed in seven divisions, the wearying army entered Northumbria some distance east of the royal manor of Conisbrough, probably early on the Saturday after the battle at Fulford. Moving north-west, the troops crossed the Don near Doncaster, and pushed on to ford the Aire near the junction of that river with the Calder, at present-day Castleford. Beyond the Aire, the road ran due north for several miles, then turned sharply north-east to reach the Wharfe at Tadcaster. On Sunday, the twenty-fourth of September, the English king came to the little river-town and halted his host before the final stage of the journey to York. Like other great captains whose successes have been founded on mobility, Harold Godwinsson possessed the ability to manoeuvre with a rapidity almost inconceivable to more static commanders. This aspect of generalship has seldom been so vividly demonstrated as in the campaign of King Harold against the Norse invaders. In little more than a week, the English army had covered more than a hundred and eighty miles. Their presence in the north was unknown and unlooked-for. The swiftness of the march had cloaked the operation with an open secrecy, and had ensured for Harold's later actions the powerful tactical advantage of surprise.

This was the contingency for which the Norse leaders had not allowed in their plan of conquest. When the English forces were fully assembled at Tadcaster, King Harold drew them up in order of battle. Refugees from York informed the king of the capitulation of the city. If Harald Hardraada were aware of the coming of the southern English, now would be the time for him to attack, before his challengers were rested after the rigours of their march. But there was no Norse onslaught along the ten-mile *High Street* from York. The Norwegian king had not even posted outriders on the approaches to the northern capital; no possible threat to his mastery of the north could have arisen in the four days since his destruction of the Northumbrian and Mercian fyrd. The hours of Sunday passed, and it became clear that no immediate danger menaced the exhausted English troops. The men stood down, and sentries were posted. That same evening, leaving the majority of his army encamped at Tadcaster, King Harold rode on with his housecarls to York. The northern progress he had made with Bishop Wulstan in the early months of his reign now bore fruit. The city which so recently had given its bludgeoned assent to the peace terms of the conqueror welcomed the king with joy. Guards were set so that no intelligence could leak to the enemy, and Harold sat again in council with the Northumbrian lords.

* * * * *

The morning of Monday, the twenty-fifth of September, was fine and promised, once the early mists had risen, to be unusually sunny and very warm. The Norsemen were wakened at dawn and breakfasted hurriedly, for there were some fourteen miles to travel before the business of the day could begin. The gemot which was to establish the rule of Harald Sigurdsson in Northumbria was unlikely to be other than peaceful; but English representatives who had not been at Fulford or York on Wednesday would meet at Stamford Bridge, and Hardraada and Tostig intended that they recognise fully the power of the invaders. They ordered two-thirds of the Norse and Flemish warriors to accompany their commanders to the council, the others to remain by the ships at Riccall. The trumpets were sounded for landing; and when the men were all ashore, King Harald chose his companions. Tostig and most of the allied leaders went with the king. In titular charge of the fleet, Harald left his young son, Olaf, and to advise the prince, the earls Paul and Erlend of Orkney, Eystein Orre, the 'gorcock', and Eystein's brother, Nicholas Thorbergsson.

The day promised well. It was to be no more than a cheerful parade in the autumn sun, a show of strength and military arrogance. Without weapons the Norsemen would have been naked; they took with them from the ships their helmets and shields, their spears, swords and axes, and many carried bows and arrows. But the morning was brightening rapidly, and before the men were ready to march, armour became uncomfortable. Ignoring the objections of Tostig, who had small cause to trust the Northumbrians, all but a few of the soldiers laid aside their byrnies, the knee-length coats of leather, sewn with iron rings and studs, which were the standard harness of the age throughout western Europe. King Harald himself set the example, discarding the mail-coat which he called Emma. The trumpets sounded again. Across the fields to the Derwent and along the west bank of the river, the army moved north to the crossing at Kexby, and so north again, east of the river, to Stamford Bridge.[28]

The place chosen for the gemot lies about eight miles north-east of York, on the road which runs from the city through Gate Helmsley towards Bridlington. Here the river Derwent, narrow above and below, broadens suddenly into shallows in a valley approximately a quarter of a mile wide. On either side of the reeded and sluggish stream the land rises to featureless plateaus little more than fifty feet above the Derwent. To the west the slope is very gradual, reaching the brow of the ridge at Gate Helmsley a mile or so away. On the left bank the rise is more rapid to the higher ground still known as Battle Flats. The construction of a weir at the east end of the village and of a lock a few miles downstream has made the river deeper than it was in the eleventh century; but the shallows are still fordable, and there lie the stones which gave the crossing its oldest name of Stamford. The present bridge was built in the eighteenth century south-west of the village, replacing a mediaeval structure which bridged the western end of the shallows. The first bridge, however, was almost certainly built by the Romans at a considerable distance from either of these, to cross the narrower course of the Derwent some way north of the shallows. The engineers of the legions disliked unnecessary detours, and the site can be placed fairly accurately on the line of the Bridlington road which follows the Roman highway before and after the village. The events of the battle suggest that the wooden bridge of 1066 occupied the same site as its predecessor.

Stamford Bridge, farther from Riccall than York, seems at first an awkward choice of meeting-place for the submission of Northumbria. There were, however, several likely reasons for its selection. Until the harrying of the north by the Norman barbarian in 1069, the Vale of York was relatively densely populated, and Stamford Bridge offered an excellent centre both for the gathering of fresh supplies and for the reception of the promised hostages from the distant parts of the province. At least five Roman roads converged on the crossing. West of the river, the highway from York was joined by another from

Northallerton and the western districts of the North Riding. East of the bridge, the York road ran on to Bridlington and Holderness, while the route from the north-west continued south-east through Market Weighton and past the western slopes of the Wolds to Brough on the Humber. A little over a mile from the crossing, a branch of the Bridlington road led north-eastwards to Malton and thence to the rich Vale of Pickering, beyond the northern limits of the Wolds. There were other considerations to inspire the choice of Stamford Bridge. The chronicles indicate that the business of the gemot was to include the formal surrender of York. If, as seems likely, the armistice-terms agreed after Gate Fulford guaranteed the city against sack, the move gave added protection from the Norse soldiery, plunder-hungry and never easily controllable even by such a commander as Harald Hardraada. Again, less than three miles above the bridge, on a mound overlooking the Derwent, there stood an ancient palace of the Northumbrian kings; this may have been designated as the residence and headquarters of the allied leaders during their stay in the north.

It was about mid-morning when the conquerors reached Stamford Bridge. The sun was now high, and the air shimmered in the heat of the day. The Northumbrian representatives had not yet arrived at the meeting-place; but it was early, and there was no cause for anxiety. The long walk from Riccall was over, and Hardraada gave the men leave to rest. At ease and confident, the Norsemen threw themselves down on the warm grass, drinking in the autumn sunshine, or wandered by the river, or up on the flats where far to the east the Wolds glimmered against the sky-line. In the pastures beside the Derwent cattle were grazing, and the more energetic of the troops scattered to herd them in. Discipline was relaxed; neither scouts nor guards were posted; and while the leaders and their attendants and the larger part of the army remained east of the river, many of the herders crossed the ford and the bridge to carry off the cattle on the slopes of the right bank. But battle-gear is cumbersome, and shields and spears could only hinder the chase. Most of the hunters left some at least of their accoutrements in the care of their less active comrades. The late morning passed lazily; the laughter and the eager cries of the herdsmen rang across the leas; and it was nearing midday when the keenest of the watchers saw above the crest of the rise a mile to the west a growing cloud of dust.

The dust-cloud thickened and spread as men on horseback spilled down over the ridge, and in the gathering haze the noon sun flashed on shields and armour. Unsure of what he saw, King Harald Sigurdsson called Earl Tostig to his side. The dark-browed exile was bitter: the Norsemen had disregarded his warnings; now they would learn how his countrymen were to be trusted. Still the king waited in indecision, unwilling or unable to believe that he would have to fight again to hold his conquest, less than five days after the northern resistance had shattered against his shield-wall at Fulford. But the unknown horsemen rode swiftly, and behind them pressed foot-soldiers, column upon column, until the glitter of their weapons seemed to sheet the western slopes with ice. The thunder of the hooves could be heard now, and on the far side of the river the laughter of the cattle-gatherers died and they turned to look westwards in dismay. Even yet Harald hesitated, until at last the banners that waved above the riders became clear to the sight. There in the sunlight shone the devices of the English king, the golden dragon of Wessex and the fighting man of Harold Godwinsson, *woven in threads of purest gold*;[29] and Hardraada knew that he had to face the one enemy whose power could challenge his own, the enemy he had dismissed as a distant threat, to be met on a field far to the south and on a day of the Viking's choosing.

The surprise was complete. When the English army passed through York on that Monday morning, King Harold of England had already wrested the initiative from his namesake; and when the vanguard of the fyrd crested the ridge at Gate Helmsley, the loyalty of the northern subjects of the king was proved. The invaders were taken unaware, caught wholly unprepared for battle and carelessly dispersed on both sides of the Derwent. A mere hundred or so wore body-armour; there were few horses; and many of the Norsemen on the west bank of the river, in the full path of the advancing English, were only lightly weaponed. The host that came against them was well equipped and seriously outnumbered the allies; and it was led by a strong force of heavy cavalry, the only antagonists whom the Vikings feared, the housecarls of the English king and the southern earls. In a hurried council of war, Tostig advised retreat: if the Norsemen could reach their ships they could rearm and confront the enemy with their whole power; at the same time, the fleet would provide shelter and nullify the advantage of the opposing cavalry. But a retreat presented difficulties that were in effect insurmountable: the probability of regaining Riccall without being forced to fight was negligible: the withdrawal would be paralleled on the far side of the Derwent by the main mass of the English army, while part of the mounted elite subjected the Norsemen to flank and rear attacks, and the remainder of the housecarls raced ahead to seize the crossing at Kexby.

There was no alternative but to accept battle. The Norsemen beyond the river were scurrying back now to the ford and the bridge, and they were already under attack. Hardraada could have attempted to defend the Derwent, but the numerical superiority of the English made it certain that sooner or later the line would be turned, and the plight of the defenders would then be hopeless. On the rise to the east, however, the allies could form a shield-wall, and the slight slope of the ground would be in their favour. Outnumbered and outarmed, the Norwegian king could count still on one unchanging strength, the wild courage of his followers. They would fall where they fought, but they would not fly. While the shield-wall held, the battle was not lost; at worst, the English would pay dearly to break the ring of Norse steel; at best, the coming of reinforcements might snatch victory from the English grasp. The debate ended. Three of the best riders in the host were mounted on the fastest available horses and sent to summon Eystein gorcock and the men who had been left at Riccall. The trumpets sounded; the paralysis that had gripped the invaders passed; they hurried to join the king on the flats above the river. *Then King Harald ordered his banner Landravager to be set up, and Fridrek was the name of him who bore the banner.*[30]

Beyond the Derwent, men were dying. Thrusting down from the west, the English horsemen rode among the fugitives on the right bank, hewing and slashing. Knowing they were doomed, the half-armed Norsemen bought with their lives the time necessary for their comrades to reach the eastward ridge, and rally about their king. Forming themselves into a crude battle-array, the survivors of the first assault fell back to the river, giving ground, but not breaking. Those who reached the ford fought on the bank, in the shallows, and in the deeper water too, until the sheer weight of the attack took its toll, and the last of the living were driven across the stream over the bodies of their dead companions, and corpses dammed the flow. While the defenders of the ford were making their desperate stand, those of the cattle-gatherers who had retreated to the north-east were keeping the bridge with equal stubbornness. One by one they died, until a single Viking remained, holding the narrow passage against the English onslaught. One of the few who had borne mail on the sun-drenched march from Riccall, the Norseman beat off attack after attack, wielding an axe, and killing more than forty assailants. The English archers were no more able to dislodge the axeman than the men-at-arms, and the wooden bridge may have been roofed; but covered or not, it was rudely built. The timbers of the flooring lay unevenly, and this at last brought an end to the defence. In a small boat, or perhaps nothing more manageable than a salting-tub, an Englishman manoeuvred himself below the tired and unsuspecting invader. Reaching up through a gap between the floor-timbers, he speared the Viking through beneath his byrnie.[31]

The taking of the crossings of the Derwent marked the close of the first phase of the battle. While the few Norse survivors of the fights at the river stumbled exhaustedly and thankfully up the eastern slope to a precarious refuge, the English host surged across the ford and the bridge to the left bank, where the marshals halted them. On the higher flats, little more than two arrow-flights from the jubilant English, the shield-wall was taking shape. *King Harald arranged his army, and made the line of battle long, but not deep. He bent both wings of it back, so that they met together; and formed a wide ring equally thick all round, shield to shield, both in the front and rear ranks.*[32] By the king's orders, the men of the outer ring set their spears butt to the ground, while those behind thrust theirs forward between the shields of the first rank, so that the double line of targes, their gay painting marred by the scars of Fulford, bristled with blades in a hedge of steel. The bowmen of the army were stationed inside the circle, and what horses the Norwegians had were tethered there too. The leaders themselves were not in the defensive lines. On horseback, Hardraada waited beside the Landravager with his retinue and a band of chosen warriors, ready to give support at any threatened point of the line. Under his personal banner, and with the elite of his own followers, Tostig was similarly positioned at another pole of the ring of spears.

The shield-wall was completed, while the English marshals were still ordering their troops. The assault would come soon, but not yet. Mounted on a black horse with a white blaze on its brow, Hardraada rode slowly round his army, assessing the strength of each part of the circle. The ground was uneven; the horse stumbled, throwing its rider. The king rose quickly and turned aside what might have been accounted yet another omen of disaster: a fall, he said, is lucky for a traveller. It is easy to believe that those who heard laughed with Hardraada. But down by the Derwent, where King Harold of England waited and watched the preparations of the Norsemen, the accident was also seen, and the interpretation differed. There were Norsemen standing with the English king, captives or deserters from the invading host, and Harold turned to them. Who, he asked, was the man who fell from his horse, the tall man with the blue mantle and the decorated helmet? They told him it was the Norwegian king himself. Hardraada was a great man, the king said, and his appearance was stately; but now his luck had left him.

On the river-bank below the Norse array, the dead and the dying had been dragged away, and the fyrd was reforming. The force which Harold had led from York was immense: it numbered possibly twenty thousand men, of whom perhaps a quarter were mounted, and it included the majority of the skilled archers of the southern earldoms. To oppose the English host, Hardraada had immediately available at most ten thousand men: the victory at Gate Fulford had been expensively won, and the Norwegian king faced his rival with only two-thirds of an army already weakened by heavy casualties. The effective strength of the invaders was further reduced by the legacy of the morning's carelessness: the disparity in equipment between the armies was as marked as their disparity in numbers. The overwhelming superiority of his troops enabled the English commander to dictate the tactics of the coming battle. It was a restricted freedom. The military genius of Harold Godwinsson had been demonstrated in his Welsh campaigns, in his massive defence of the south coast throughout the past summer, and in his reaction to the invasion of the north: he was an innovator in several aspects of contemporary warfare: but the adaptability of his means and methods was limited by the circumstances of the age in which he lived.

In the eleventh century, the use of the striking power of both the bowman and the cavalryman was imperfectly understood. Not until the great days of Edward III and his son was the longbow to come into its own, when the English archers stepped forward in serried ranks and loosed their arrows in unified, controlled flights to transfix and maim the myth of French chivalry. The French knights who died at Crecy and Poitiers were themselves the inheritors of a tactical tradition which dated only from the late twelfth century: the close-ordered charge of armoured horsemen with levelled lances firmly couched. In 1066, the heavy lance had not yet been developed, and the standard weapon of the mounted soldier was a light throwing-spear. Under Saxon, Norseman, or Norman, skirmishes between parties of cavalry were uncommon, and when they occurred the horsemen fought with the weapons which they would have used unmounted. On the battlefield the horse was employed, even in attack, primarily as a defensive arm; in an action against a superior force it was usually abandoned in favour of a static defence, which had reached a temporary apogee in the shieldwall. In an offensive situation, harassing an opponent arrayed defensively, the horsemen rode in small groups within spear-shot of the enemy, cast their javelins, and sped out of range of retaliation. If the attacks, frequently repeated and supported by archers, succeeded in breaking the defensive line, the fragments of the enemy could be destroyed in detail by combined cavalry and infantry assaults. If the attacks failed, the horse-soldiers dismounted and added their weight to a hand-to-hand onslaught on foot.[33]

In the lull, while the English regrouped, a sudden activity beside the Derwent brought Earl Tostig to Hardraada's side. From the press of the housecarls and up the slope rode twenty horsemen, armoured, but clearly on a mission of peace. The Norse shield-ring opened, and Tostig went to meet the truce-party. One of the riders, wearing a gilded helm and carrying a red shield embossed with a golden hawk, spoke. He gave the renegade the greetings of his brother and an offer of reconciliation: if Tostig would return to his natural allegiance, Harold would not only restore to him his forfeited earldom, but would appoint him joint-ruler of a third of the kingdom. The terms were more than generous; but the exile had been too often accused of faithlessness, and the accusations rankled. What, he asked, would be granted to King Harald Sigurdsson? The horse-man answered quickly: *'Seven feet of English ground, or as much more as he may be taller than other men.'* [34] With the dark pride that had contributed to his earlier ruin, Tostig refused his brother's embassy: both offers came too late, and he would not now betray the one ally who had befriended him. The parley ended, and as the horsemen rode off, the earl rejoined Hardraada. Not until the Englishmen were beyond the reach of the Norse king's vengeance did Tostig tell Hardraada that the am-bassador who had spoken so well had been Harold Godwinsson himself. The Viking's anger at the deception subsided almost as it kindled. The Norwegian giant looked down towards his enemy with a brief comment: the English king was a small man, yet he sat firmly in his stirrups.

Harold and his attendants rode among the waiting troops, now ranged for battle. The orders were given, and the relative quiet that had followed the taking of the bridge was split by a clamour of war-cries as the advance began. Through the afternoon air, the shouts of 'God Almighty!' and 'Holy Cross!' rang over the little valley, and the archers and foot-soldiers moved slowly forward, while ahead of them the housecarls led the assault, coming to a gallop and dividing to encircle the enemy as they neared the shield-wall. Hardraada had bidden his men to stand fast, and not to fight too hotly; but the hail of spears and arrows that the Norsemen launched was powerful enough to keep the English at a distance. Crouching low in the saddle, the riders came

swiftly in, threw their javelins, and sheered away. The engagement was general now, as the English horsemen circled the Norse
ring; but it was still *loose and light*,[35] and the only weapons in
play were missiles. It seems certain that Harold had halted the
infantry advance until the success or failure of the mounted
attack was decided. But hotheads among the Viking defenders
misread the English commander's purpose. The cavalry battle
had been in progress for some time, inconclusively; losses on
both sides grew, but the shield-wall held firm, the attackers
could make no headway against the ring of spears, and each
assault broke under the fire of the Norse bowmen and javelineers.
King Harold may or may not have known that some fourteen
miles to the south reinforcements were hurriedly making ready
to come to Hardraada's aid; but the decision to commit his foot-
soldiers could not have been postponed much longer, when the
one gift the English leader could not have looked for was suddenly presented to him.

*Now when the Northmen thought they perceived that the
enemy were making but weak assaults, they set after them, and
would drive them into flight.*[36] Unrehearsed and unsignalled,
the hour had come that was to be the turning-point of the
battle, the beginning of the end for King Harald Sigurdsson,
and the doom of Tostig's hopes. The berserk fury had seized
the invaders; discipline gave place to disorder; and Hardraada's
bidding was forgotten. In wave after wave, the English cavalry
had been beaten off, until at last the Norsemen themselves, mistaking prudence for cowardice, had done what their opponents
had failed to accomplish. Without understanding of the larger
meaning of their leader's strategy, the strong defence that might
stave off defeat until Eystein gorcock could reach the field, they
saw only an enemy who seemed to flee before them. The unaccustomed, unwilling restraint snapped; the Vikings streamed
outwards; and in part of the circle at least, the rampart of shields
was broken. If Hardraada and his officers could have made
their voices heard above the din of battle, and if the English had
held off, there might have been time to recall the killing-hungry
defenders to their posts. But there was no time : the voices were
unheard : and Harold Godwinsson's commands were unneeded.
The housecarls and thegns turned their horses and rode upon

the pursuers from all sides, spears flying, swords and axes swinging. And farther down the slope to the river, the English battle-cries rose in triumph, and on again came the waiting mass of the foot-soldiers of the fyrd.

The Norse advance slowed and stopped, and the salient it had created splintered under the growing pressure on front and flanks. Infiltrated and scattered by the opposing cavalry, the Norsemen who had led the charge were struggling for their lives in small, isolated groups. With the whole English army now committed to the attack, Hardraada could no longer hold back his reserves. But the men who stood with the king were the picked warriors of the allied host; if fighting ability alone could force a withdrawal by the enemy, the respite gained might give time for the repair of the broken line. With the royal banner beside him, Hardraada left behind the black horse that had failed him less than his shield-men, and led his chosen troop *into the fray where the greatest crash of weapons was; and there was a sharp conflict, in which many people fell on both sides. King Harald then was in a rage, and ran out in front of the array, and hewed down with both hands; so that neither helmet nor armour could withstand him, and all who were nearest gave way before him.*[37] But the king's anger had made him reckless, and the towering figure beneath the Landravager loomed starkly over the melee. Axeman and spearman dropped before him, and all about him cleared a swathe where no Englishman could enter and live; yet there were enemies whom his sword could not reach, and whose blows he could not parry. Closing in now to a range where the weakest could not miss the quarry, the archers of the fyrd bent their bows on the Norse giant; the strings sang, the arrows flashed briefly in the bright September sunlight, and Hardraada fell, pierced through cheek and throat.

It was the finish of the dream of Norwegian dominion over all the northern lands, the dream that had brought King Harald Sigurdsson a thousand miles from Nidaros to the river-crossing that the English called Stamford Bridge. While about him the royal bodyguard fought to protect their fallen lord, Harald Hardraada lay choking in his own blood on a desolate Northumbrian flat, his head pillowed on the knee of Thiodolf the skald, the bard who had come to make the song of triumph that would never be sung. A shiver of despair ran through the Norse array with the word of King Harald's fall; but the Landravager still waved above the king, and from his distant post Tostig hurried to Hardraada's side. The Norwegian adventurer had seen too much death not to recognise his own. With what breath was left to him, the dying man bade his ally accept whatever terms King Harold of England would offer : for his part he would ask no more than what had been granted already. But bitterness was too deeply rooted in the exile : he would not sue now for the reconciliation he had refused before : if victory was to be denied the invaders, Hardraada and he would be guests in the same lodging that night. There would be no truce. The blood bubbled in the Viking's throat and lungs and drowned him, and King Harald Sigurdsson was dead.

It was about mid-afternoon when Harald Hardraada died. There was no time for obsequies; the fierce fighting about the Landravager continued, but the warriors whom the Norwegian king had led into the fray were thinning rapidly. Tostig took the Norse banner and fell back to the shield-wall with those of the royal bodyguard who had survived. Crowding them closely, the English swept up to the blood-boltered corpse, and a roar of triumph rose from the attackers as the leading troops recognised the sprawled body and torn features of the dead giant. Scenting victory in the defender's dismay, the men of the fyrd hurled themselves on the still disorganised Norsemen. The conflict was short. For Harold Godwinsson, Tostig was even now his brother and the nearest of all his kin; and the English king valued the saving of his own people above the killing of his enemies. Needless slaughter held no lure for Harold, and with the fall of Hardraada, the heart of the invasion had perished. In this second phase of the battle, losses in both armies had mounted quickly, and the best men on each side had borne the brunt of the struggle. Swift orders were issued; the fyrd broke off the attack; and once again an English embassy rode near to the Norse lines and called out to Earl Tostig. The terms were less generous than they had been before to the renegade, more so to his companions. No dominion was offered now to the earl; but if the invaders surrendered, there would be peace in his brother's kingdom for

Tostig and quarter for his allies, provided reparation was made for the harm done to English lives and property.

The pause in the fighting lengthened, while Norse and English regrouped, and King Harold awaited the return of his ambassadors. Although the dead lay heaped about the invaders, morale was high; and *the Northmen called out all of them together that they would rather fall, one across the other, than accept of quarter from the Englishmen.*[38] But the decision rested with Tostig. The withdrawal of the earl and his followers would force surrender on the surviving Norsemen, or mean certain annihilation if they refused to submit. There was no sign yet of Eystein Orre, but the gorcock would come; and the influx of the men from the ships, fresh, well armed and armoured, might tip the scales of battle in the allies' favour. If the English exiles and the Flemings stayed true to their compact, the ring of shields might stand until Eystein's five thousand warriors arrived to rescue the dying army. All this must have passed through Tostig's mind; but his decision had little to do with strategy. The choice lay between death and obscurity. If he lived, it would be as a conqueror, not as a pensioner of either Flemish count or English king. The pride that had driven him beyond kinship, beyond reason, and beyond hope, now brought Tostig at last beyond despair. The decision had been taken long ago and reaffirmed beside the ruined body of the earl's lost ally. Tostig grasped the banner of Hardraada and sent his defiance to the waiting embassy: while he was still able to fight, all the Norse leaders were not fallen.

War-cries were rising from the Norse lines as the housecarls rode back to the English array. The ambassadors gave the earl's answer to his brother; there was nothing more the king could do to end the slaying, and reluctantly Harold ordered the advance. The Englishmen cheered, and once more the shouts of 'Holy Cross!' and 'God Almighty!' resounded through the army as the fyrd moved forward against the Norsemen. This time there was no fretting of the enemy with flying attacks by the cavalry. All along the weakened front of the invading host, the English thrust in with swords and axes, hacking apart the spears and shields of the outer rampart of the defence, while above them the arrows whistled down on the rear ranks of the defenders, and rents grew in the beleagured lines. Now there were no eager reserves to fill the gaps, and the assailants tore their way through the allied ring over the corpses of the fallen. The shield-wall broke and vanished under the tide of attack, and the battle split into scattered knots of conflict. With victory again in their grasp, the English pressed even more fiercely, and it was nearing the end for the Norsemen when the bowmen of the fyrd struck again. In the rain of arrows that dropped on the guardians grouped about the Landravager, one hit Tostig, and the exile fell, killed instantly.

When King Harold heard that his brother was dead, he offered peace once more to the Norsemen; but the offer was unheard. Almost as Tostig died, over the rises to the south came the help for which he and Hardraada had looked in vain. Led by the sons of Thorberg, Eystein Orre and Nicholas, and the Orkney earls, the men from the ships sped across the southern approaches to the flats and threw themselves on the surprised English. The struggle that followed was the most bitter of the day, and so ferocious *that ever since in England 'gorcock's storm' is used to mean great peril of men*.[39] The surprise may have been complete, for it seems possible that in the first minutes of the 'gorcock's bout' the English were close to rout. But the new-comers had hurried all the way from Riccall in full armour through the heat of the afternoon, and they were near exhaustion before they reached the battlefield. Though Eystein broke through to the Norse standard, the impetus of the attack failed; the fyrd rallied to face the unexpected threat; and the moment that might have brought defeat to King Harold was past. Still the desperate fighting continued, until the fury of the Norsemen themselves gave back the advantage to their enemies. Distracted by heat and fatigue, and to gain greater freedom of movement, the Vikings threw off their byrnies, *and then the Englishmen could easily lay their blows at them; and many fell from weariness, and died without a wound*.[40] The afternoon drew on to evening, and the brightness and warmth faded from the air; the clash of arms persisted, but the outcome of the battle was decided. Nicholas Thorbergsson died, and the strife went on; until at last the victorious English cut down the defenders of the Landravager, and Eystein gorcock fell with his company. With the death of Eystein, the Norse resistance cracked, and the surviving invaders fled; *and darkness fell before the slaughter was altogether ended.*[41]

King Harold had possession of the place of battle; while part of the army chased the fleeing remnants of the enemy to Kexby, and on through the September dusk to Riccall, the weary king counted the cost of victory. It was dearer than he knew, or would know before another month began. Harold Godwinsson had brought down a conqueror beside whom William of Normandy was no more than a petty princeling and a novice in war. Bearing a military reputation unequalled in his own age, Harald Hardraada had sailed against England with a host larger, more coherent and more experienced than all Duke William's promises and bribes could muster; Northumbria had surrendered to him almost at the first challenge; then, in the flush of success, he had been out-generalled, out-manouevred and out-fought by the Englishman whose throne he had vowed to topple. But to accomplish the destruction of the invader, King Harold had stripped the southern provinces of his realm of defenders, and many of the best of these lay dead on the flats above the Derwent. The struggle had been drawn out and bloody; lightly armed though the Norsemen might be, the veterans of the Danish wars did not give away their lives easily. In the breaking of the shield-wall, the burden of the attack had fallen inevitably on the better armoured Englishmen, the housecarls and thegns, and these had borne also the burden of the losses. For Harold, the campaign had been unavoidable: Hardraada was a more dangerous foe than the Norman duke could be; the wound torn by the Vikings in northern England had to be cauterised as swiftly as possible. But the price of victory had been high; and the consequences were to be catastrophic.

The lot of the defeated was terrible. Harried by the pursuing English, the fugitives stumbled through night-darkened fields in a strange land, some to be cut down by the hunters, or more horribly by the peasants they had plundered, others to be driven into the Derwent or the Ouse to drown. Some of the few who reached Riccall were burned to death when their ships were fired by the English, before the last attackers were called off by their officers. But the great mass of the Norsemen had already died; less than a twelfth of the huge army survived the battle. Most of the allied leaders lay with their followers beside the Derwent: King Harald Sigurdsson and Earl Tostig; the lendermen, Eystein Orre and Nicholas Thorbergsson; the unnamed Irish king, and uncounted others unnamed among the Norwegian and Flemish lords. Some escaped, their names remembered through later references: Skule and Ketel, the young sons of Tostig, who probably remained at the ships throughout the day with the Norse prince, Olaf Haraldsson, and the Norwegian bishop who had sailed with Hardraada; the earls Paul and Erlend of Orkney regained the ships after the final collapse; Copsig, Tostig's lieutenant; the Icelander, Godred Crouan.[42] Styrkar the marshal made off on a horse, a helmet on his head, his sword still in his hand, but clad in little more than a shirt. It was a chill evening, and the Norseman was beginning to feel the cold when he met an English wagoner in a lined skin-coat. Recognising Styrkar's accent, the peasant not only refused to sell the coat, but regretted he could not kill the Viking instead. His honesty was not politic. Styrkar swept off his head, took the coat for nothing, and rode on to the shore.

The surviving defenders of the ships lived only by the grace of King Harold of England. The remains of Harald Sigurdsson were borne to Riccall and carried home to Norway, again by the grant of the English king. The body of Earl Tostig, identified by distinctive marks between the shoulder-blades, was taken by his brother's command to be buried in York. The thousands of lesser dead, however, were left where they had fallen, and even in the eighteenth century bones and weapons were occasionally turned up on what by then had come to be called 'Battle Flats'. Stamford Bridge was a decisive battle. It has been overshadowed by the conflict that followed, the results of which were more cataclysmic. Yet Senlac was a minor affray by comparison with the earlier engagement, and the outcome of the Norman invasion was largely a consequence of the preceding campaign in Northumbria.

The defeat at Stamford Bridge broke the power of the Norwegian kings for several decades, and ended the long age of Viking conquest. It confirmed the circumspect reign of Swegen Estrithsson in Denmark, established the national divisions of the

Scandinavian kingdoms, removed the fear of the Norsemen from the southern coasts of Britain and western Europe, and shifted the political centre of gravity in the west irrevocably southwards. The victors had exacted a fearful vengeance from the pillagers of Scarborough and Holderness, and they had shattered the Nordic dream of re-establishing the empire of Canute. The dead totalled almost a third of the full fighting strength of Norway, and the fall of Hardraada and the other Viking leaders exposed the Norwegian people to the perils of minority rule under the guidance of aging jarls. In the days following the battle, the English king remained in York, and there he received the formal surrender of the enemy. From the ships at Riccall, Olaf Haraldsson *was brought to King Harold. He begged for mercy and promised tribute. Harold received his homage, and from all the others he took good and valued hostages.*[43] The loot taken from the Norsemen was huge: it included not only the gold brought by Hardraada from Norway, but the plunder seized by the invaders in England. The greater part of the allied fleet too passed into the hands of the English. For the time being, King Harold kept the gathered treasure under his own control. Much would be needed to repair the damage done by the Vikings, but recompense and resettlement were of small urgency. The emergency was over; the king's lost brother lay quiet at last in the city he had once ruled so turbulently; the Norse emissaries were dismissed, and Harold Godwinsson relaxed among his triumphant captains.

The sad cavalcade moved slowly southwards over the stubbled fields, back to the ships and the long voyage home. The king had been handsome and nobly built, more than seven feet tall; the hair and the long moustaches, the short beard and the eyebrows, one higher than the other, were yellow; the hands and feet were large, but well made. Now the strong hands were crossed in death, the blood had been washed from the yellow hair, and the giant frame lay stiffly on the rude bier. Harsh to his enemies, but generous to his friends, the last of the Norse conquerors had been *of the highest understanding, bold in arms, and greedy of power and property; of great courage, but not acquainted with the way of winning the favour of the people; zealous in governing, and severe in revenge.*[44] King Harald Sigurdsson was returning to

Nidaros, borne by the followers he had led to disaster. The procession came to the moorings on the Ouse, and the corpse was brought on board the royal 'dragon'. Under the watchful eyes of the English guards, in only twenty-four ships of the three hundred that had met in the Tyne, the residue of the Norse host moved out into the current, to follow the ebbing tide to the Humber and the distant sea.

*   *   *   *   *

The morning of Wednesday, the twenty-seventh of September, dawned clear and calm at St. Valery. In the Channel, the north wind had died, and the rain-clouds had passed over. Expectantly, Duke William watched the weather-cock above the abbey-church, and in the early afternoon his prayers were answered. The vane turned about, and the south wind blew. The duke gave orders for immediate embarkation. The troops needed little encouragement: after the inaction of the late weeks, the excitement of doing something was enough to banish their fears of the sea and the unknown, and even the happenings of the voyage from the Dives were forgotten. The only dread that concerned the soldiers now was of being left on shore. Discipline surrendered almost to a panic not to be the last aboard. Oblivious of comrades and subordinates, supplies and equipment, the Normans and their allies hurried to the waiting vessels, while the duke and his officers came behind them, reprimanding and spurring on the laggards. Somehow order was brought out of chaos. The horses were led into the transports. Coats of mail, the equivalents of the English and Norse byrnies, were strung on poles and hoisted on the shoulders of bearers, with bundles of swords and spears. Others of the serving men drew wagons loaded with more spears, and casks of wine.

While the final preparations were being made, Duke William again visited the shrine of St. Valery and made a last offering to the relics. His conscience cleansed, the Norman leader hastened to the *Mora* and issued his sailing orders. It was already late in the afternoon, and the sky had clouded over. It would soon be dark, and there would be little moonlight to help the voyagers. The fleet was to sail now, while the wind was steady, using the last of the daylight to reach the open sea; but after the coming of night, they would not chance the uncertain dangers of enemy waters, anchoring instead in close formation in the Channel until dawn was near. The signal to proceed would be the lighting of a beacon at the mast-head of the duke's ship and the sounding of a trumpet. Each vessel would then mount a lantern on the mast and follow the duke's lead. William gave the command; the bugles were blown; and the *Mora* moved out into the centre of the roadstead. Ship by ship, the mooring lines were freed, and the fleet stood out to join their leader in mid-channel. After the losses of the earlier voyage, there were now not quite a thousand vessels gathered in the Somme estuary, and of these about seven hundred were transports of the larger type, the remainder being the smaller boats used normally in river and coastal traffic. They carried some five thousand horses; the army of the duke now numbered approximately twelve thousand men, of whom perhaps two-thirds were combatants, with their necessary servants, grooms and craftsmen.

In the failing light, the fleet passed out of the estuary and headed west of north into the Channel. The wind was mild, and there was only a gentle swell in the waters that had been lashed by storms a day or two before. The darkness came down, and Duke William gave orders to anchor. The chains were slipped, the sails were furled, and the invaders rested. It was some time before dawn when the beacon flared above the *Mora* and the duke's trumpeters alerted the fleet. Hurriedly by torchlight, the ships were readied. The lanterns were lit and hauled to the tops of the masts; the anchors were drawn in, and the sails were raised; the signal was given, and the armada moved off. The voyage had so far gone smoothly; but in the moonless dark, the inexperience of his sailors briefly jeopardised William's careful planning. The early success of the expedition hung upon the Norman's ability to strike with his full force at one point, establishing a beach-head before the defenders could rally to destroy him. If the fleet became dispersed, not only would the isolated units of the invaders be vulnerable to enemy attack, but there would be little likelihood of the ships being regrouped, and the attempt on England might come to nothing almost as it began. In the darkness before dawn, contact between the duke and his followers was lost. Less heavily laden and faster than the other vessels, the *Mora* was allowed by her pilot to out-distance her companions. Skilled in navigation as Stephen, son of Airadri, may have been, his captaincy had not previously entailed the leading of a convoy. When day broke, the *Mora* was alone in the empty Channel, and a seaman sent aloft could see only waves and sky as far as the horizon.

Before alarm could change to panic, the Norman leader acted with calm assurance and authority. *Immediately they cast anchor, and so that fear and sadness should not overtake his attendants, the intrepid duke, just as if he had been at home in his own dining-hall, ate a copious meal, helped down with spiced and honeyed wine and with memorable gaiety of spirit, affirming that the other ships would not be long in coming, under the guidance of God to whose keeping he had committed them.*[45] William's self-control was quickly rewarded : breakfast was scarcely taken when the look-out called down that four sails had appeared on the sky-line, and before long so many ships had come into view that their masts looked like a thick forest on the sea. The duke gave thanks, and soon the fleet had reassembled about the waiting *Mora*. It was intact, except for two vessels which had either lagged far behind, overloaded and in danger of foundering, or mistaken their course in the darkness. The wind was still southerly, and the Channel was quiet; swiftly, the invaders pushed on. It was early in the day when the English coast rose above the horizon; and shortly before nine o'clock on the morning of Thursday, the twenty-eighth of September, the eve of Michaelmas, the Norman fleet sailed into the lagoon of Pevensey.

The ships moved in below the long walls of the ancient Roman fortress of Anderida, still guarding the south-west corner of the broad lagoon, but deserted and neglected through five and a half centuries, since the South Saxon invaders had swept away the last British garrison. In the Norman fleet, the elation of the preceding day had hardened to a taut expectancy. Without certain knowledge of the whereabouts of Harold and the English fyrd, the allied commanders were prepared to meet resistance even on the Sussex shore : by the duke's orders, the soldiers were armed and ready before the coast was reached. Side by side, the transports closed to the shore; the keels touched bottom; and the lightly harnessed troops, archers and men-at-arms, leapt down to the shingle, spreading immediately to scour the beaches and the nearer countryside. As they sped outwards, the horses were being led ashore. The knights followed, wearing helmets and coats of mail, swords girded on, shields slung about their necks; and with them came the leaders of the expedition. Thousands watched as Duke William stepped on to the land he claimed as his own. The sloping shingle was treacherous: the duke slipped and fell, grasping at the alien earth with outstretched hands. When he rose, there was blood on his face; and a murmur of dismay at the unlucky chance went round the onlookers. But the seneschal, fitzOsbern, who had landed with William and stood nearby, cried out that the omen was fortunate: the duke, he called, had taken hold of England with both hands, and he had guaranteed it to his descendants with his blood. The moment of tension passed. The knights mounted; and the unloading of supplies and equipment began.

The knights were formed in battle-order, but they were un-needed. The forward scouts returned without having seen any trace of the enemy in arms. The surrounding country, however, was sparsely populated; and the foot-soldiers had found a cheerful outlet for their pent-up blood-lust in the killing of un-armed peasants and the firing of their houses. The smoke of the burning thatches rose in the clear September air, but the Normans had little fear of either reprisal or reprimand: many had served the duke before, and they knew well his policy to-wards invaded territories. But though the first harryings had brought no retaliation, there was as yet no surety that the beach-head would escape attack. The shallow waters of the lagoon formed a superb anchorage; but except on the slight eminence where the ruined fortress stood, the shore was not easily defen-sible. All were commanded to stay close to the beaches; and William ordered the digging of entrenchments and the throwing-up of temporary fortifications about the landing-place. While the pioneers set about their tasks, the discharged ships were drawn ashore and dismantled, steering-oars and masts unstepped, sails furled and stored away. The day was passing; the unloading had taken several hours; and it was long since the men had eaten. Field-kitchens were built, fires were lit, and the cooks prepared a meal. The defence-works were completed; the foragers and booty-hunters were recalled; and the tired and hungry army sat down to dinner.

After some thirty-six hours in which he can have had little sleep, William was at ease. He had landed in England, unchallenged, and with evening drawing on there was still no sign of the enemy. Before the fleet had left the Somme, a clerk who claimed an understanding of astrology had predicted a safe crossing, and he had assured the duke that England would be won without a battle. The first part of the prophecy had been fulfilled, and the Norman leader called for the seer. The clerk, however, was not in the camp: he had sailed in one of the missing ships. William dismissed both diviner and divination: he could see no profit in believing the words of one so little gifted that he could not even foretell his own death, let alone avoid it. There were important matters to be discussed, and the duke took council with his half-brothers, Odo of Bayeux and Robert of Mortain. Pevensey was clearly no position to hold as a base for the operations that must come. It was evident now that the reports of the disbanding of the great fyrd were accurate; therefore a developing English attack would almost certainly originate from London, thrusting against the invaders from the north-east. The beach-entrenchments were vulnerable from sea and land, and their situation allowed no latitude for the deployment of cavalry. Roman Anderida could be occupied, and the walls were strong; but if the host retired there, the enemy onslaught would sweep over the landing-place, and the loss of the ships was inevitable. A few miles east of Pevensey, however, lay the small port of Hastings. The peninsula on which it stood would offer a good defence; and stationed there, the army could afford indirect protection to the fleet, an English force striking against the lagoon from the Andredsweald being open to flank attack from the peninsula.

On the morning of Friday, the twenty-ninth of September, the main bulk of the allies marched eastwards from Pevensey to Hastings, leaving only a small detachment of knights to guard the ships. Pushing inland a little way, they passed north of the haven of Bulverhythe and the marshes that bordered the chosen defensive area on the west, and turned south-east towards the port. Within the Hastings peninsula as without, the coastline was then much more sharply indented than it is today, and the Saxon town was built on the slopes of the more westerly of two gorges that cut in from the Channel to the Fairlight ridge. Between the inlets rose a hill which fell steeply to the sea at its southern limit, and which had been entrenched since Neolithic times. In the summer months, the port and the earth-works on the cliff had been garrisoned by the fyrd; but the fortifications had been levelled, the defenders were gone, and the inhabitants had no power to oppose the invaders. Hastings surrendered without resistance. The town itself was unsuitable as headquarters for the campaign, and William established his camp on the height above, commanding the landward and seaward approaches to the port. A deep trench was dug, a mound was raised, and on the summit the duke's engineers erected a wooden castle, one of the prefabricated structures transported sectionally from Normandy, its walls shaped, framed and pierced, ready for the linking pins. The construction and wardenship of the stronghold were given into the care of a Norman baron, Humphrey of Tilleul.

It is unlikely that Duke William knew of the coming of Hardraada and Tostig prior to the departure from Ponthieu; he may have learned of the earlier invasion and the northward march of King Harold only after the taking of Hastings. But it was now clear that the Norman had time at least to consolidate his landing before he must confront an enemy. William cannot have known yet of the doom of the Norwegian king; but unlike Harald Sigurdsson, he had no intention of hazarding his army on a venture into unfamiliar territory far from the fleet and his one route of escape. Sooner or later, the duke must meet one of two powerful enemies : while either of these remained in the field, their numbers and location unsure, he had no alternative but to stay close to a well protected base. Against reasonable odds, William was ready to chance battle; but the English or the Norse might attack in such strength that defeat would become more than a possibility. Trapped inland, the Normans would risk annihilation; at Hastings, they might ward off the assailants long enough for the ships from Pevensey to come to the rescue. At the same time, the duke could not safely assume that Wessex was wholly unguarded. Although eastern Sussex had been abandoned to an invader, there was no surety that this was the case with rich districts farther to the east. Perhaps the opposite was true: from the men of Hastings, William may have discovered the fate of some of his lost followers. Less than twenty miles north-east of the captured town lay the sister-port of Romney; later events suggest that one at least of the missing transports had strayed there, the troops aboard attempting a defended shore and being cut to pieces.

But waiting could prove as dangerous as seeking out the enemy. Surrender would ultimately be forced on the Normans if the English blockaded them, the army containing the invaders, the navy cutting communications between Sussex and Normandy. The return of Harold from the north would speed the refitting of the ships lying at London; and William knew well that his sea-scows could not survive a second encounter with the English fleet when the weather was fair. If the Norse invasion had been overcome, the duke's best hope lay in provoking an early attack by the king: his chosen weapon was terror. The Norman set about a systematic ravaging of the land he had come to liberate. His foragers pillaged the countryside of provisions and goods, killing and burning, while the Saxons fled before them, driving off their cattle, quitting their homes, and finding little safety even in churchyards. The resistance was minimal. With an escort of only twenty-five knights, William himself reconnoitred the vicinity and its inhabitants, over ground so rough that the party was driven to return on foot. The devastation was thorough: some villages disappeared, never to rise again. It served subsidiary purposes as well: the rapidly diminishing stores of the allied encampment were replenished; a desert area was created about Hastings, a belt of wasteland offering no sustenance, through which the avengers must pass before they could reach the Norman defences.

It was perhaps on the last day of the month that a messenger was brought to the duke. He had been sent by Robert fitzWymarc, the staller who had stood with Harold beside the deathbed of King Edward. A possible kinsman of William, yet seemingly a loyal subject of the English king, fitzWymarc owned extensive lands in Essex and he may have held an estate near Pevensey. Now he sought to end the strife between his kinsman and his lord before it began. The Norman learned at last the

identity of the enemy he must face. The duke, said Robert, had
overreached himself. He had come to England with too slight a
force to accomplish what he had undertaken. King Harold had
fought and slain his own brother and the king of Norway, *the
bravest warrior under Heaven*,[46] and had destroyed their powerful army. He was returning at the head of a strong and confident host, against whom the Normans would *avail no more
than so many miserable dogs*.[47] Bluntly, fitzWymarc counselled
the duke. Till now, William had been considered a prudent
leader, in peace and in war : let him avoid an engagement with
the English, and go back to his own land before the king should
arrive, lest misled by rashness he found himself in a snare from
which there would be no escape. The duke replied shortly and
proudly : he thanked the messenger for his master's advice,
though it would have been more seemly without insult; but he
had no misgivings, and he would remain in England. William
had come to claim a right, and he would claim it; whatever the
numbers on either side, he would fight with Harold as soon as
possible, and with God's help he would crush him.

* * * * *

The courier who brought the news of Stamford Bridge to
London may have passed, on his way, another rider, northward
bound with grimmer tidings. The landing at Pevensey had been
witnessed. A thegn of Sussex, lying unseen behind a rock beside
the beach, had watched the disembarkation, the early harrying
of the shore-lands, and the digging of the first entrenchments. He
had heard the cries of the peasants and the wailing of the
children who saw their fathers die. When he had observed
enough, he hurried to his home, took his sword and spear, and
rode off, leaving word that he went to the king. While far to
the north, beyond the Humber, King Harold celebrated his great
victory, and in the south the Norman terror spread through
Sussex, the horseman rode on day and night. The remnant of
Hardraada's fleet crept past Holderness and Cleveland, the
coasts the Norsemen had so recently pillaged; the emissary of
Robert fitzWymarc returned to his master with the Norman
duke's retort; and the South-Saxon thegn neared the border of
Northumbria and his king.

OCTOBER

THE victory celebrations in York had lasted almost a week. These had been the supreme days of Harold's reign, when it seemed that at last he sat securely on the throne of England, and *when the king might have thought that all his enemies were wiped out.*[1] In London, Eadric's ships were still refitting after the Channel battle, but the work progressed without haste; the Normans had been defeated, and their routed fleet had fled before the storm-wind, eastward and out of English reckoning. In the north, many thegns and housecarls had been killed; yet the slaughter at Gate Fulford had been savagely avenged, and the men of the fyrd who had fallen in the meadows by the Derwent had taken with them many more than their number of the Norsemen. The new month began; King Harold lingered in the northern city, triumphant among his people, and confident in the belief that in all the realm of England his rule was un-challenged. Not the wind, but English arms, had dispersed his rivals; and the future that had been dark and unsure now glittered with promise. In the early evening of Sunday, the first of October, a rider, weary and travel-stained, spurred his flagging horse to the gates of York, and pushed his way through the narrow streets to the hall where the king sat. Only a week before, the walls of the city had been guarded, and the streets had been silent, while the king and his captains waited to make an end of Harald Hardraada. Now York thronged with merry-makers, and Harold was at dinner when the messenger brought him word of the coming of William the Bastard.

The Normans had landed, and with them had come many Frenchmen and Bretons. They had fortified the Pevensey shore, and were devastating the land around. They had carried off the cattle, and were leading away as captives the children and widows of the men they had killed. Unless Harold acted quickly to defend his kingdom, England was lost. Less than a month ago, the trusted seamen of the king had assured him that his southern enemy was destroyed; now that same enemy was pillaging the undefended coast of Sussex, the coast where before the sea-battle, if the legend is true, Harold had planned to counter this very threat. The first shock passed, and the king spoke. The words he is said to have uttered hold a deep and bitter sadness.[2] He was sorry, said the king, that he had not been in the south when the Normans arrived. It might have been better to have lost all that Tostig had demanded, so that Harold might have been at Pevensey when Duke William reached the shore. The enemy would have been driven into the sea and drowned, never to accomplish a landing, nor to touch anything English; nor would they have escaped death even if the sea had not taken them. *But thus it pleased the Heavenly King: I could not be everywhere at once.*

The surprise achieved by William was as powerful as that won by Harold over the Norse invaders. An evaluation of the historical probabilities underlying the accepted sequence of events in September and October, 1066, leads to three interdependent conclusions: firstly, that after mid-September a Norman landing was totally unexpected by the English king; secondly, that when the landing had been made, Harold believed the marauders to be much weaker than in fact they were; and thirdly, that even when the strength of the invaders was manifest, the king remained confident of their swift expulsion. It is clear that up till the actual eve of battle the king considered the enemy to be in no position to launch any attack beyond the closest limits of the beach-head. It is also clear that from the beginning of his campaign Harold intended a containing operation against the invaders, until the whole forces of England, naval and military, could be assembled to crush them.

When the South Saxon had spoken, Harold summoned at once the English leaders who were gathered in York; and in an armed gemot the king addressed his captains. They were his guard, his wall and his aid, the king said, and with their help he had overcome the enemy from the northland, the Norwegian who had borne the same name as himself, and the Englishman whom the breasts of his own mother had nourished. Now another raider had entered the realm, plundering, impoverishing and despoiling. But Harold had known this Norman who sought

to subdue the people of England. Though Duke William brought
with him a high reputation, he had a timorous heart; yet provided he might do so easily, the duke would try to seize power
in the land. William was sly, greedy and excessively haughty;
and he knew how to keep neither peace nor his word of honour.
Grief and pain, calamity and darkness would fall on an England
under Norman rule. If the English loved life, they had no choice
now but to fight once more for the saving of their country. When
Harold had finished speaking, there was a brief silence; then a
cry rose up loudly from the whole gemot, and *all had but a
single voice*: '*We would rather have war, or die as a result of it,
than place our necks beneath the yoke of another king*'.[3]

The king thanked his followers, and took counsel from those
of both higher and lower degree on the campaign to be waged
against the southern intruder. With the Normans already entrenched in Sussex, there was no time to be wasted; two hundred
and fifty miles separated the opposing commanders, and Harold's
forces lay more than three times farther than the invading army
from London, the prize of the realm. The deliberations were
swift and decisive. The battles of the past weeks had greatly
reduced the number of troops available to the king: the fyrds
of Northumbria and Mercia had disintegrated after Gate Fulford, and much of the strength of the south had been dissipated
at Stamford Bridge. Little immediate help could be expected
from the north or the midlands, and even in Wessex and East
Anglia the summoning of a third muster within half a year
would tax the resources of the provinces. Yet Harold was determined to march without delay. The king would set out at once
for London with the surviving housecarls and such others as
would be able to keep pace with him. Couriers would ride ahead,
to the east and south-west, calling out all who could bear arms,
with only illness as an excuse for absence. Edwin and Morkere
would remain in the north to scour their earldoms for fighting-
men; but when they had gathered what reinforcements they
could, they would lead them southwards to join the king. In the
absence of the earls, the guardianship of their territories was
given into the care of Marleswegen, sheriff of Lincolnshire, and
a landowner from Cornwall to Yorkshire.

The treasure taken from the Norsemen had still to be disposed

of, stored against the future need of the kingdom, and Harold
entrusted its safe keeping to Archbishop Eldred. Later it was
written that many were resentful of this, and that the plunder
should have been distributed among those who had fought to
win it. There may have been malcontents in the English host,
men who could not see beyond the greed of the moment; but
the authority for the claim is slight,[4] and the housecarls, whose
resentment might have been greatest, stayed with Harold to the
end. The affairs of the north were set in order, and throughout
the city soldiers were making ready to ride with the king. The
couriers were leaving, and with them went one with a more
special mission: a monk, cautious in speech and chosen by the
gemot, rode swiftly south as envoy of the king to the camp of
the Norman duke. The message the cleric carried, *the terrible
words beneath his black cassock,*[5] was less terrible than it might
have been. Though Harold was prepared for war, he had no
wish for it. Too many had died already, and time was needed
for England to recuperate. Before battle became inevitable.
Harold wanted to make a gesture of conciliation to the invader.
If Duke William would offer a treaty of peace satisfactory to the
English, the king would not refuse it; otherwise the duke would
leave England not of his own arranging. The choice lay with
the Norman: let him abandon the enterprise he had embarked
on, or take the consequences; if he must seek a kingdom, let him
find it beyond the Channel. Early on October the second, the
king and his followers rode from York, southward towards London and the last enemy.

*   *   *   *   *

The Norman terror continued in Sussex; the stench of burning
and death fouled the air; but still the radius of the devastation
was small, and the harriers did not wander far from the fortified camp above Hastings. Despite the high tone of Duke
William's reply to fitzWymarc, the activity of the allied army
followed at least in part the advice of the Anglo-Norman,
and had done so even before the staller's message reached the
encampment. William had as yet no sure knowledge of the location of his enemy, nor of the strength which the king would
muster against him. Until he could be certain of security in the

wilderness which the foragers had created about his base, the duke was circumspect, and *he remained so perfectly quiet that he seemed to think of nothing less than war.*[6] By now, the reports of the scouts and the duke's own reconnaissance had pointed to the dangers of the peninsular position, and the original disposition of the allied forces had been modified: some of the ships which had been drawn ashore and dismantled at Pevensey had been reassembled and brought to the harbour at Hastings; although no more than a fraction of the fleet could have anchored in the port, the ships provided a possibility of escape to the survivors of the invading host, if the peninsula should be over-run.

It was towards the end of the first week of October, when the cowled messenger passed the southern outskirts of the Andredsweald and rode wearily down the last miles of the Fairlight ridge to the allied encampment. When the ambassador reached the cliff fortress, the duke was in the town below, by the harbour side, inspecting the guard which had been set over the ships. The arrival was announced to William, and the Norman leader went to meet the newcomer in person. The duke found the English monk still asking for an introduction to the commandant of the camp; and William is said to have made use of the stranger's ignorance of his identity: '*No one approaches William, duke of the Normans*', he began, '*more closely than his seneschal. You will have no way of speaking to him except through me. Tell me therefore the message you bear. He will willingly acquaint himself with it through my mediation, for no one is dearer to him than I am. You will be able to come afterwards at a convenient time and talk to him as you wish.*'[7] If this trick was in fact played, William may have believed that more might be revealed incautiously to a follower than to the leader of the invading host himself. The monk, however, chosen for his prudence, is unlikely to have satisfied the Norman's hope, although it was in his interest to make clear the purpose of his coming. When the duke learned the official status of the embassy, he saw to it immediately that the envoy was well lodged, and gave orders that the Englishman be treated courteously. *Meanwhile he turned over in his own mind and with his council what would be the suitable reply to such a message.*[8]

On the following day, the English ambassador was brought before the duke and his advisers. Seated among his barons, the 'seneschal' of the previous afternoon said to the startled advocate: '*It is I who am William, by the grace of God, prince of the Normans. Repeat now, in the presence of those gathered here, what you reported to me yesterday*'.[9] This, said the monk, was what Harold the king wished him to convey. By audacity or temerity, the duke had invaded the realm of the English. He must now quit the country; the king and his chief men, who together disposed of the royal power, ordered the intruder to return to his own land *quicker than a word*.[10] The Norman was to give up forthwith the prisoners he had taken, and whatever else he had seized by force. On his part, Harold was prepared to overlook the other injuries inflicted by the invaders, ascribing the recklessness of William's actions to immaturity and the essential fickleness of his character. If, however, the duke refused this offer, or were slow in returning the king's possessions, all treaties between England and Normandy were void, and William was responsible for the war which must follow. He urged the duke to be cautious, for only with difficulty was Harold able to hold in check his soldiers and his people.

The duke was angered. Harold's words, he retorted, were not those of a wise man. William had ceased to be a boy; it was neither the lightness of youth, nor daring, nor injustice which had led him to invade the territory of the English, but mature reflection and a sense of equity. The kingdom was his by right, he had been made heir by King Edward for his own worthiness, and in return for the honours and services which his forebears had rendered to the king and his father, Ethelred; Harold had broken the pact of friendship between himself and the Norman by taking possession of what was legally owed to William. As for the recommendation to go back to Normandy, it demanded the impossible : the season of the year and the difficulty of the voyage combined to prevent such a move. It is probable that by now the delayed equinoctial gales had begun to blow in the Channel; these the English king had counted on, less than a month before, to lock his rival in the harbours of the dukedom, and they would have made the crossing hazardous in the extreme for the shallow vessels of the allied fleet. If storms forbade a Norman sailing, however, they gave at least added reason for courage to the invaders; their effect on Harold's planning would be more far-reaching. But this lay still in the future; and Duke William had no intention of withdrawing. Not only the weather prevented him : in retreat, William would lose face before Rome and the princes of Europe more ignominiously than in any defeat, while a return to Normandy with a half-mercenary army, unrewarded and unsatisfied, would put an end to the duke's ambitions for much more than a winter, and might bring about the ruin of the dukedom.

William asked the monk if he would be willing to conduct a Norman embassy to the king. The Englishman promised to look after the safety of the messenger as he would his own, and the duke ended the audience. While the English envoy made ready for departure, the council of the allies chose as ambassador to Harold another cleric of proven bravery and eloquence. Of the great monastic houses of Normandy, none had closer ties with both England and the duke than the Abbey of the Holy Trinity at Fécamp. Edward had made numerous gifts of land to the monastery, and these were to be confirmed by William. The manor of Steyning in Sussex, less than a day's travel to the west of Hastings, had been the subject of a writ issued by the duke even before his sailing, confirming the estate to the monastery, if God granted a Norman victory.[11] As early as 1054, William had entrusted a mission to England to the abbot of Fécamp, and now his choice of envoy fell on a monk of the abbey, Huon Margot, *a learned man, well known and much valued.*[12] The Norman was given his instructions, the Englishman was recalled, and the fellow-clerics set off for London and the court of King Harold. Meanwhile, William strengthened the guard on his camp. The duke knew the military craft of his adversary; and much as he might sneer before the unsophisticated captains of his motley army at an enemy whose practice was *to conquer by guile and not by might,*[13] he recognised the danger that guile presented. With Harold already probably no more than two days' march from the Norman encampment, the duke's attention to security grew even greater.

*   *   *   *   *

The king and his following entered London about the same time as the English emissary to Duke William rode into the Hastings camp. Harold and his mounted elite had covered a hundred and ninety miles in little over four days, averaging more than forty miles a day. In the shires the riders had passed through, other horsemen had hurried to join them. Elsewhere, the men of England were responding again to the national danger: in Northumbria and Mercia, the grandsons of Earl Leofric were collecting fresh contingents to augment the survivors of the September battles; the distant areas of Wessex and East Anglia were already mustering the last of their warrior-representatives; from all points of the compass, along the roads converging on London, bodies of Englishmen were hastening to the aid of their king. In London welcome intelligence awaited the king: in the anchorage below London bridge, Danish ships were moored, and the captains of the troops the ships had carried greeted Harold's return. The coming of the Danes was not expected. Swegen of Denmark can have had no knowledge of the Norman landing when these auxiliaries were embarked for England, and clearly they were intended to buttress Harold's operations against the earlier invader, the special enemy of King Swegen. Arriving too late to take part in the Northumbrian campaign, the Danes remained now to help the conqueror of Hardraada in the struggle with his southern rival. But precious days would be lost before the English reinforcements could reach London, and even with the Danish auxiliaries, the forces which Harold commanded were still pitifully few, a fragment of the huge host which had marched north a fortnight earlier along the Roman way to York.

There could be no rest after the journey for the English leaders. The conciliatory mood of York was ended, and now Harold feared only that the pillagers might escape him. In conference with the English and Danish commanders, the king forswore every agreement between himself and the enemy, and *he ordered his men to prepare themselves with all speed, that he might come upon the Normans, with their leader William, before they could flee from England.*[14] There was much to be done. Since May, part of the national fyrd had been almost continuously in arms, and the stores of the country had been exhausted in its maintenance; now the fyrd was needed again, and new supplies must be requisitioned. King Harold and his brothers, with the witan who were at Westminster, immediately started organising the destruction of the invaders. Work on the warships docked in the port of London was speeded up: the king's plan included the fleet, and in less than a week upward of three hundred vessels were to be cleared for sea. In and about the city, quarters and provisions were needed for the soldiery from the provinces.

It was probably on Monday, the ninth of October, that the Norman embassy crossed the Thames and came to Thorney Island. The English envoy brought Huon Margot to the king. The monk of Fécamp was an ill choice as ambassador, unless it was Duke William's intention deliberately to incense his opponent. Worthy and learned the Norman cleric may have been, but he lacked both discretion and courtesy, the absence of these being balanced by an excess of self-righteousness and an exaggerated sense of his own importance. Margot began as he meant to go on, not deigning to dignify the 'usurper' with even a borrowed title of nobility: *'Harold!' said he, 'hearken to me! I am a messenger, hear you from whom?'*[15] Had Harold forgotten the oath he had sworn to the duke? Did he not know that he had committed perjury? If the Englishman wished to be saved, he must redress the wrong done by him, and give up to William the crown that was not his by ancestry, neither by heritage, nor through any man of his lineage. Margot left the question of descent, which could be at best an embarrassing subject where Duke William was concerned. King Edward, the Norman said, of his own free will had given his land and realm to William. The great nobles of England had confirmed the grant, and Harold himself, when the duke had saved his life, had sworn to maintain it: he had become a Norman vassal, *by the tradition of hands*,[16] and had guaranteed his faith to the duke. William was ready to show mercy; let Harold restore the kingdom he had seized; but woe betide him if he tried to hold it.

King Harold was restrained with difficulty from making a violent reply. The manner of the messenger can only have reminded the Englishman of the ravages being carired out in his land by the barbarian who spoke so glibly of mercy and the redressing of wrong. Gyrth stepped between his brother and the monk, and dismissed the Norman. Huon Margot left the English court at once, without taking leave. It is said that, close on Margot's heels, Harold sent a second envoy to Hastings, one *who knew the language of France*.[17] This ambassador was charged with presenting to Duke William a reasoned statement of the English case: if an oath was sworn by Harold, it was extorted from him under duress; if an agreement was made between Harold and William, it concerned the Englishman only as a private individual, and could not prejudice his actions as the elected leader of his nation; if King Edward had at first resolved to make the Norman his heir, the pledge was cancelled by his dying nomination of Harold. If this message was delivered, the king forebore to point out that in the contract between himself and the duke, the clauses now dwelt upon by William were subsidiary and had been drafted when the circumstances of the two leaders were very different; the main clauses, by which the treaty stood or fell, were already void. It is, however, unlikely that a second approach was made: the time available almost precludes it as a possibility; and the temper of the king no longer sought peace through arbitration.

Harold was anxious to bring the invaders to battle, *before the people following on from Normandy could come to their defence*.[18] But the king's impetuosity perturbed his closer advisers. His mother, Gytha, still grieving over the death of Tostig, tried to dissuade Harold from risking the lives of her remaining sons. It was Gyrth who put forward the most cogent argument. The fourth son of Godwin, and since the crowning of his brother the second man in England, he begged Harold to let him lead the fyrd against the Normans, while the king watched over the defences of London. The Northumbrian campaign had been arduous, and Harold was weary. So many of their best warriors had been killed, *when God did justice on the Norwegians*,[19] and so few had been gathered as yet to replace them, that it would be folly for the king to command the army in person, if all was to be hazarded on a single encounter. There were no ties on Gyrth. However much the provisions of the covenant with Duke William had been distorted by the Norman, Harold had sworn a form of fealty to the duke; however nebulous the benefits conferred might have been, he had done homage. Though the oath was perjured by William himself, it had been given and taken. Though the king of England was not the earl of Wessex, and Harold crowned was not the fugitive suitor of two years earlier, it was better that the English defiance in arms be issued by one whose honour could not be called in question. The allegiance of Gyrth was owed only to Harold, as brother and king, and the earl could fight freely to protect his native land.

It might happen that there would be no need to come to blows: in that event, the leadership of the fyrd was a matter of no importance. But England could not afford the loss of the king: if war must be waged, and if Harold led the Saxon array, he would place in jeopardy not only his own life, but the strength of the nation and *the untarnished liberty of the English people.*[20] On the other hand, should Gyrth command and conquer, all trouble would cease, and the kingdom would be at peace as readily as if Harold himself had fought. And if disaster overtook the earl, at least the king would not be taken, not all the nobility would perish, and the whole power of England would not have been wagered and lost in one battle. Though Gyrth lay dead or in captivity, Harold could rally the defeated, raise a new army, and avenge or rescue his brother. The earl knew Harold too well to suggest that the king rest idly in London through the days of decision. While the younger Godwinsson marched against the enemy, the earl proposed, let the elder scour the country in the path of the Normans, burning houses and destroying villages, wasting the land and carrying off all stores of foodstuffs and all livestock. Then, even if the Normans were victorious, they would find nowhere the means to live. Weakened by the fighting, and starved by the activity of the king, the invaders would be driven back with ease. Faced by the full might of England, and unable to maintain his hungry troops in the wilderness he had helped to create, Duke William would have no alternative but to retire empty-handed to his own dominions.

Gyrth had given his advice, and all who were with the brothers held that it was good counsel and wished the king to accept it. But Harold was in no mood to admit even by default any justice in the Norman allegations, nor could he follow a course that would slight his manhood and bring despair to those who looked to him for protection. Whatever had been promised to Duke William, the one oath that bound Harold was the vow he had taken on the day of his coronation, pledging his duty to the people of England, as they had pledged theirs to him. The king answered: *'It may be, brother, that you are better fitted to fight with William; but I have not been wont to lie in a lair when other men fought, and William the Bastard shall not hear that I dare not look him in the face'.*[21] None would go into the field, or do battle without him, the king swore, nor would the earth of England be scorched by his orders. Fourteen years before, Harold had plundered and harried the Somerset coast at Porlock: but as the king had been willing to condone William's ravages as the deeds of immaturity, so now Harold could not act as the exile of a half-forgotten time had acted. *'How,'* said he, *'can I harm the people that I should govern? I cannot destroy nor injure those who should prosper under me.'*[22]

*　　*　　*　　*　　*

The mainland of Scotland and the Skerries had been left behind, and the mourning fleet came at last to Orkney. The sails were furled, and the oarsmen took the ships through the channels of the south-eastern islands into Scapa Flow. The first stage of the long voyage home was almost completed; and the ships moved into the shore, where, a few miles to the north-west, still hidden beyond the low hills and lochs of Hrossey, lay the Brock of Birsay and the castle of the Orkney earls. In the weeks of waiting, the islet fortress had sheltered Harald Sigurdsson's queen, the princess Ingigerd, and the king's first-born, the princess Maria, the daughter of whom men had said that she and Harald had but one life between them. With the earls Paul and Erlend, Skule and Ketel Krok, the sons of Tostig, Styrkar and the other survivors of the Norse defeat, Olaf Haraldsson landed on the mainland, to bring the news of defeat to the Lady Elizabeth and his half-sisters. The prince had learned the lesson of his father's final campaign and the capitulation: in later years, the younger son of Harald Hardraada was to be known as Olaf Kyrre, Olaf the Quiet, and in his long kingship *Olaf reigned in a peace unknown before in Norway.*[23] But death had not finished with the Norsemen: the refugees crossed Hrossey to the castle on the Brock, *and there they heard these tidings, that on that day and at that very hour when Harald fell, his daughter Maria died a sudden death.*[24] The one life was ended. The Norwegians had no will to continue their journey. Though word must have been sent to Nidaros of all that had taken place, Olaf, the queen and Ingigerd, with their retinue, remained at Birsay under the protection of the Orkney earls.

*   *   *   *   *

In the last days before he marched south to seek the Norman challenger, the king left Westminster and rode into Essex to make his devotions and his plea for victory in the church which had been the object of his special reverence for so many years. Riding from Thorney probably in the afternoon of Tuesday, the tenth of October, Harold made his way to the minster of the Holy Cross early on the following day with his escort and the canons and other clergy of Waltham. The king went first to his own chapel, and brought forth the relics which he had gathered there; these he took to the high altar, and laid down as an earnest of the vow that he would make. The king knelt in prayer. If war must come, and God granted success to the arms of England, Harold promised, he would confer upon the church wealth beyond measure, many estates, and the service of a multitude of clerics. More than this, he would pledge his own homage to the church forever, as the ransomed servant of the Lord.

King Harold rose. The procession formed in front of the king, and passed slowly along the nave, within the double row of fluted columns, massive and inlaid with gold, towards the great west door. As the worshippers moved away, one man remained behind: it was the duty of Thurkill, the sacristan, to guard the holy relics and to return them to the royal chapel, when the king was gone. The sacristan waited beside the altar, watching the clergy and the laymen of the escort file out. Thurkill was to witness an event beyond explanation, eerie as the omens that had shadowed the sailing of the Norse fleet. In the years since the finding of the Holy Rood, the cross of Tofig the Proud had become a crucifix: to the marble of the cross had been fixed a painted, wooden image of the Christ, the head erect, the eyes raised up to Heaven. The king's companions had left, and Thurkill and Harold were alone in the church, when the king turned again to face the rood, and threw himself prostrate before it in a last prayer, his arms outflung like the arms of the cross itself. And while Harold prayed, to the astonishment of the sacristan, the figure on the crucifix lowered its face towards the king, *as if sad, wood to which had been given foreknowledge of happenings to come.*[25] The story is strange, and might be dismissed as legend : but from that day forward, the head of the Christ on the Holy Rood at Waltham drooped, and as many as knew the image in those later days had seen it as it formerly stood.

The king was determined to bring the invaders to battle before the week was out, and by Thursday at the latest, the English host had to leave London. Outside the minster that Harold had founded and where he would finally rest the king's retinue mounted and the company rode off swiftly in the direction of the city. But in the church where the king and his followers had prayed for grace in the struggle to come, there was confusion. When Harold had risen and left the church, Thurkill recovered his wits, and hurried to the dean and chapter of the college. The sacristan told what he had seen, and the other clerics went with him to the minster. They looked up at the stooping figure on the cross, and the omen was clear. *Shrinking with many a grief,*[26] the canons chose two of their number to go to the king at Westminster, and to travel with him into Sussex. The representatives were Osegod Cnoppe and Ailric the Childmaster, both elders and distinguished among the brothers; and their allotted mission was to give to the body of King Harold the care of their office, *when the outcome of these events should be known.*[27]

*   *   *   *   *

At Hastings, the duke waited inside the strong defences of the camp. By now, William must have learned the fate of the ships which had strayed to Romney; but he made no move against the neighbouring port. Knowing the skill and vigour of his opponent, and dreading a sudden attack, the Norman lingered behind his entrenchments, extending only little by little

the range of his foragers, as stores dwindled under the huge
demands of the allied army. Huon Margot had returned, in-
dignant and complaining, but without any useful information.
The duke knew that he must discover more about the operations
of his enemy. A second proposal to the English leader was hurriedly drafted, and again a monk was chosen as envoy. When
the Norman messenger set out, half as ambassador, half as spy,
King Harold and his army were already on the march.

*   *   *   *   *

On Wednesday, the eleventh of October, soon after the return
from Waltham, Harold decided not to wait any longer for the
reinforcements from the North. The thegns and freemen of many
counties had answered the king's summons. *The men of London
had come at once, and those of Kent, of Hertford and of Essex;
of Surrey and of Sussex; of St. Edmund and of Suffolk; of
Norwich and of Norfolk; of Cambridge and of Stamford; and
thither they came from Bedfordshire, and thither those of
Huntingdon. The men of Northampton also came; and those of
York and of Buckingham, of Bedford and of Nottingham; of
Lindsey and of Lincoln, came all those who heard the summons.
There came also from the west many people; from Salisbury
and from Dorset, from Bath and from Somerset. Many came
too from about Gloucester, and many from Worcester, from
Winchester, from Hampshire and from the county of Berkshire;
and many more from other places and shires, parts of the country
that we have not named, nor can name all, nor wish to recount.
All who could bear arms and had learned the news of the duke's
arrival, came to defend the land against those who wished to
seize it.*[28] Fighting-men had flocked into London, from the earldoms of Harold and his brothers, and of Waltheof, and from
the counties through which the king had ridden on his southward
journey. The king had now some three or four thousand trained
soldiers under his command, including about fifteen hundred
housecarls and the auxiliaries sent by Swegen. It was as yet no
more than a nucleus, a fraction of the seven divisions that
Harold had led to meet the Norsemen; but the impatient king
believed that, with the shire-levies that would rally to the host
during the march to Hastings, and with the close support of the

fleet, he should have a sufficient force to wage the defensive campaign which he planned.

It was a question of time. Though it appeared probable that the invading army was larger than Harold had at first considered possible, hesitation by the English leader could only magnify the power of the duke. The delay was already more than Harold had envisaged; the news from Sussex was increasingly disquieting, and every day lost added to the likelihood of fresh accessions to the Normans; the fleet was cleared for sea, and the king was eager to bring an end to uncertainty before winter set in. Once the duke was expelled, England would be safe until the spring and another summer would find the realm strengthened. Yet the English numbers were small; five months of military activity had drained the reserves of the southern and central counties; Mercia and Northumbria had suffered heavily in the war with Hardraada, and the northern contingents of the fyrd were those who had left York with the king.

Gyrth's advice had been nicely judged but though *the intermediate part of his army had not yet assembled, as it was earlier able to do,*[29] Harold would not wait. It must have been in the afternoon or evening of Wednesday that the couriers rode from London, calling the men of the south-eastern shires to meet two days later, on Caldbec Hill between the Andredsweald and the Hastings isthmus, *at the hoar apple-tree.*[30]

The king's strategy depended on the co-operation of the fleet, and it seems that in the last days before the departure of the fyrd, the reports of the weather in the Channel were poor. Yet Harold was prepared now to risk everything on a single venture, and by the late hours of the eleventh of October, all was ready. The ships were gone, making their way along the estuary of the Thames towards the Wantsum and the uncertain waters beyond. In the encampments about London, in the city itself, and in the palace on Thorney, the soldiers of the king arranged their affairs and put their equipment in order. Earl and thegn, monk and yeoman, these were men who would fight for no special reward. Few of the companions of Harold can be identified, even fewer than those who can be named in the host of Duke William; and the greater number are commemorated solely in the dry records of their forfeiture of life and lands. Of the earls, certainly Gyrth and Leofwine were with their brother, and Waltheof may also have taken part in the campaign; but Edwin and Morkere were still far from London, and there is no trace of the shadowy figure of Oswulf. The king's stewards, the stallers, were thinly represented: after the exchange of messages in the first days after the Norman landing, Robert fitzWymarc seems to have stood aloof from both sides; Bondig appears to have lingered in the north, perhaps to assist the earls in their muster; the whereabouts of Eadnoth are unreported; only Ansgar, the grandson of Tofig the Proud, was definitely with the king.

These were the most powerful laymen in England; and Ansgar was the chief of the Londoners who marched with Harold, for as well as being staller, he was sheriff of Middlesex. Another sheriff led the men of his county into Sussex: Godric, lord of Fyfield near Abingdon, and sheriff of Berkshire, was one of the wealthiest landholders in central Wessex, and he may have been sheriff also of Buckinghamshire. With Godric came his neighbour, Thurkill, tenant of the manor of Kingston Bagpuze and of other estates in Berkshire. Two of the lesser men of Wessex, who fought for the king, may have been Eadnoth and Eadwig, joint-occupants of a small acreage in Hampshire, who died about this time, and whose lands were taken by William. Not only the laity among the West Saxons followed their former earl: the aging abbot of the New Minster at Winchester, Aelfwig, brother of Earl Godwin, came with twelve of his order to support in arms his crowned nephew. Another churchman of similar birth and rank arrived from the earldom of Waltheof: Leofric, abbot of Peterborough and nephew of Earl Leofric, set the need of his country above that of the monastery he had so enriched in his thirteen years rule *that men called it the 'golden borough'*.[31] Under Waltheof's leadership too was a thegn of Huntingdonshire, Aelfric of Yelling and Hemingford, in the flat country between Huntingdon and Cambridge. Presumably in the train of Gyrth were two East Anglians, Breme, a freeman of King Edward, and Eadric the deacon, a minor churchman: the former was the possessor of land at 'Dagaworda' in Suffolk; the latter held acres at Cavendish near Sudbury.

There is a strange and improbable story that may mask the

presence at Senlac of one of the richest of the English thegns. According to the legend, Brihtric Mau, the son of Aelfgar, was sent as ambassador to the court of Flanders in the early years of the reign of King Edward. At Bruges, Matilda, daughter of the Flemish count, fell in love with the ambassador and offered herself to him in marriage. But the Englishman found the young woman less attractive than the Norman duke was to do, and refused her advances. Brihtric returned to England, Matilda married William the Bastard, and the years passed; until, at length, the duke usurped a crown, and his duchess became a queen. Matilda asked her husband for revenge; William could not refuse, and although the Englishman had already made his peace with the Norman, Brihtric paid the penalty of his earlier indiscretion. Arrested at his manor of Hanley in Gloucestershire, the thegn was brought to Winchester and there murdered in prison, while his heritage was seized and divided between Matilda and a Norman baron, Robert fitzHamon. The only certain facts about Brihtric Mau, however, are that his father's name was Aelfgar; that he owned extensive territories in western England, from Dorset to Cornwall and north to Worcestershire; and that, by 1086, all his properties had passed into other hands, principally those of the queen. The tale of Matilda's spurning and revenge may have a basis in truth, but it may equally have arisen from the later history of the forfeited estates. In the latter case, the confiscations may well have been the result of Brihtric's participation in King Harold's last campaign.

Soon after dawn, on the morning of October the twelfth, the fyrd gathered, presumably in Southwark, beyond the bridge. With the uncle and brothers of the king may have come his nephew: Hakon the son of Swegen, he may have spent his early years as a hostage in Normandy, but he is said to have returned to England with Harold in 1064. Probably the eldest of Godwin's grandsons, he would almost certainly have ridden to Sussex beside his kinsmen. In the English assembly, non-combatants were few. Though women could only hamper the operations of the army there is evidence to suggest that his mother and wife were both with Harold, and that Gytha and Edith Swan-Neck watched the battle with the monks of Waltham. But on that Thursday morning, the English leaders were more concerned with the rigours of the march ahead than with the fighting. More than sixty miles had to be covered on the most practicable route to the rendezvous, and Harold was determined to occupy his chosen position by the evening of Friday. There could be no delays, and stragglers could only be left to make their own way after the main force.

The first stage of the march brought the English army to Crayford, through flat and open country, seldom far from the Thames. From there the divisions pushed on to cross the Medway at Rochester, where they turned south along the branch highway to Hastings. In the October day, there were no more than twelve hours of light; the moon was entering its last quarter, and would not rise till late. Within an hour and a half of sunset, further travel would be impossible, and it must have been nearing dusk when the rearmost troops reached Rochester. The king hurried along the Hastings way south to Maidstone, until a mile or so beyond the town, where the Andredsweald thickened about the old road: even in twilight, the clustering trees would have made it difficult to go on. The king halted at last; a temporary camp was established and the soldiers rested.

* * * * *

William's messenger stumbled across the English encampment before dawn on the morning of Friday: *the envoy, turning aside through trackless parts, came unaware to where the king lurked in secret.*[32] The fyrd was stirring and its commanders were preparing to set out at first light. The Norman mission was ill-timed and a cowled colleague of Huon Margot could hardly look for a welcome from the king whom his precursor had insulted. But the message and the manner of the second Norman ambassador were more circumspect. The monk hailed the king on behalf of the duke, and *gave him his choice, which he would take of three things. Either he should give up England to the duke and take his daughter in marriage; or submit himself to the good judgment of the Apostle and his people; or meet the duke singly and fight body to body, on the condition that he who could kill the other, or overcome and take him captive, should hold England in peace, no other person being injured.*[33] The embassy offered, in effect, a choice of three impossibilities; and it can

221

only be considered a further attempt by William to confuse the issue. Harold Godwinson was king of the English by the elective will of the witan, the crown was not his to dispose of, and he was married before the church and the people; an appeal to Rome was inevitably pre-judged, Hildebrand's power in the curia was undiminished, and Harold was as aware as William of the partiality of the Holy See; the challenge to trial by combat could scarcely have been meant seriously, or have been taken so by any but the most juvenile of its hearers.

The Norman was given scant attention in the bustle of the morning. The king was occupied with more pressing matters and there was no time to spare for social courtesies. As far as Harold was concerned, the debate in words with the invader was already concluded. While the monk prattled, the king continued with the urgent business in hand. Harold's lack of interest, however, was interpreted by the envoy as a numbness induced by fear, and he persisted in his demands for a reply to the duke's propositions. It is not difficult to picture the scene, with the English leader moving among his men, overseeing the preparations for the march, and the obstinate cleric following the king about the camp, with a growing awareness of the futility of his mission, as statesman if not as spy. Phrases uttered by Harold were to be remembered and reported as the inconsequent answers of a disturbed mind : those quoted by the chronicler[34] are more reasonably explicable as directions to the English captains. But the perseverance of the messenger finally provoked a response. Angrily, the king turned on the Norman, *and said to the envoy: 'Go back, fool! Tomorrow, as God is our judge, my just share of the kingdom will be made apparent: the holy hand of God will make an equitable division'.*[35] The Norman had his reply. He hurried to the duke to tell of all that he had seen and heard.

It was in the mid-afternoon of Friday at the earliest that the ambassador regained the Norman encampment. Duke William questioned him closely. The duke was more interested in what the monk had learned of the English dispositions than in the outcome of the embassy, and the first answers told him what he most needed to discover : the king, said the churchman, was approaching with a vast army, and he was not far away. With only the sketchiest knowledge of the country through which he had passed, the envoy could hardly have been expected to be more specific. But the information satisfied the duke : he knew now that within a day, Harold would come against him. The military value of the monk's estimate of the strength of the fyrd was limited, and William could not yet have been sure of his opponent's power, or have anticipated Harold's tactical purpose. The presence at sea, reported by the monk, of an English fleet sent by the king to cut off a Norman retreat implied neither siege nor storm by the land forces, but could support either. It was clear, however, that the English had been making ready to strike camp when the mesenger found them; and it was possible that, as the monk claimed, the king had hoped to catch the invaders off guard, and to overwhelm them in a sudden assault. Though the arrival of the ambassador must have driven the king to abandon such a hope, Harold was unlikely to have halted his advance in consequence, and his forward troops could not have been far behind the returning envoy. Within hours, direct observation would bring the duke the insight he required, and he would settle his plans accordingly. For the time being, the Norman position was probably secure : it was late in the day for battle, and the time of year and the phase of the moon would hamper night operations, now that surprise could not be achieved.

*   *   *   *   *

The fyrd pushed southwards on the old road into the Andredsweald. The forest thickened about the column, dulling the sounds of the marching and the voices of the marchers. The numbers had grown as the Kentish levies came to join the king, some with arms and armour, some equipped with nothing more than primitive clubs, stones lashed to handles of wood. The Romans had built well : though broken here and there, the road was still good, and the soldiers made swift progress. For about fifteen miles their way led through the woodland, which stretched from the outcrops of the North Downs almost to the great lagoon that reached inland to the Isle of Oxney and the broad channel of the River Rother. In the late morning or early afternoon, the English vanguard emerged from the forest a mile

or so north of Bodiam, to pass the Rother and move on towards Sedlescombe and Hastings. In the open country beyond
the Andredsweald, Harold paused, to rest and regroup; the last
miles of the journey were travelled away from the metalled highways of the legions, on pitted tracks that tired the marchers. At
Sedlescombe, the Roman road crossed the Brede, the river that
formed the northern boundary of the Hastings peninsula. Here,
in the eleventh century, the Brede was tidal and more than two
hundred yards wide, flowing eastwards to meet open water near
the site of modern Winchelsea. The ferrying of the army would
have been arduous, length and dangerous. With warning of the
king's coming, Duke William might already have set a guard
on the southern bank of the river, and it was essential now that
Harold reach the meeting-place and the ground of battle as
quickly as possible.

At Cripps Corner, two miles north of Sedlescombe, an ancient
folkway left the Roman road, branching west towards the
southern rises of the Weald. This was probably the point at
which the fyrd turned away from the direct route to Hastings.
A little over a mile west of Cripps Corner, at Vinehall, the way
to the west was joined by a local track from the south; here the
line of march turned again, with Caldbec Hill in sight to the
south-west and less than three miles distant. The dark mass of
the forest blanketed the northern horizon to within a few hundred yards of the road but trees were sparse now in the path of
the army and the beaten earth track ran through brush and long
grass, broken by streams and gullies. The narrowing Brede was
forded at Whatlington, and in the failing light of the October
afternoon, the weary troops came at last to Caldbec Hill and the
final mustering. The rendezvous was well chosen: it was a
known location, easily reached and easily recognised; several
trackways met there, from east, west, north and south, and it
seems likely that the hoar apple-tree itself served as a landmark,
fixing the junction of three Sussex 'hundreds'.[36] From the crest
of the hill, there was a fair view of the open country to the south,
across the full width of the isthmus of the peninsula. Less than
eight miles away lay Hastings and the Norman base; and half a
mile from Caldbec, commanding the one road out of the peninsula, was a defensive position that no outward thrust by the

invaders could by-pass. The halt at the meeting-place was brief. When the main body of the army had gathered, the marshals led their men from the hill, along the neck of land on which the High Street of the town of Battle would be built in a later age, to the ridge above Senlac.

*   *   *   *   *

The English must still have been deploying when the first of the Norman scouts rode into the Hastings encampment and hurried to the duke with word of the arrival of the fyrd. The intelligence brought by the monk was confirmed : King Harold had come, and at the head of a large army. Despite the abrupt dismissals of his previous embassies, William decided to attempt yet another approach to his enemy. But the mood this time was to be wholly conciliatory, in so far as William could amend his arrogance without total loss of face. It seems more than possible that the earliest reports from the Norman outposts exaggerated the English strength; that conditions at sea remained stormy; and that briefly the duke may have doubted his destiny. William had not, however, lost belief in his personal power of persuasion, and he determined to be his own ambassador on this occasion. In a hasty council, the duke told his barons that he *would himself speak with Harold, and summon him with his own mouth to give up that of which he had cheated him.*[37] He would accuse the Englishman of perjury, William said, and charge him to fulfil the terms of his pledge. If the English leader would not restore the dignities which rightfully belonged to the Norman, there would be no recourse but battle. But if Harold yielded, and if the allied council consented, the duke proposed a division of the kingdom between himself and the 'usurper'. It was a remarkable come-down from the attitudes adopted by the challenger at Lillebonne and Rome.

The barons approved the plan. A division of England between William and Harold would still offer a fair return for their investment, and the only alternatives were to fight immediately, without means of escape if they were defeated, or to wait with dwindling stores while the English forces grew to irresistible proportions. One thing the barons wished to say : if nothing else could be done, and battle was not to be averted, let the Normans attack promptly; further delay could only injure the allies, for they had nothing to wait for, while the English numbers would increase daily. William promised that he would hold back no longer, and made preparations for the meeting with Harold. Twenty knights were mounted, armed with swords and accompanied by squires who bore their other weapons. These rode out some way from the camp towards the designated meeting-place. A hundred knights were then mounted and armed, and they were stationed where they could hasten, if required, to the aid of the twenty. A thousand knights gave similar support to the hundred. Lastly, a herald was sent to the enemy lines to convey the duke's proposal to Harold.

The English sentinels brought the herald to the king. Harold may still have been on the ridge with his men; but if Gytha and Edith had in fact ridden with the fyrd, the king and his brothers may have quitted the forward position once the occupation was completed and a guard had been established. On the westward slopes of Caldbec Hill, until the middle years of the twentieth century, there stood an isolated and aged tree known locally as the 'Watch Oak'. Traditionally, this was the site from which the king's mother and mistress, with their attendants, witnessed the eclipse of Anglo-Saxon England. Most of the crest of the ridge could be seen from the oak; and it is reasonable to assume that here Harold retired when it became evident that no Norman attack was likely to develop that evening. As soon as the rendezvous was reached, scouts were sent out by the English commander: it is said that one group of reconnoitrers reported of the army of the duke, *that almost all his soldiers had the appearance of priests*;[38] and that the king smiled at a simplicity which confused an absence of beards and moustaches with a religious vocation. But the herald came before the king and *desired him to come into the field and speak with the duke, and to fear nothing, but to bring with him whom he would, that they might talk of an arrangement.*[39] Gyrth, however, was with his brother and did not wait for Harold to answer. The earl sprang to his feet and spoke for the king: Harold would go to no solitary meeting with the duke; if William wanted to make any arrangement, let him send his terms plainly detailed to the full council of the English army.

The messenger left and the king called together the leaders of the fyrd. The Norman returned shortly with Duke William's proposition: if Harold would abide by his former covenant, the duke would grant to the Englishman as an independent kingship, *all Northumbria and whatever belonged to the realm beyond the Humber*;[40] William offered also to give to Gyrth the lands which Godwin had held, within the part of the kingdom to be ruled by the Norman. The messenger went on to exercise again the tired arguments of Harold's perjury, his slighting of the duke's daughter, and the promise of the crown to William. But the audience remained silent, and the voice of the herald hardened. If Harold would not accept the duke's generosity, more than merely war was the doom of the English. The Norman played his master's trump card: Duke William *desired that the English should know, and take notice, that all who came with Harold against the duke, or stood by him in this situation, were excommunicated by the Apostle and the clergy.*[41] The benediction of Rome had been purchased at a heavy price; but it was a potent weapon even against the inheritors of a church that antedated the Holy See. The listeners were troubled: though the chosen attitude of the curia must already have been known in England, the direct threat of excommunication was fearful. There were murmurs among the members of the gemot, and anxious consultations: courageous as the commanders of the fyrd were, the omens had been unpropitious, and all would gladly have avoided battle.

It was once again Gyrth who brought reason to bear on the discussion. He could see, the earl said, that the English notables dreaded the coming struggle and would have preferred to reach some form of agreement with the invader. His own fear was as great as theirs, or greater. But Gyrth had another fear: of Duke William, whose every act was treacherous. They had heard the duke's offer: how low he rated the English, that he would give them only what portion he chose of a land which was not his to give. If the English accepted the treaty, if they went beyond the Humber, William's desires would not be satisfied: he would push them farther and farther, watching them at all times, and bringing them to ruin in the end. Once in control, the Norman would try to seize everything. He wanted to cheat them into taking, instead of a rich country, a meagre part of one; and soon he would have even that. Gyrth could easily secure his own fortune : his fears were on behalf of his hearers. If they surrendered to the Norman, their lands were already forfeited : there was not a knight in the enemy host to whom William had not promised territory in England; there was not an earldom or manor that he had not pledged away; he had even taken homage from his supporters for the inheritances of the English. Under the duke's licence and protection, his barons would chase the men of England from their estates, hunt them down, and kill them. Their vassals would be pillaged, their sons and daughters degraded. The invaders did not come merely for plunder : their purpose was to destroy the English and their heritage.

Gyrth rallied his audience. Let the followers of the king defend themselves, their children, and all that belonged to them, while it was still possible. His brother had never given away, nor agreed to give away, the great lordships, the honours or lands of their ancestors : earls had remained earls, and thegns had enjoyed their rights; sons had held the estates of their fathers; the tranquillity of the kingdom had not been disturbed. This was how matters should be in England, and how they should continue to be; and this was what all must determine to preserve. But if the lords of the realm abandoned their houses, their manors, and their other possessions, the country which had nourished them all their lives, what would they become, and what would they do? In what land would they go begging, and where would they seek a place to rest? When they had lost in such a manner their own honour, how should they look for it in others? After the earl had made his peroration, Harold spoke, pledging anew his service to his people. Gyrth had aroused and excited the spirits of the English : the doubts that had divided the council were swept aside, and the menaces of Normandy and Rome were forgotten in an upsurge of national pride. The men who so recently had dreaded battle and sought an urgent end to hostility, regained their courage and were eager to fight. The fervour of the gemot was so high that any man who had talked of peace would have been shouted down, and hesitancy would have brought instant censure.

The Norman messenger returned to his master. The last embassy had been rejected, and battle was now unavoidable. William had promised that there would be no further delay, and the duke and his men retired to their tents to make ready for the morrow. In every part of the camp, men were straightening lances, stringing bows, filling quivers, tending to saddles and stirrups, and adjusting the fit of hauberks and helmets. The duke had decided to begin his advance at dawn, and the soldiers were ordered to stand to throughout the night. Though the sky was very dark and the moon obscured by cloud, the steady watch guarded also against a sudden attack by the enemy. By this time, William must have known that the fyrd, while stronger in number, was weaker in arms than the invaders, and that fewer than half of the English were drawn from social ranks equipped and trained for war. Yet even in a darkness that made organised movement almost impossible, there could be no relaxation of alertness : weakness had not prevented Harold from rejecting every diplomatic approach by the duke; and it would not hinder any operation planned by the Englishman. All remained awake. Two bishops, Odo of Bayeux and Geoffrey of Coutances, had accompanied William from Normandy, and with them had come many lesser clergy. In the encampment, numerous chapels and confessionals had been set up; and when their weapons and armour were in order, the soldiers went to the priests for absolution, penances and blessings. The priets passed the night in prayer and in hearing confessions; and in the early hours of the morning, the bishops administered the mass. Under the still-dark sky, the duke and his followers knelt before the altars and received the sacrament.

There was as little sleep on the ridge where the English rested in their battle-stations. Chronicles tell of singing and drinking that went on all night among the men of the fyrd,[42] of dancing and shouts of 'waes-hail' and 'drink-hail'. Among the rustics who made up the greater part of the army, excitement may well have led to an unthinking frivolity. But the leaders and the experienced soldiers had small inducement to merriment. The seriousness of their situation and the hazards that they would face in the succeeding hours were patent. The general campaign design had failed. No word had come from the fleet, and no English ships challenged the seaward defences of the enemy base. Far to the east, the wind had interfered again with the destiny of England :[43] the wind that had brought Tostig in May; that had held the Normans land-locked in the late summer months when Harold stood ready to crush them; and that had sped their crossing at the one juncture of the year when the king and the main power of England were away from the south. In the north-eastern reaches of the Channel, the English fleet beat unavailingly against adverse storms; and in Sussex, the scouts on the rises in front of the English position looked vainly towards an empty sea for the support that did not come. It must have been clear by now, too, that the invaders were stronger than Harold had believed. The decision would be close. There could be no thought of attack by the fyrd : the shock troops of the housecarls were reduced and battle-worn; and a charge of the levies would break irrecoverably before a firm opposition. Already the horses of the army had been sent to the rear, and defensive lines had been fixed. In the short time allowed, primitive entrenchments may have been dug, though the protection they gave would have been more moral than physical. Yet the terrain was advantageous to the English, and while the fyrd held, the Normans could not conquer.

* * * * *

On Saturday, the fourteenth of October, 1066, dawn broke at about half past five. Southwards, the waning moon hung low. Light touched the tops of Caldbec Hill and Telham Hill, south of the English position, and crept over the ridge where preparations for the day were beginning. The location was ideally suited to Harold's purpose. The fighting qualities of the shire-levies did not match their ardour, and they could not be expected to function effectively, even as infantry in a static defensive line without a strengthening leaven of trained soldiers. The surviving housecarls and thegns were too few to be spared for service as other than rallying centres and anchors to the mass of the levies. Hence, the king could afford to field neither a cavalry attack force nor a mounted reserve. At the same time, most of the archers had necessarily been left behind in the precipitate return from York. Even in the great days of the English longbow, the archer came commonly from the poorer classes : this was true in

the eleventh century, and few of the bowmen who had marched
to meet the Norsemen could have owned horses. The fyrd, therefore, was weak in precisely those arms which were most powerfully developed in the enemy array. The situation of Stamford
Bridge was reversed. But Hardraada had been given no opportunity to choose his ground of battle, and the flats beside the
Derwent had been perfect for cavalry manoeuvres and archery
attack. At Senlac, the English position had been carefully
selected: the imposed angle of fire would seriously reduce the
effectiveness of the Norman bowmen, and Harold could hope to
beat off indefinitely the loosely disciplined charges in column of
the allied knights. Though losses might be heavy, each held
assault would weaken the enemy proportionately, and every day
of confinement within the peninsula would lessen his resources,
until reinforcements to the fyrd had swung the balance over-
whelmingly against the invaders.

From Caldbec Hill, the level of the ground dropped to about
two hundred and fifty feet southwards across the isthmus to the
spur of the downs where the English were to make their stand.
Here, the level rose slightly again, and the isthmus broadened
suddenly from a width of less than two hundred yards to form a
cross ridge some eight hundred yards in length. From its western
extremity, the spine of the ridge ran north of east by a few
degrees; its height remained fairly constant, except centrally,
where it mounted to a low summit, approximately twenty-five
feet above the surrounding ground. The southern rim of the spur
followed more or less the two hundred and fifty foot contour line
from the west end to a point immediately in front of the summit;
from there it dropped at a very gentle gradient to a small hillock
which marked the east end. The front was almost straight,
slightly convex to the south. The steepest faces of the ridge were
to the north, where ravines separated the arms of the spur from
the isthmus: to the north-west the slope was one in six, and to the
north-east, one in four. Four hundred yards west of the summit,
the height of the northern bank was already over thirty feet, while
the equivalent height to the east was over fifty feet, and the fear
of any cavalry assault from the rear, east or west, was negligible.
The forward southern slopes were less exaggerated: the gradient
was sharpest before the summit, where the level fell away at one

in fifteen to a second isthmus or saddle, some forty feet below the rim, linking the ridge to the northern rises of Telham Hill; at the south-east end of the spur, the slope was one in twenty-two; at the south-west end, it was no more than one in thirty-three.

The ridge alone would have been a formidable obstacle to an army of the time. But it was not merely the configuration of the land that had led Harold to choose his site of battle. The ridge was a watershed. About it, behind and in front, several small streams rose, flowing east and west from both the isthmus to the north and the saddle to the south. The country around was rough and broken, uninhabited and wholly uncultivated, except possibly on the slopes of Telham Hill south-west of the saddle, where lay the 'sand-lake' which was to give the coming encounter its less accepted but more definitive name of Senlac. On the isthmus, the ridge itself, and the saddle, the ground was firm : open heathland with scattered bushes of gorse and broom. Behind the spur, the streams ran in the gullies that bordered the ridge to the north, and here the undergrowth was probably thicker, with brambles and other bushes masking the steepness of the banks. South of the ridge, however, there was little brush; marshes spread along the courses of the streams and the lower ground on either side of the saddle was a quagmire. Both flanks of the position were therefore protected, and the only approach lay across the saddle from Telham Hill, on the route of the trackway from the coast, which was also the only outlet from the Hastings peninsula for an army marching to the north.

On the summit of the ridge, the road from Hastings crossed another track which followed the crest of the spur. At this crossroads, where the gradual slope to the south-east began, the royal headquarters were set up, and the standards of Wessex and King Harold were raised. Below and some fifty yards in advance of the command, the English lines extended east and west on the southern rim of the ridge, curving very slightly with the curve of the position along the eight hundred yards front, with the extreme flanks turned sharply back to rest on the banks of the gullies behind the spur. In full length, the foremost rank of the fyrd must have measured between eight hundred and fifty and nine hundred yards, and the total strength numbered now something more than eight thousand five hundred men. Not all the king's supporters had yet arrived; there were stragglers in the forest and on the ways to Caldbec Hill, and it seems probable that late-comers continued to reach the ridge throughout the day. Nevertheless, arrayed in a depth of possibly ten ranks, with perhaps half of the three thousand or so experienced warriors in the forward ranks and the remainder grouped around the standards, the English crowded the hill-top. The position may indeed have been so compressed that *in as much as the English were drawn up in a narrow place, many withdrew from the battle line.*[44] The reports of desertions are exaggerated, and it is certainly not true that *very few remained stout of heart,*[45] but what runaways there were may have found additional cause for their defection in Harold's chosen strategy: a policy of defence without attack could scarcely have been attractive to the men whose homes lay close to the terror wrought by the invaders.

Soon after dawn, the English were in their stations, armed and ready.[46] On the right wing of the line, to the west where the slope of the ridge was easiest and the ground was less of a marsh than to the east, there stood the Kentish thegns with the levies of their shire behind them: *for they say that the men of Kent are entitled to strike first,*[47] and here the enemy was most likely to launch his attack. Centrally, with the household troops of the king and his brothers, the representatives of the London burghers faced the Norman advance: for they say too that *the right of the men of London is to defend the king's person, to place themselves around him, and to guard his standard.*[48] It was a very different army from the host which Harold had led to victory in the north. Less than a third wore the full armour of the times, byrnies and helmets with nose-pieces and leather neck-guards. Others wore shorter leather jerkins strengthened with iron studs or rings. The jerkins of many, however, were unprotected, and a high proportion of the mustered peasantry were dressed only in the tunics and thonged leggings of everyday wear. The armoured warriors mostly carried the yard-long, kite-shaped shields of lime wood which had become standard; but it seems likely that some, whose shields had been damaged beyond repair at Stamford Bridge, had refurnished themselves from the Norwegian dead and bore the obsolescent round targes of an earlier age. Among the men of the levies, there were shields of both types; but there were also many improvised from planks of wood and other materials and the poorest were without protection of any kind. The weapons of the fyrd were yet more varied : the housecarls and thegns were equipped with spears and throwing-axes, long, two-edged swords, and the dreaded battle axes; the arms of the countrymen ranged from javelins, axes, bills and clubs, to slings, scythes, pitch-forks and the rude, stone-headed hatchets and hammers.

*   *   *   *   *

In the first glimmer of dawn, the Norman army assembled; and before the day was fully lit, the duke moved out of the encampment with his forces. In no particular formation as yet, the host made its way along the road to Senlac; and a little over an hour after leaving the camp, the head of the column reached Blackhorse Hill, then known as Hechelande or Hedgeland,[49] above the northern spurs of Telham Hill. Here the duke halted to prepare his order of battle. Though the English position was not yet in sight, there were only some two miles still to be covered, and the soldiers donned their armour. A coat of mail was brought for William, and again an omen seemed to presage disaster. By a strange accident, the hauberk was handed to the duke reversed, and he put it on unthinkingly back to front. There was a chorus of dismay from those who stood about the duke. But one of William's attendants called out quickly : this was a token of good fortune, he swore, and foretold that he who wore the coat would turn from a duke to a king. William was apparently unmoved. He removed the mail and put it on again correctly. Then he spoke to his companions. As a true Christian, the duke said, he had never given heed to omens or to sorcery in any shape. However, because he trusted in God and His aid, and to reassure those who were to risk their lives on his behalf, he would make a vow : if the Normans conquered that day, he would found a monastery for the salvation of all his followers, and especially of those who fell; and the house would be built on the place of battle. Among those who heard the vow was the former smith, William Faber, monk of Marmoutiers in the Loire Valley. He came to the duke and asked that the raised monastery should be dedicated to St. Martin, the apostle of the Gauls. The request was immediately granted.[50]

The army was now drawn up in three great divisions: the first was composed of the French and Flemish auxiliaries, but under the command of a Norman, the seneschal, William fitzOsbern; the second comprised the men of Britanny, Poitou, and Maine, and was led by Alan the Red, Count of Britanny; the third consisted of the Normans themselves, with the duke at their head. Subordinate to fitzOsbern were Eustace of Boulogne and Gilbert of Ghent. With Alan the Red rode Aimeri of Thouars and Ralph of Gael and probably Count Brian of Britanny, brother of Alan. But the majority of the names that were to live in English history were grouped about Duke William: Odo of Bayeux, Robert of Mortain, and the lords and barons of Normandy. The field army numbered some eight thousand men, of whom rather more than half were Normans; the balance of strength between the allied divisions lay with the Bretons. Each division included bowmen, heavy infantry, and armoured knights; and there were possibly a thousand archers, four thousand men-at-arms, and three thousand cavalry. Among the invaders, there was a considerably greater uniformity of weapons and harness than in the fyrd. The knights wore armour similar to that of the English housecarls and carried lances, cutting swords, maces and the yard-long shields of the day; their horses, however, were unprotected. Many of the men-at-arms wore chain-mail shirts and conical, iron helmets with nose-pieces, and the rest wore caps and jerkins of stout leather; they were armed with broadswords, spears and daggers, and a few carried axes. The archers were lightly clothed in jerkins and caps; their bows were primitive, short and of limited power, with an effective range scarcely above one hundred yards.

His army ready the duke called for his commanders. A knight named Vital, a follower of Bishop Odo, had scouted the ground ahead and seen the English array and reported to the duke the presence on the ridge of Harold's personal banner. Even in the final hours, the king might have withdrawn, leaving the immediate battle to his subordinates: he had not done so, and William knew at last with certainty that this was to be the decisive engagement. When the allied leaders had gathered around the duke, he *urged them, both by persuasion and promises, to acquit themselves faithfully in the conflict.*[51] He reminded them of their country, their good name, and the many dangers they had passed througn under his leadership. William had no illusions about the fate of his forces in defeat. *'It is now,'* he said, *'that your hands should prove the power with which you are endowed, and the courage which spurs you on. Henceforward, it is no longer a question of living as masters, but of escaping alive from imminent peril. If you fight like men, victory, honour and riches will be yours: if not, you will either let yourselves be killed, or you will be taken prisoner and serve the whims of the cruellest of enemies. Add to that the eternal dishonour which you will incur. No way lies open for flight: on the one hand, battle and unknown enemy territory bar the way; on the other, the sea and yet again battle.*[52] The duke went on to speak of the meaninglessness of numbers in the field. The English had been conquered before; the Normans, never. The exhortation ended and *when everything was in order, the ensign was unfurled which the Pope had sent from the Holy Church at Rome. This done, and all being assembled, the whole of them, spears in hand, marched against their mortal enemies.*[53]

* * * * *

When Vital was making his report to Duke William, an English scout brought word of the Norman advance to King Harold. It seems possible that he found the king by the Watch Oak, taking his farewells of those who would await the outcome of the day on the slopes of Caldbec Hill. Mounted and already armed the king hurried back to the ridge. Harold moved among the fyrd, and explained simply the tactics which he had adopted. *The duke,* he said, *ought to seek him, as he wanted to conquer England; and it became him to abide the attack, who had to defend the land.*[54] His battle orders were equally simple. Whatever happened elsewhere, the English were to stand firm, each defending his own place. While they kept together and remained steady, the enemy would achieve little against them; but if they broke ranks and became separated, they would with difficulty recover themselves. They must not under-rate their opponents: the Normans were good soldiers and well armed, and they numbered almost man for man the strength of the fyrd. But the weapons of the English were sufficient and the king was confident of their ability to repel any assault. The lines were dressed, and the ranks closed, and *when Harold had made all ready, and given his orders, he came into the midst of the English, and dismounted by the standard.*[55] Gyrth and Leofwine stood with Harold; and about the brothers were the others of their kin, and the nobles who were their friends. Above them, the early morning light glittered on the gem-encrusted gonfanon of the Fighting Man which was so soon to be lost irretrievably in the vaults of Rome, and on the golden Dragon, which would not wave again over an English army for three hundred years.[56] Across the valley to the south, the first ranks of the Franco-Flemish division came into sight over the brow of the hill, and as they advanced downwards towards the west of the saddle, the English leaders offered their last prayers for God's help.

The earliest point from which the English position could have been seen by the invaders lay almost due south-east of the standard, where the road from Hastings turned more steeply down over a three hundred foot shoulder of Telham Hill towards the saddle. The allies had marched about a mile and a half from Blackhorse Hill and were now half a mile from the Senlac ridge. But the column was long, and when the vanguard began the descent into the valley, the duke was still a mile or more behind them. In the past fortnight, however, William must have studied the topography of the peninsula thoroughly, and the order of the deployment of his forces was planned, if to a certain extent hazardous. The broken ground, and the marshes on either side of the saddle, prevented an advance in line from Telham Hill. An attack on the narrow front of the saddle alone was out of the question. There was no alternative but to deploy beyond the saddle, forming first on the right, where the line of approach was more direct, and taking all possible advantage of the less swampy surfaces to the west in the stationing of the left wing. Though this would entail a flank movement by the Breton division across the face of an enemy less than two hundred yards distant, William gambled that the English would not seize the opportunity to exploit the weaknesses of the manoeuvre. The Norman scouts must already have given the duke a fairly accurate estimate of the strength and structure of the fyrd; the nature of

Harold's strategy was by now to some extent evident; and once the French and Flemish contingents were drawn up, they would give a measure of protection to the Breton march.

It was about eight a.m. when the first troops of the leading division reached the saddle. *Those on foot led the way with serried ranks, bearing their bows. The knights rode next, supporting the bowmen from behind. Thus both horse and foot kept their course and order of march as they began; in close ranks at a gentle pace, that the one might not pass or separate from the others.*[57] The French and Flemings moved northwards over the saddle and took up a position curving slightly to the north-east, facing the left wing of the English. The Breton auxiliaries followed. They crossed the valley and wheeled to the west, spreading along the northern side of the marsh, to confront the far right wing of the fyrd. Close behind them came the main body of the army, the Normans, and in the midst of his barons, Duke William himself, armed with an iron mace and mounted on the warhorse that had been the gift of the Spanish king. The Normans advanced across the saddle and extended to fill the great gap between the wings already formed. With his personal attendants William remained south of the saddle and the papal standard was raised on a knoll overlooking the allied dispositions and some three hundred yards to the rear of the line. The priests and servants of the army occupied neighbouring hillocks. It seems likely that the duke's half-brothers held back with him, Odo wearing a hauberk over his white alb and carrying, like William, a mace. The consecrated banner was borne by a knight of Caux, Turstin fitzRou; it was an unenvied task, and had been twice refused, by Ralph of Toesni, the hereditary standard-bearer of the Norman duke, and Walter Giffard, aged and failing, but still eager to wield a sword rather than a gonfanon.

The allied divisions were drawn up, the archers nearest to the defenders of the ridge, the men-at-arms in close support, and the knights stationed behind the foot-soldiers. It appears probable that the bowmen mingled with the forward ranks of the men-at-arms, and that there were altogether some six lines of infantry, with the cavalry massed four deep in the rear. William's tactics were designed primarily to hold his least expendable troops, the armoured knights, in reserve to exploit a break-through and to destroy his opponents, broken and in defeat, before they could reach the shelter of the Andredsweald. The archers and slingers were to use their missiles to harass the English, and if possible to throw the shield-wall into disorder. When their quivers were exhausted, the archers would retire, and the heavy infantry would launch an assault against the weakened front of the fyrd, breaching the defences and allowing the cavalry to play their part with optimum effect. From his command post, the duke would exercise control over every phase of the action. It was as good a basic plan as could be devised in the circumstances: an immediate charge by the knights, up the slopes of the ridge and into reach of the axes of the housecarls within their rampart of shields, would have invited disaster. But while William's experience of war was extensive, his experience of battle was limited: he had fought only two previous engagements, both on the plains of Normandy, and only at the second of these had he commanded; Val-ès-dunes in 1047 was largely a cavalry encounter, and Varaville in 1057 was the massacre of a baggage-laden rearguard by immensely superior forces. At Senlac, though the duke had recognised and accepted the paralysis of his principal arm, there were factors which he had either overlooked or ignored: the trajectory of the archers' fire, sending the Norman arrows harmlessly on to the defending shields, or over the English lines; and the effect on morale of the slaughter that would greet the allied infantry on the embattled crest of the ridge.

Shorly before nine, the third hour of the Christian day, the allied deployment was completed. On the ridge, the front ranks of the fyrd waited, shields raised, swords girt, axes resting on shoulders, spears and clubs held ready to rain down in answer to the missiles from the slopes below. Tension was mounting and the air was ringing with the shouted defiances and war-cries of both hosts, when suddenly the Norman lines parted, and the shouting faltered as a single horseman rode out into the clear ground between the armies. During the advance, Taillefer, the minstrel, had ridden before the duke, singing the song of Roland. Now he hoped to win glory by an exhibition of bravery, over-awing the English and rousing the ardour of his comrades. *He took his lance by the butt, as if it were a truncheon. He threw it very high and caught it again by the blade. Three times thus he threw his lance, then the fourth time he advanced quite near and aimed it at the English ranks, wounding one of the men. Then drawing his sword, he came into the open space, and threw the sword that he held on high, and then caught it again. Those who saw this said to one another, that this was magic which he did before the folk.*[58] Unfortunately for the juggler, his horse was as spirited a performer as its rider. Trained by Taillefer to charge with its jaws gaping fearsomely, the animal took its cue from its master. The minstrel had tossed and grasped the sword again three times, when abruptly and without warning the horse bolted, bringing the helpless Norman right into the English position. The invader struck with his sword at one Englishman, and then at another, but that was the end of the adventure. Attacked on all sides, Taillefer and his charger fell and died, under a shower of spears and darts.

The first blood had been spilt, and Taillefer, the 'Cleaver of Iron', had earned himself a kind of immortality. But the gesture was soon to be made empty by the more serious business of the time. *About the third hour of the day, the battle began.*[59] Through the clamour of the morning, the clash of brandished arms, and the cries of 'Holy Cross!' and 'Dex aïe!' there cut the shrill blasts of the Norman trumpets and the answering challenge from the ridge. On the summit, under the waving banners, Harold called to his captains to stand firm, and the English ranks stiffened as the cry echoed along the line. Up the slopes towards the waiting fyrd came the enemy bowmen. Still out of range of the English hand-missiles, though less than a hundred yards from the crest, the archers halted and loosed their first volley. All along the eight hundred yard front, there rose the eerie hiss of a thousand arrows in flight. The shafts sped upwards and here and there on the hill-top a man screamed where a gap was found between the closely hedged shields; but most of the arrows thrummed ineffectually against the lime-wood barricade, or whistled above the heads of the defenders, to fall into the ravines behind the spur. Again the archers bent their bows, the arrows flew and in the serried ranks on the ridge occasional figures staggered and dropped, plucking at the shafts that had struck through the rings and leather of their harness. Again, and yet again, without reply, each hit bringing cheers from the allied lines. But the arrows were flimsy and the hits were few and for every Englishman who fell there was another ready to take his place. Quivers were emptied, and there were no responding volleys to replenish the bowmen's stocks. The firing dwindled, and one by one the archers retired. On the hillock where he watched Duke William knew that the first stage of his battle plan had failed.

The opening attack had lasted half an hour or more, and it was now the turn of the invaders to endure the hail of missiles. The archers withdrew, and William ordered a general advance of his footmen. Through an unending shower of *javelins and all kinds of darts, the most murderous axes, and stones fixed to pieces of wood,*[60] the allied men-at-arms struggled up the slopes of the spur to reach the unbroken shield-wall. But the housecarls were waiting, and they had the deaths of comrades to avenge, when the English had stood helpless, but unflinching, under the storm of the arrows. The housecarls waited and poised over their heads they held the great double-handed battle-axes that no shield or armour could resist. On the easier gradients to the west, the Bretons were the first to feel the impact of the terrible weapon which the Danes had brought to England. To their right, the Normans, with the French and Flemish infantry beyond them, toiled their way up the steeper rises of the central and eastern faces of the ridge. The din was tumultuous. *Loud and far resounded the braying of trumpets, and the shock of spears, the mighty strokes of clubs, and the quick clashing of swords. Sometimes the English pushed forward, sometimes they fell back; while the men from oversea charged onwards, and at other times retreated. The Normans shouted 'God help us!' and the English people, 'Out!'.*[61] From both sides, taunts and defiances rose, to little purpose since neither army understood the speech of their opponents. Yet though rank after rank of the invaders pressed to the attack and at places the defenders gave ground, few of the attackers who came within the sweep of the axes lived, and each assault was beaten back at deadly cost. Half the morning passed, and still the English lines held; the litter of bodies below and on the crest of the ridge grew, the screams of the wounded shrilled above the battle-cries, and the tempo of the onslaught slackened, slowly but inevitably.

Time was slipping away, and even from the distance of the knoll it was clear that the allied attacks were losing strength, and that weariness and the steady drain of life were affecting the duke's men-at-arms. The second and crucial phase of the invader's tactical design was breaking in fragments against the steadfast defence of the ridge. There was no alternative but to admit the superiority of the English foot-soldiers and the Norman commander was driven to realise that in continuing his chosen plan could lead only to ruin. The decision was taken; messengers hurried to the cavalry squadrons of the three divisions; and new sounds were added to the noise of battle : the neighing of spurred horses and the drumming of hooves. Into the mêlée on the hill-top charged the flower of William's army, the armoured knights of Normandy, France, Flanders and Britanny. There was no room for manoeuvre : the horsemen cast their spears ahead, and plunged through the wilting line of the footmen, sword in hand. All the duke's forces were now committed, and the full power of the fyrd was likewise engaged. Right and left, housecarl, thegn and peasant fought their assailants to a stand-still; and down from the summit where the standards stood thrust the royal guard, the king's brothers, and Harold himself, his axe cleaving through helmet and hauberk, striking down both horse and man with one blow. *Then the carnage was so general until past noon, that neither from sharp spears, glittering lances, piercing swords, well-ground axes, nor pointed arrows, did any think to escape or to survive.*[62] Soldier and horse stumbled, labouring to find foot-holds in the knee-high grass, slippery with blood. The earth steamed, the weapons clashed and the cries of the wounded rose ceaselessly; and still the Dragon of Wessex and the Fighting Man waved undefeated above the heights of Senlac.

The unbending will of the English king and the resolution of his followers had countered every effort of the invaders, and shortly after midday they brought the Norman challenge to the brink of disaster. Now and then, the tired defenders faltered, and small groups of the enemy burst through the forward ranks of the fyrd but the penetrations were short-lived and achieved little and the few survivors extricated themselves with difficulty. It may have been a larger break-through by the Breton knights on the allied left that precipitated the sequence of events which led the attackers almost to rout. At its western end, the spur was narrowest, and the drop to the gully and stream behind was sheer compared with the southern ascent to the crest. The impetus that carried a strong and compactly wedged body of horsemen past the shields, spears and axes of the veteran troops lining the outer rim of the ridge would not easily be braked and as the squadron swept through the yielding ranks of the shire-levies, the leading riders would be on the edge of the ravine before they realised their danger. Then came the sudden fear, and too late the reining back, the animals rearing and twisting, the unheard warning cries, the hooves scrambling for purchase; and crashing into the confusion, the other chargers, the victims of their own inertia, carried all together over the verge. There are indications that something like this happened;[63] and that the screams of the falling horses and men triggered dismay through-out the left wing of the duke's army. Whatever the cause, after some three hours of struggle, panic seized the Breton division, and *the foot-soldiers and cavalry of Britanny, as well as all the auxiliaries who constituted the left wing, broke in flight.*[64]

All order lost, and leaderless, the Bretons and their com-panions fled from the terror of the ridge, down the western slopes in a mess of men and horses, to the swampy bottom of the valley. On their right, the Normans too began to retreat, their flank exposed and vulnerable. Ignorant of the cause of the debacle, some cried out that the duke had been killed. The cry was taken up, and the panic spread, until the French and Flemings on the right were also falling back, and the entire allied army was disorganised and close to rout. From their vantage-points, the king and the duke watched the collapse of the Norman line, while the fortune of war seemed to swing at last one way: in favour of England. But on the English right, the men of the fyrd were effecting the break in the defence that all the enemy attacks of the morning had not been able to create. Forgetful of the strict orders of the king, and conscious only of the flight of their foes before them, the shire-levies burst from their position, thrusting aside the housecarls who had guarded them, to hurry after the fleers, hacking and killing. Caught in the marshes, the western allies of Normandy floundered and died. And the English militia pressed on to the attack, unaware of the danger they brought upon themselves and the whole hope of England. In the command post by the standards there were no illusions of early victory; and it seems likely that Harold sent a force of housecarls under the leadership of Gyrth and Leofwine to recall the pursuers to their stations. The rescue-party, however, was already too late.

The contagion of terror had reached even the youths set to guard the allied baggage-train, and they were beginning to desert. But Duke William had reacted as quickly as his rival. While Odo of Bayeux hastened to reassure the serving-youths, the duke galloped down into the valley to meet and turn back the fugitives. With Turstin bearing the papal banner beside him, William rode among the defeated troops, pushing away the helmet from his face and calling out, '*Look at me! I am alive and will conquer, with God's help! What madness has taken hold of you, that you flee in this way? What path will lie open before your retreat? Those whom you have it in your power to sacrifice like a herd of cattle drive you back and kill you. You abandon victory and undying glory, and rush headlong to your own destruction and everlasting dishonour. By flight, not one of you will escape death.*'[65] The rout was stemmed. Bishop Odo, mace in hand, had now rejoined the duke; and Eustace of Boulogne with typical courage had spurred his horse out of the fighting line and through the mêlée to beg the Norman to retire. Brushing aside the count and his plea, William led his shamed troops in a charge against the English in the floor of the valley. The attack was met by the king's brothers and their company, and for a time the defence was ferocious. Swords and axes bit through shields and helmets, and the duke himself was unhorsed by a spear, possibly twice. But the housecarls were outnumbered, and on the level, they fought at a serious disadvantage. One by one the veterans fell, and among them died Gyrth and Leofwine. The men of the levies, who had so rashly advanced, now felt the weight of the Norman counter-attack. Without armour, and poorly weaponed, they stood no chance against the enemy. Though some tried to hold out on a low hillock a little way south-west of the ridge, the entire body that had surged in pursuit of the fleeing Bretons was cut to pieces.

The duke rested grimly on his borrowed horse among the dead.

On the hill above, the king mourned the fall of his brothers. It was a time of respite that neither Harold nor William could deny his followers. A grievous loss had been inflicted on the defenders of the ridge, though it no more than balanced the losses incurred by the invaders during the attacks of the morning. Though it was not yet defeated, the fyrd had been weakened; but the advantage lay, if anywhere, still with the English. Through dust-rimmed eyes, the duke looked out over an army disorganised by retreat, a cavalry shaken by an opposition they had not expected to encounter, and an infantry shredded by that opposition, and no longer to be considered as a striking arm. Yet all the arguments in favour of early battle remained good, and withdrawal behind the fortifications at Hastings could only bring the ultimate annihilation of the allied host. While their men took breath, and ate and drank their scanty rations, the rival commanders re-ordered their plans and redistributed their forces. There was little for Harold to do. Though the English casualties may already have exceeded two thousand, and there were many wounded among the survivors, the ranks stood even now six or seven deep along the chosen front, and the gaps in the shield-wall were filled with warriors drawn from the reserve massed about the standards. The courage of the fyrd was unimpaired; and the deaths of kin and friends were added incentives to the king's companions, as the killing of Gyrth and Leofwine was to Harold. Across the valley, the duke had summoned his captains. With no road back, there was no way to go but forward. The allies would return to the attack. But the assault would be made by the one arm that might meet the housecarls on even terms: the men-at-arms, decimated and demoralised, would be held as a reserve, while the whole strength of the knights rode against the still unswerving English line.

Two hours or more had passed since the collapse of the combined assault on the English position. The allied leaders rode back to their divisions, and the cavalry squadrons formed again. The trumpets blew, and with a determination born of desperation, the knights spurred their frightened mounts through the renewed hail of missiles to the upper slopes of the ridge. Still so densely packed that there was hardly room for the slain to fall, the defenders met the charge with the same ferocity that had

crushed the earlier onsets. Mace clashed with sword, and sword
with axe, and the English and Norman battle-cries sounded over
the hill. But the strength of England had been bled. The line was
no longer impregnable, and at places the heavier attacks
smashed through the wall of shields to harry the softer rear of
the fyrd. On the right particularly, where the daring of Robert
of Beaumont won the young Norman distinction in his first
battle, inroads were made and the English were driven back.
Nevertheless, each local retreat brought a counter-charge, the
breaches were repaired, and every assault was once more beaten
off. At length it became evident even to the jealous duke that the
partial successes achieved were not enough, and that the
attackers were failing. At about three o'clock, in the centre,
where the invaders had faced the main power of the English and
the casualties had been most damaging, the exhausted knights of
the Norman division began to withdraw; and all along the front,
the tenor of the fighting diminshed as, man by man, the élite of
the allied army joined the retreat. Though it did not seem so, it
was the prologue to tragedy.

It is impossible today to define with any certainty the cause
of what followed the Norman disengagement. As the shire-levies
of the English right had done some three hours before, the ranks
of the centre now broke in pursuit of the retreating cavalry. The
least likely explanation is that coined by the Norman panegyrists : that once again the simple islanders were lured by the
cunning of the duke.[66] More possibly, the sortie may have been
intended for the recovery of spears, hatchets and other missiles,
thrown during the early stages of the enemy attack : by this time,
such weapons must have been in short supply, and it could not
be doubted that they would be needed in later action. It is also
possible that Harold saw in the withdrawal the opportunity for
a limited counter-offensive against his most stubborn opponents.
The most credible interpretation would seem to combine the
latter possibilities, and to assume that the purpose of the raid was
two-fold : to replenish the missile-stocks, and to reduce further
the duke's people. Whatever the king's aim, it was a major
tactical blunder. The order made no allowance for the revenge-
hunger of men who had withstood six hours of almost constant
warfare, and who saw the enemy in flight below them. The

Normans fled, and the English hunted them, as heedless as the levies in the first sally; and *when the duke saw his men fall back, and the English too much rejoicing, his spirits rose high, and he seized his shield by the straps and his lance, which a servant handed to him, and took post by his gonfanon. Then those who kept close guard by the duke, and rode where he rode, being about a thousand armed men, came and rushed with closed ranks upon the English; and with the weight of their good horses, and the blows that the knights gave, broke the press of the enemy and scattered the crowd before them.*[67]

Few of the English escaped the slaughter, and fewer regained the ridge. The losses were fatal. Though the banners of England still waved above Senlac, Harold's strategic design had failed. None could have known this better than the soldier who had conquered Wales and defeated Hardraada, the captain who had determined to hold William the Bastard imprisoned within the fifty square miles of the Hastings peninsula. But all was not lost. If the hill-top could be held until nightfall, it might be possible to pull out under the cover of darkness. But this was the one hope for England: the victory that had seemed probable less than an hour ago was now beyond Harold's grasp. With the killing on the saddle and the southern gradients of the spur, the advantage of the terrain had been sacrificed, for an extended line could no longer be maintained by the depleted fyrd. During the hour and a half of daylight that remained, the king could plan to hold in strength only the higher central and eastern sector of the front; and Harold had no option but to draw his surviving troops more tightly about the summit and the standards. The way to the ridge was open to the enemy. The western slopes, where the first attack of the morning had been shattered, were clear of defenders; and although the assault could never be easy on the narrow crest, there would be from the west an almost level approach to the outer ranks of the English array. Yet there was no wavering, and up till the last the supporters of the king stood loyally to their posts.

The allied infantry had been cut to ribbons, and the cavalry had been sorely hurt; but if a Norman victory was to be secured, the time had come when a final and decisive assault must be made. Duke William decided to wager the full force left to him on a concerted action against the English position. While the knights, many if not most dismounted, and the men-at-arms attacked together on the face and both flanks of the contracted line, the archers would follow closely, giving covering fire. To achieve this most effectively, the duke gave an order which was to prove the most successful stratagem of the day, and was to bring a reward past valuing: he *commanded his bowmen not to aim their arrows straight at the enemy, but to shoot them in the air, that their cloud might spread darkness over the enemy ranks.*[68] Up the slopes strewn with the bodies of the fallen, through the grass greasy with the blood of the dead and the dying, the weary soldiers advanced, the archers behind them, fresher and with quivers refilled. Battle was rejoined all along the front, and *the arrows flew thicker than rain before the wind.*[69] Steeply among the hard pressed English the shafts fell, piercing helmets and tearing heads and faces; and for a while the fighting swayed back and forth, the issue in doubt. *Then it was that an arrow, which was shot towards the sky, struck Harold above the right eye, and that one of his eyes it put out.*[70] Convulsed with pain, the axe falling from his grasp, the king wrenched the arrow from the wound; breaking the shaft between his hands, Harold threw it from him, and bent down over his shield in agony. It was shortly after four o'clock on the afternoon of October the fourteenth, 1066, and the turning-point in English history.

The battle was not yet over, but the English resistance began to falter. The shield-wall was crumbling, even where the house-carls of the royal guard clustered about the summit, their axes still swinging in defence of the king. Despite his wound, Harold too fought on; but pain and shock must have slowed his movements and dissipated his strength, curbing the suddenness and power of the blows that had hewn down both horse and man. East, west and south, the invaders were hacking their way towards the English command; and the Norman duke himself was on the hill, thrusting against the exposed right flank of the fyrd. With the sure knowledge that victory was at last within his reach, William summoned Eustace of Boulogne, with the troops he led, to the aid of those whose task was the destruction of the king and the taking of the English banners. One Norman had already attempted the capture of the ensigns: Robert fitzErneis, the kinsman of Ralph of Tesson, had galloped, sword in hand, among the housecarls on the summit; his body was to be found stretched at the feet of the standards. A party of twenty knights had now sworn to carve a path to the heart of the English position. Cutting and slashing, they pushed through the weakening defenders; and though most paid for the venture with their lives, four survived to achieve the goal. Two were Norman, and two, French: Hugh of Montfort, and Walter Giffard the younger; Eustace of Boulogne, and Ivo, the heir to the county of Ponthieu. They threw themselves on the wounded king. The first drove his spear through Harold's shield and into his breast. The second felled him to the earth with a sword-stroke below the lacings of his helmet. As the dying king struggled to rise, the third disemboweled him with a spear. Harold was dead when the fourth struck at the prostrate body with a sword, laying open the thigh, down to the bone.

For the last, cowardly act, the 'noble heir of Ponthieu' *was branded with ignominy by William, and expelled from the army*;[71] and Ivo, son of Count Guy, was one of the few followers of the duke to return from England without great reward. But the twenty knights had accomplished the Norman leader's dearest purpose. The royal Dragon had been beaten to the ground, and the golden emblem of the Fighting Man had been borne off in triumph. And Harold Godwinsson, king of the English, lay dead on Senlac ridge. In the gathering October twilight the king was beyond hurt, beyond attack, beyond treason. There was grief and pain for others, for Gytha and Edith, for the children doomed to exile or captivity, and for many thousands of his countrymen; but for Harold these were past. The legacy of Tostig had been realised in full; and except for one half-forgotten prisoner of the Norman duke, all the sons of Godwin were dead. Nineteen days after Tostig had fallen beside the Landravager of Norway, the vengeance he had sought so strenuously had been wreaked by the ally who had rejected him. The exile lay forgotten, in a grave soon to be lost; yet there would have been no victory for Duke William without the intervention of the dark-browed renegade. Whatever had been, or would be, Harold had paid his reckoning; and the nine month nine day reign of little stillness had run its course.

The fighting on the hill-top had now become chaotic, the fyrd split into groups assailed on all sides. The rumour that Harold had been killed spread rapidly, and the capture of the standards gave confirmation. With the death of the king, the day was lost, and a general flight of the English began. On horseback and on foot, by roads and byways, those who could escape fled; and though the king's housecarls may have fought on, as their custom was, dying to a man round the corpse of their commander, by sunset the ridge was in the possession of the invaders. It was about five o'clock, and some eight hours had passed since the start of the conflict. But while there was English blood to spill, the duke was unsatisfied. Despite the uncertain light and the difficult country ahead, William ordered the cavalry to pursue the fleeing enemy. Two, and perhaps three, horses had been killed under the duke; his helmet and his shield had been dented by heavy blows; and the spear he carried was broken. Nevertheless, he rode after the hunters through the dusk to Caldbec Hill. On the rises where, little more than a day before, the fyrd of Wessex and East Anglia had gathered about King Harold and his brothers, the Norman paused. And out of the gloom of the valley below came Eustace of Boulogne, hurrying up the slopes at the head of fifty horsemen, and calling out to the duke to stay, for it was certain death to proceed. Angrily, William halted the runaways : to learn that even now victory was not complete, and that English arms were still ready and able to strike down the rasher among his pursuing troops.

A quarter of a mile or so north of Caldbec lies the ravine of Oak Wood Gyll. The gyll breaks suddenly across the gently rolling land that courses down from the hill to Oak Wood; and in the eleventh century, the sides of the ravine fell away steeply beneath high banks, to a buried causeway that ran along the deep bottom. The rim of the southern bank was covered by long grass, and the slightly higher northern bank was similarly masked. The entire chasm was overgrown with bushes and brambles, and on an October evening, the gully must have been almost invisible to horsemen approaching from the south. The level ground north of the ravine marked the southern boundary of the Andredsweald, and it offered a good natural defence, protected on the right by marsh and on the left by the ditches of several streams. Here a detachment of the English had established themselves, in a last stand against the pursuers; and mistaking them for fresh reinforcements to the fyrd, Count Eustace had abandoned the chase and beat a hasty retreat. But on Caldbec Hill, even as he begged the duke to withdraw, a blow from an unseen enemy struck the count between the shoulders and sent him reeling into the arms of his companions, half-dead and bleeding from nose and mouth. The injury had come too close to William. He ordered an immediate attack. The cavalry formed again and set their steeds in a gallop, straight for the waiting English. Disordered and ignorant of their danger, the knights charged up to and over the edge of the hidden gyll, plunging to their deaths in the abyss that was to be named from the disaster: Malfosse, the 'evil ditch'.[72]

On the invaders who survived the fall, the English showered down spears and stones; and few of the many who had tumbled into the gyll lived to leave it. The extent of the catastrophe could not have been known till the succeeding day; but the numbers who died in the Malfosse left a memory of horror that would not be erased for many years. Limited and local as it was, the last victory had been given to the English. The duke rallied those attackers who had drawn back in time from the grass-grown verge, and led them round the ravine against the English position. But the defenders had already achieved more than they could have dreamed possible. The remnant of the largely peasant army that had so nearly crushed the assembled feudal power and chivalry of Normandy and its allies melted into the obscurity of the Andredsweald. Duke William recalled his men, and rode back through the deepening night to Senlac ridge. The battle was over.

*   *   *   *   *

Although strategically little more than a postscript to the campaign of Stamford Bridge, and militarily a trivial affair by comparison with the earlier engagament, the political and historical consequences of Senlac were to be profound. Despite the crudity of the tactics employed by both sides, and the tragedy of errors that alone had given it a positive result, it was to be included in every listing of the decisive battles of the world. The cut-and-thrust, hand-to-hand slugging, enjoined by an attacker of limited repertoire, and a defender of equally limited means, bought and sold a kingdom. Years of struggle still faced Duke William, before he could claim full possession of the realm of his predecessor; but from this night forward, the conquest of England was assured. Though the Norman dynasty endured less than a century, the duke and his sons sat on the throne of Athelstan, Edward and Harold, and an alien nobility occupied the highest places in the land. If Harold had survived the battle, or if there had been another Englishman able to take his place, even the destruction wrought at Senlac might not have won William the crown. But there was none. In the crucial months ahead, factional jealousies divided the leaders of the English, and they were allowed no later opportunity to unite; and though armed risings were to crowd the first years of the Norman's rule, William never again met a rival commanding the allegiance of a national army. Within a generation, men would be saying of this feastday of St. Calixtus, that this was *the fatal day of England, the sad overthrow of the dear country, the day of the handing over to new masters.*[73]

As the October night settled over the battlefield, none of the exhausted, allied host were yet aware of how final their victory was. By six-thirty, it was pitch-dark; and torches flared on the ridge as Duke William and his company rode up the northern slopes to dismount on the crest. Except for the talk, hushed by weariness, of the soldiers who waited for the duke's return, it was still on the hill-top: the allied wounded had been removed to the care of their comrades; and by the order of the vengeful duke, men of the fyrd found still alive had been summarily dispatched. All around lay the bodies of the fallen, English and Norman, and nowhere more thickly than on the summit, where the king had died and the standard of Wessex had been trampled down. There, in the flickering torchlight, William knelt and returned his thanks to God. He ordered the consecrated banner to be brought and raised where the English standard had stood and directed his attendants to set up his tent beside the gonfanon and to prepare his supper there. The old baron, Walter Giffard, remonstrated with the duke. Hidden amidst the corpses, Englishmen must be lying, blood-smeared and wounded perhaps, but shamming death only, to evade the Norman executioners. Though they might hope to escape in the darkness, the killing of the duke would be a lure none could resist, a revenge worth giving a life for. William should sleep elsewhere, and under strong guard. William was once more supremely confident. He rejected Giffard's advice: his safety was in the keeping of Heaven. The battered armour was removed, and the duke gave thanks again to God, and to the knights around him. *And he ate and drank among the dead, and made his bed that night upon the field.*[74]

* * * * *

The invaders spent the night on the hill; and in the early morning of Sunday, as soon as he had breakfasted, the duke went over the field of battle with his staff. The tour of inspection completed, the arms and armour of the slain were collected, and whatever booty had been left by the English was gathered. Then the allied dead were separated and taken for burial. It seems likely that most, if not all, were interred in a common grave in Beauport Park, three miles or so south-east of Senlac. The corpses of the defenders, however, were *left to be eaten by worms and wolves, by birds and dogs,*[75] though it appears that William may have allowed priests and families to seek out at least the local fallen and remove them to more fitting places of rest. Not all the English dead were unobserved by the victor: the corpses of Abbot Aelfwig and the twelve monks of the New Minster at Winchester were to cost the abbey dear in confiscations.[76] But the one body that William sought was not to be easily found: tossed unceremoniously aside in the raising of the duke's tent, the nephew of the abbot of Hyde lay lost, mutilated and disfigured, the royal insignia stripped away, his armour looted, among the heaped cadavers on the summit. Others were looking for Harold. When the fyrd had broken on the previous evening, the party by the Watch Oak had probably retreated with the fugitives to the safety of the forest; but in the morning, the urgency of their mission overcame their fear, and Osegod Cnoppe and Ailric the Childmaster went humbly to William. They bore the offer of Gytha of the weight in gold of Harold's corpse, if the invader would permit the remains of the king to be carried to Waltham, to his chosen grave in the church of his own foundation. The duke refused the gold; but, concealing his real intentions, he gave the canons leave to search for the body.

The churchmen moved among the slain; but most had been terribly wounded, and it proved impossible for Osegod and Ailric to identify the king. At length the canons gave up, and Osegod hurried back to Gytha and her companions, to fetch the one person who might hope to recognise the body of Harold among so many. It can hardly have been a task welcome to the woman who had loved Harold and borne his children and who had followed her lord into Sussex, to be with him in the last days of his life. Nevertheless, Edith Swan-Neck returned with Osegod to the ridge; and there, amid the carnage, *by her knowledge of secret tokens which they could not have known from his outer parts,*[77] Edith did her last service to her lover. It was less of a service than she knew. Duke William did not intend to create by his victory a royal martyr or a place of pilgrimage for the defeated enemy. When the body had been found and sworn to, the duke dismissed his English suitors peremptorily : there would be no interment in hallowed ground for the rival who had opposed the ambition of Normandy. Harold had sought to hold the sea and the shore against the invaders : let him guard it still. The mangled corpse of the king, torn by thirteen wounds, was taken up, wrapped in a shroud of purple linen, and carried to the encampment at Hastings. There it was entrusted for burial to William Malet, the half-English lord of Graville-in-Caux, who was the trusted vassal of Duke William, the kinsman of the earls Edwin and Morkere, and had known Harold and may have been counted by him a friend. What the Norman could do in pity he did; he laid the king to rest under a stone on a high point of the cliffs of Fairlight.

* * * * *

When he had paid a last tribute to those who had fallen in his service, and given alms for distribution to the poor, the duke returned to the camp at Hastings. Though the death of the 'usurper' had advanced him more than a step nearer to the crown, William could not yet be sure of the future. He had won a battle, not a war. His dominion stretched no farther than it had before the coming of Harold. For the time being, the Normans were safe from attack, but safe only where they were. Though the terror of the victory at Senlac would weaken English resistance in later stages of the campaign, the allied losses had been heavy beyond estimation, and the invaders were in effect crippled. Reinforcements were expected any day from Normandy, lured by the news of the allies' success; but until his forces were strengthened the duke could make no move to exploit the destruction of the southern fyrd. There was no alternative but to wait. Yet William knew already how vital this one battle had been; how essential to the unity of the enemy had been the single will of the king. For thirteen years, the arbiter of policy, the guiding hand in government, general of the army and the best captain in England, Harold had been in his own person the centre and front of English power. With the fall of Harold, William was prepared even now to receive the surrender of the remaining English leaders. His hope was to be disappointed; but while he awaited the arrival of the troops from Normandy, the duke was also waiting to see if his future subjects would submit to him without further violence.

The days passed, but without bringing any English embassies to Hastings. Meanwhile, as so often in this remarkable year, the weather was again changing in the Norman favour: the storms were dying out in the Channel, and a southerly wind blew. No sails cut the horizon yet, however, and no fleet, Norman or English, neared the Sussex cliffs. The time was not wasted. The army that had conquered at Senlac was reduced in strength as well as in number. The infantry in particular had been weakened by the axes and swords of the shield-wall. Rest was essential. Weapons and armour were also in a poor state, and though some was replaced by equipment taken from the fallen of both armies, the circumstances of the victory suggest that its condition was poor. Throughout the stay at Hastings, the smiths and armourers were busily employed, refurbishing mail, restoring shafts, re-edging blades.

Duke William's pledge before the battle had been no empty propitiation: the abbey he had vowed would be built on the site of his victory, and the duke intended to establish it richly, *showering on it in abundance all the wealth that it could possibly*

need, on behalf of the slain on both sides.[78] The position of
the high altar had already been chosen : it was to be raised where
the king's standard had stood, and the place was marked for
the architects who were to come there from Normandy. On
Caldbec Hill, too, a memorial was erected : the cairn of stones
that the Normans called a 'mountjoy', and made to commemor-
ate the success of their arms.[79]

Before a week was over the expected reinforcements arrived.
They came in such numbers, and with such promises of future
augmentation, that William felt strong enough to launch a full
campaign against England; strong enough not merely to confront any army which the English could put into the field against
him, but to divide his forces in a two-pronged attack against the
heart-land of the enemy. A garrison was to be left in the Hastings
entrenchments, and the watch on the Norman beach-head was
entrusted to Humphrey of Tilleul. The allied rear secured, the
duke would lead the main part of the army eastwards towards
Dover and Canterbury, turning thence north-west for London.
While William thrust at the English seat of government, his
namesake and seneschal, fitzOsbern, would take command of the
fleet and the remainder of the host; sailing westwards, the seneschal was to continue the reduction of the south coast as far
as Wight, where he would await the coming of the second wave
of reinforcements. When his troops were rested and the later
recruits had reached him, fitzOsbern was to land on the mainland
in Hampshire and to strike north through the eastern outgrowths
of the Hampshire forest for Winchester, the ancient capital and
still the second city of England. There, if the circumstances war-
ranted it, the duke would meet him, and the divisions of the
army would unite. Five days after the battle, the arrangements
were finalised; the fleet and the army were ready; and a ship
had been sent to Normandy to guide the new musters to fitz-
Osbern. On Friday, the twentieth of October, Duke William
rode from the encampment, north-westwards along the Fairlight
spur to Blackhorse Hill and Telham Hill, and on over the
desolate ridge above Senlac, still guarded by the English dead.

*   *   *   *   *

The survivors were flocking into London, in such a press, said one of the chroniclers,[80] that the bridge broke under them and many were drowned. Everything had been abandoned in the flight,[81] and most were wounded. Ansgar the staller had been so disabled that he came home on a litter; and Leofric, the abbot of Peterborough, near to death, paused in the city on his way back to the 'golden borough'. Not all the English leaders had died: apart from Ansgar, Waltheof and Hakon had escaped with their lives, if indeed they had fought at Senlac. Word of the defeat had met Edwin and Morkere on their southward journey, and the northern earls had hastened their march; their first act on reaching London was to send their sister, the queen, now nearing her time, swiftly north to comparative safety within the distant walls of Chester. From all the counties under the immediate threat of invasion, men hurried to the Thames-side city. The fleet, too, had returned, its efforts to come to the aid of the king abandoned. One paramount need faced the gathered witan: Harold was dead, and a successor had to be named, behind whom the nation could form a common front against the enemy. The candidates were few, and there was no one man who, by birth and merit, could count on the unanimous support of the English. The greatness of the house of Godwin had died at Senlac. The queen's child was yet unborn, and there could be no guarantee that Alditha would bear a boy. But even had there been a legitimate son of Harold, an infant could not have commanded the allegiance of the people. The sons of Edith Swan-Neck had no recognisable claim to the crown. The descendants of Leofric and Siward were equally barred from the accession; and though Edwin and Morkere solicited strenuously the raising of one or other of them to the throne, there were no real qualifications for kingship to which they could appeal.

There was one candidate only, whose credit was reasonable in the eyes of most Englishmen. Though still a youth, and without experience of either government or war, the Atheling Edgar was of the blood-royal of Wessex, and by direct descent in the elder line the great-grandson of Ethelred. When Edwin and Morkere were at last persuaded that their own ambitions were fruitless, and that the elevation of the atheling was a necessity, if the kingdom was to be saved, the election was ensured; under the aegis of the archbishops, the earls of Mercia and Northumbria, and others of the chief magnates, with the support of the citizens of London and the seamen, Edgar was chosen king. The choice was not universally popular. Certain of the bishops withheld their assent, at least until the urgency of the danger was made clear to them. The decision of the witan was the best compromise solution of the problem facing England. It appears likely that Edgar was never crowned, and that he was therefore never king in the fullest sense of the term; but even as king-elect, he gave a focus to English resistance, and his lineage weakened the flimsy title of the Norman duke. The English leaders now prepared to resume the war. Though the toll of Gate Fulford, Stamford Bridge and Senlac had been severe, and the housecarls, the primary striking force of the fyrd, had been practically wiped out, the strength of England was not broken. Nevertheless, no plans were made as yet to oppose William again in the field; and for the time being, the defensive power of the nation was concentrated in London, under the command of the wounded Ansgar.

*   *   *   *   *

Hemmed between the Andredsweald and the vast stretch of open water and swamp that reached inland to the estuary of the Rother and the isle of Oxney, the allied army marched eastwards into Kent. William's first objective was Romney, where the stragglers of the Norman fleet had been cut to pieces in the last days of September. Swinging south-east near Appledore, along the Kentish shore of the great bay, the duke brought terrible retribution to the port in the marshes and its inhabitants, taking *what vengeance he would for the slaughter of his men*.[82] There was no long delay, for the town could have offered little opposition to the massed enemy; and within hours, the avengers were pushing on towards Dover. The policy of terror continued. Harrying, burning and killing, the Normans came, probably in the late afternoon of Saturday, to the port which had been a stronghold since the time of the Romans, and which was the key to south-eastern England. Lying, like Hastings, in a valley between cliffs, the port was protected by powerful defence-works on the height to the east. Here, commanding the sea approaches, the valley and the town, the early conquerors had built a lighthouse and a fort. The lighthouse had outlasted its builders; and in the eleventh century, as earl of Wessex, Harold Godwinsson had restored the fortifications, embracing the pharos and the church of St. Mary, which had probably been constructed in the reign of Canute from the ruins of the Roman walls. Though nothing remains today of the earl's works, except the fortress mound and a well still known as 'Harold's Well', they consisted of an oval enclosure surrounded by a fosse, and a motte topped by a palisade; within the enclosure, besides the church and the lighthouse, lay garrison barracks and other structures. Accounted impregnable, the castle had become crowded in the past days with refugees from the Norman terror.

Under a determined guard, the citadel on the cliffs might well have withstood every assault. But as the invaders neared Dover, resistance to the duke melted. The strength of any fortress depends ultimately on the will of its defenders; and it seems likely that the garrison posted in the Kentish stronghold by Harold had been summoned with the other soldiers of the shire to the hoar apple-tree, to fight and die with the king at Senlac, and that the men now gathered in the castle were little more than a rabble, without military skill or leadership. Negotiations for surrender had already begun when the first of the allied troops entered the port; and it is possible that William intended the occupation to be as peaceful as the circumstances permitted. His wishes were forestalled, however, by the followers whose earlier pillagings he had encouraged, if not ordered : eager as ever for plunder, the Normans fired the town, and the damage had spread widely before the blaze could be checked. When the submission was finally agreed and accepted, the duke promised indemnity to those whose property had been destroyed; but as soon as the defences were in his possession, he took over the castle and evicted the English from their houses, to provide lodgings for the army. With Dover now firmly in his hands, and fear of the invaders spreading to the farthest quarters of Kent, the duke set about preparing a second base in England. The fortifications were extended by the erection of a bastion to the north-west, and a raised bank was added beyond Harold's entrenchments, reaching to the edge of the cliff.

The work on the fortress was under way, when the duke's

forces were attacked by an enemy against which the strongest walls could afford no protection. Striking down knights and footmen, nobles and commoners, a wave of dysentery swept through the army. Many died, and many more were in danger of dying. But nothing now could be allowed to interfere with the Norman advance. Within a week, the engineers had completed their task; and on or about the twenty-ninth of the month, the invaders marched north-westwards from Dover on the road to Canterbury, leaving behind a garrison in the castle and those too ill to travel. The terror had achieved its purpose. Not far from Dover, William was met by representatives of the first city in Kent, the city of Augustine and the religious centre of England. The citizens of Canterbury made full submission to the duke, swearing fealty and giving hostages and tribute. Accompanied by the envoys, the duke continued his march; and on the following day, the thirtieth of October, the allied host reached the Kentish capital. While camps were set up for the soldiery in the surrounding villages, William entered the city, to take up residence in the ancient hospice that a Norman chronicler called the 'broken tower',[83] standing on the site of the later West Gate of Canterbury.

* * * * *

The longest month of the year was ending, the month which had found the king triumphant, and left him, torn and disfigured, robbed of everything save honour, lying beneath a stone on a lonely cliff above the shore he had given his life to defend. Harold was gone, and with him the hope of England. When October began, Duke William had been little better than an adventurer, tied to the few miles about his camp, dreading to go forward and unable to go back. Now, he had destroyed the rival whose crown he had challenged; town by town, the shires of Wessex were surrendering to his arms; and the opponents of his power were divided under the leadership of an unblooded boy. In London, the magnates bickered about the king-elect, while a sick man directed the defence of the last bastion of English liberty. Dead were the housecarls, and with them the Vikings whom the king's cousin had sent to his aid. Dead were the earls Gyrth and Leofwine, Godric the sheriff, and the greater part of the southern thegnhood. Abbot Aelfwig had fallen with his nephew; and in the 'golden borough', Abbot Leofric was nearing his end. There was fear in England, far beyond the reach of a Norman spear. And as the late hours of the month passed, there was fear in Canterbury also. In the last day of October, Duke William fell sick of the dysentery that had struck the soldiers at Dover, and lay ill in the 'broken tower'.

NOVEMBER

ON the first of November, the festival of All Saints, Abbot Leofric died in Peterborough. His adherence to the cause of the last Anglo-Saxon king had cost the abbot his life, and it was to bring a time of sorrow on the great house which he had administered so fruitfully. As successor to Leofric, the monks of the 'golden borough' chose the provost of the monastery, Brand, and sent him for confirmation to Edgar Atheling, *for that the people of the land expected that he should become king.*[1] The witan approved the election, and Edgar gave the staff of office to the new abbot. But the atheling was never to be crowned, and the acknowledgement of his kingship by the house was to require expiation in the reign of his supplanter. Although the Norman was already in the realm, and had defeated and killed his predecessor, and although the centre of religious life in England had accepted William's overlordship, the monks of Peterborough had dared publicly to flout his authority. *When that King William heard that saying he was very wroth, and said that the abbot had slighted him. Then good men went between them and reconciled them, for that the abbot was a good man. Then he gave the king forty marks of gold in recompense.*[2] It was a light fee for Norman forgiveness; and the treatment of Peterborough was mild compared with that meted out to the New Minster in Winchester, where local history referred, uncompromisingly to the rapacious dealings of 'William the Tyrant'. For three years, the right to elect an abbot of Hyde was refused, and many properties of the house were confiscated and given to the followers of the invader. In a grim joke, the Norman king is said to have remarked that Abbot Aelfwig was surely worth a barony, and each of the monks who went with him to war, a manor.[3] The abbey itself was not sacrosanct: part of the precinct was seized by William for the site of a new royal palace in the ancient capital of Wessex.

* * * * *

The sorrows of Peterborough and Hyde were still in the future, and meanwhile their author lay ill at Canterbury. At this juncture, illness was no more opportune for the duke than it had been for Harold in the days of the Norse ravagings in Northumbria. The prize was almost within William's grasp, but it might yet slip from him, if the English were given time to consolidate their resistance. Through the turn of the month, William was trapped in a forced inactivity, fighting the disease; *but, anxious for the welfare of the army, and fearing lest it should suffer from shortage of supplies, he refused to allow himself any respite.*[4] By now, the resources of the countryside about Canterbury were nearing exhaustion, and manors from Elmsted and Crundale to Preston and Chislet had been ruinously pillaged. Throwing off his sickness, the duke determined to launch an attack directly on London, the fulcrum of English power; and about the end of the first week of November, the allies began their march westward from the Kentish capital. Anxious to ensure that no opposition could develop in the rear of his advance and to make certain of adequate foraging, the duke divided his forces.[5] While a strong detachment took the northern road to Faversham and Chatham, the main body of the army moved south-west through Chilham to the Wye gap in the North Downs, turning then north-west between the downs and the northern outskirts of the Andredsweald towards Charing and Maidstone. Harrying the country as before, the divisions followed approximately parallel routes, north and south of the downs, in frequent communication.

The geographical factors which had already influenced Norman planning were playing an increasingly important role in the operations of the invaders. There is, to the peregrinations of the duke's forces in the two months after Senlac, a peculiarity which seems at first sight to be inconsequential, or possibly the outward show of some brilliant strategy of the allied commander. In fact, the movements of the army were neither haphazard, nor wholly contrived. Some manoeuvres were purposeful and deliberately executed; others were compelled by circumstance. Thus, the march on Dover may have been calculated, as suggested before, to provide the expedition with a second and major base and port of entry; it may equally well have been dictated by the presence across the northward road from Hastings of the almost impassable barrier of the Andredsweald. In the eleventh century, the forest of Anderida was only one of several great swathes of closely grown woodland which blanketed central and southern England. The Andredsweald reached from Petersfield in Hampshire to Ashford in Kent, and throughout most of that length it was seldom less than fifteen miles in breadth. Eastern Berkshire, part of Surrey, and a large extent of northern Hampshire was similarly wooded; so too was southern Hampshire from the Sussex border to Wiltshire and Dorset in the west. A vast forest embraced Middlesex and London on the north, stretching from the southern foothills of the Chilterns in Buckinghamshire, eastwards and north-eastwards through Hertfordshire to Cambridgeshire, and on into eastern Essex. Not far to the west were smaller forests in Oxfordshire, north-western Buckinghamshire, Northamptonshire, Bedfordshire and Huntingdonshire. These supply the key to an understanding of the wanderings of the allied host. An army, the main strength of which lay in its mounted troops, could not move easily or safely through woodland, in enemy and perhaps ambushed territory.

At Rochester and Maidstone, the invaders crossed the Medway and the Roman road which had seen the southward march of the fyrd a month earlier. While the northern wing pushed on to Dartford, the southern wing penetrated the narrow valley of the downs that leads to Sevenoaks and Oxted. Here, William again divided his forces. Sending what was probably a reconnoitring column westwards, he led the larger part of the southern division through the deep passage of the downs north of Sevenoaks to link up with the northern division at Eltham for the assault on London. About the middle of the second week of November, the duke came to the sandy banks of the Thames opposite the city and established his camp at Battersea. An advance guard of five hundred knights had driven what defenders there were south of the river back to the shelter of the city walls and, their farther progress frustrated, had burned Southwark. The fate of London bridge is unsure: the chronicler's report of its collapse under the press of fugitives from Senlac has an air of legend,[6] but it may have been destroyed when the enemy approached the city; if the bridge still stood, it must certainly have been strongly posted against both surprise and mass attack. It is clear, how-

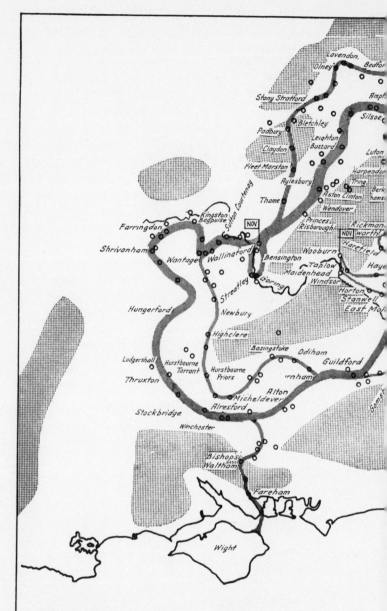

THE NORMAN MARCH THROUGH ENGLAND:
Oct., Dec, 1066

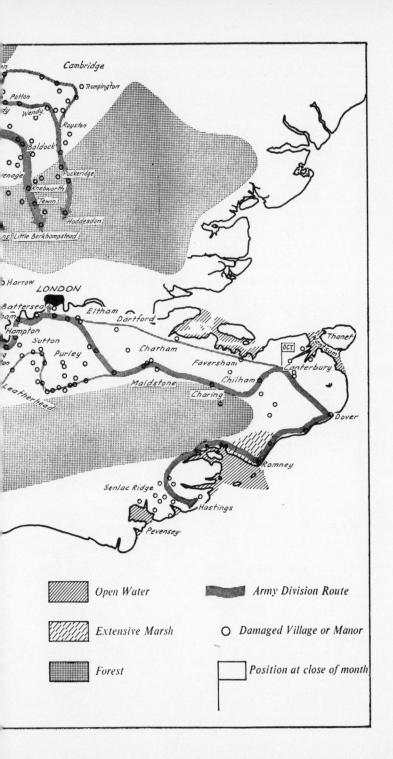

Cambridge

Trumpington

Potton
Wendy
Royston

Baldock

Puckeridge
Knebworth
Tewin

Hoddesdon

Little Berkhompstead

Harrow   LONDON

Battersea
Eltham   Dartford
Hampton
Sutton
Purley   Chatham

Leatherhead

Maidstone

Charing

Senlac Ridge

Hastings

Pevensey

Thanet

OCT.

Canterbury

Faversham
Chilham

Dover

Romney

Open Water	Army Division Route
Extensive Marsh	O Damaged Village or Manor
Forest	Position at close of month

ever, that the English had still no intention of offering open battle to the Normans. Under the leadership of Ansgar, the soldiers gathered in London were concentrating on the protection of the crossings of the Thames and the prevention of any direct onslaught upon the city. It also seems certain that the defenders encountered by the allied van were no more than outlying sentry-pickets under instruction to retire immediately the challengers came into sight. With the isle of Thorney and the king's palace just beyond the river from his camp, the duke set about the tedious business of building engines for a siege.

It soon became obvious that the English were not yet prepared to surrender to threats, or to ballistae. Though William promised that he would exact all the penalties of war from those who opposed him, that if he were granted time, he would raze the walls of the resisting city and level the houses of the inhabitants with the sand, the courage of London remained unshaken. A considerable army was gathered within the walls: the population had been swelled by the troops brought to the south by Edwin and Morkere, and by the return of the fugitives from Senlac; no mention of the Danes is made in the chronicles after the fall of the king, but foreign auxiliaries are said to have been in London when the Normans approached the city.[7] Menaces and gestures were in vain; no opportunity was allowed the invaders to confront the English in the field; and without a foothold on the north bank of the Thames, the duke's engines could accomplish little other than the harassment of the citizens, a process which has never been noted for winning compliance among the Londoners. As the failure of his military operations against the city became evident, William may have entered into negotiation with the defenders, possibly in a secert correspondence with Ansgar. The crippled sheriff may have temporised with the duke, but his purpose was no more than to gain time to strengthen still further the already strong defences of his charge. The negotiation collapsed; and as once again the supplies of the host dwindled to vanishing point, the Norman was forced to end his bargaining, to abandon his siege-works, and to withdraw from a position rapidly becoming untenable. As would-be conquerors had found in the past, and others were to find in the future, the seemingly irresistible tide of the invaders' success broke against the proud and defiant resolve of the city of London.

The allies retired westwards along the south bank of the river to Long Ditton and East Molesley; and the southern detachment which had been coming to the support of the besiegers was directed to return from Purley and Sutton through Leatherhead and Gomshall to its original course. By this time, forward scouts must have reported the nearness of the Berkshire forest, blocking the direct route to the west, and Duke William decided to move away from the Thames, heading south-west to reunite the divisions of the army in the neighbourhood of Guildford. West of Thorney, the land bordering the Thames was low-lying and extensively marshy, and this had undoubtedly contributed to the abandoning, with the siege, of any concept of a major offensive north of the river in southern Middlesex; when the main body of the army moved south, however, a probing force crossed to the left bank of the Thames to survey the country north and west into southern Buckinghamshire. Meanwhile, the duke advanced through Surrey to take Guildford and establish camp. From there, while the army rested, a courier was sent to William fitzOsbern, requiring the seneschal to bring his troops to a junction with the forces of the duke, preparatory to the start of a full campaign against London from the west or north. An embassy was also despatched into Hampshire to demand the submission of Winchester, the marriage-portion and residence of Queen Edith, widow of King Edward and daughter of Earl Godwin.

* * * * *

Protected by her sex and her title, Edith had made no effort to help her brother, the king, or to hinder or fly from the foreign duke who claimed his fallen crown. Indeed, it would be written by one of the Norman panegyrists of the duke that *this woman, endowed with manly wisdom, knowing what was just, and honouring it in her living, wished William to rule over the English.*[8] Certainly, Edith appears to have favoured Tostig among her brothers; and though it cannot be stated that she committed any overt act of treason against Harold, she was the only member of her family to retain her possessions in England under King

William. Treated with constant respect, the Lady Edith remained quietly at Winchester, in full enjoyment of the privileges of her position, until her death in 1075, when *the king had her brought to Westminster with great worship, and laid her near King Edward her husband.*[9] The later history of most of the other members of the family of Godwin is confused and indefinite. Many estates in the west of England were among the properties of Gytha and her children; and it seems likely that after her return from the vigil beside the Watch Oak, Godwin's widow lingered only a short while in London, and then retired from the city where her second son had ruled to the relative peace and security of Devon and Somerset. Her troubles were not over. In the late winter of 1067, Gytha was in Exeter when King William marched against that city. Accompanied by other noble women of the region, the aged countess fled from the advancing Normans to a desolate islet in the Bristol Channel, Flatholm, where she stayed for some time before going into exile in St. Omer. The countess may have ended her days in Flanders; but Judith, the widow of Tostig, was to remarry, and Gytha may have undertaken a final journey to the court of her nephew in Denmark.

Only three of the children of Godwin and Gytha were still alive: Wulfnoth languished in captivity until the death of William in 1087, when it seems that he was formally released, and then imprisoned again; Edith lived and died in Winchester; Gunhild fled with her mother to St. Omer, ultimately to die a nun at Bruges. Of the third generation, few were to leave distinguishable marks in the records. Hakon, son of Swegen, may have escaped to Denmark after Senlac, possibly to reappear in 1075 as an invader of Northumbria in the company of Canute, son of Swegen Estrithsson. Skule and Ketel, the sons of Tostig, returned with Olaf Kyrre to wealth and honour in Norway. Edith and Gunhild were childless, and no offspring of Gyrth, Leofwine, or Wulfnoth, are mentioned in the chronicles. Godwin, Edmund and Magnus, the illegitimate sons of Harold, may have retreated to the west with their grandmother; in the spring of 1068, they were the guests in Dublin of Dermot Mac Mael-na-mbo, who had befriended Harold and Leofwine in the exile of 1051. After apparently two abortive raids on Norman England, in the first of which one of them may have been killed, they quit the land of their father; and after the death of Dermot in 1069, one or both of the surviving brothers sought shelter with their kinsman, King Swegen. The lives of Harold's illegitimate daughters differed radically. Like her aunt and namesake, Gunhild took the veil; she was a nun at Wilton when the Breton counts sought her hand.[10] The dead king's other daughter, Gytha, made her way to Denmark. There, Swegen gave her in marriage to Vladimir, prince of Kiev. By Vladimir, Gytha had a son, named seemingly Harold, through whose daughters the blood of Harold Godwinsson, and probably of Edith Swan-Neck, reached the veins of the Scandinavian kings, and thence, centuries later. of the kings of England.

There were two other sons of Harold. One, Ulf, appears to have been captured in childhood by William, and to have been imprisoned in Normandy throughout his youth and until the death of the Norman king, when he was freed by Robert Curthose, William's eldest son and successor to the dukedom. The other, named after his father, was certainly the child of Queen Alditha and the legitimate heir to Harold's rights and titles. But as the posthumous son of a defeated king, and still an infant while William was establishing his rule, the child was without a future in England. The younger Harold's birth, probably in Chester in December, 1066, or in the first months of 1067, is recorded; but no later reference exists until 1098, when Anglesey was invaded by Magnus Barefoot, King of Norway, *with Harold, son of Harold, former king of England.*[11] It is possible that Alditha, who disappears from English history after the birth of the atheling, fled with her son before the harrying of Chester by King William in 1070, and that the flight brought the fugitive queen and prince to sanctuary in the northland. It is also possible, though unlikely, that Ulf and Harold were posthumous twins, and that Ulf was lost in the flight that carried his brother to Norway.

*   *   *   *   *

The Norman embassy came to Winchester; and the chief citizens, in consultation with the Lady Edith, accepted the duke's terms of surrender and agreed to send offerings on behalf of the queen and of the city. The ambassadors returned with the

tribute and the treaty, and the way through central Wessex was
open to the invaders. By this time, William fitzOsbern had landed
on the mainland, at Fareham in Hampshire, and word of his
landing had been brought to Guildford. The camp was struck,
and the duke moved westwards to Farnham, while the seneschal
thrust northwards through the woods of southern Hampshire
towards Bishop's Waltham. From Farnham, William sent a division of the army sweeping north by Odiham and Basingstoke,
while the main column pushed south-west to Alton, and then
west to a rendezvous with fitzOsbern at Alresford. The reinforcements from the south had harried the country beyond the
forest, north-east of Bishop's Waltham, awaiting the approach
of the duke; and the northern division was ravaging south of
Basingstoke. When the two Williams met, their combined forces
were less than ten miles from Winchester; and the detachment
from the north was converging quickly on their line of march.
The duke moved forward to camp a mile or two north of the
Wessex capital, and halted his northern reserves five or six
miles farther from the city, in the neighbourhood of Micheldever.
The representatives of the defenceless city came to meet the
duke and proffer their formal submission.

Some twenty miles north of Winchester, on the downs between
Whitchurch and Newbury, the western growth of the Berkshire
forest petered out. North and west, the hills and the wide valley
beyond were clear of dense woodland to the Chilterns, the Cots-
wolds and north-western Buckinghamshire. With the eastern and
central counties of southern England annexed, almost the whole
expeditionary army united under his leadership, and with open
country in front of him, William at last felt strong enough to
test again the English defences north of the Thames, and to
seek an alternative route of attack on London. The report of the
commanders who had pillaged through northern Hampshire had
made it clear that no direct march to the north-east would be
possible through eastern Berkshire. At the same time, communication must by now have been lost with the detachment which
had crossed the London river a week or so previously, when the
first offensive against the city had ended; and the duke could
not be confident that the valley of the Thames itself would
provide a sufficient passage for his troops, from the west to the

easier reaches of Middlesex north of the river marshes. Yet winter was nearing; and while London remained untaken, the maintenance of the army in the heart of a hostile kingdom would prove increasingly difficult. William decided to push on northwards with all speed, towards the crossings of the Thames west of the forest.

It was about the end of the third week in November, or a little later, when the invaders left Winchester. A screen of scouts rode ahead of the columns, and guides were supplied by the surrendered city; yet few of the allies could have possessed any reliable knowledge of the country before them, and the duke was too cautious a general to leave intact any possible centres of resistance on his line of retreat. A garrison was stationed in Winchester, and the deliberate devastataion and killing that had marked the progress of the Normans throughout their march was continued ruthlessly, across a broad front. The division of the army was retained; and while the right wing thrust more or less directly north, through the Hurstbournes and Highclere to cross the river Kennet at Newbury, the left wing swung far to the west, through Stockbridge and Thruxton to Ludgershall in Wiltshire, and on north-east, through the Wiltshire Downs, to pass the Kennet at Hungerford. The right wing went on from Newbury north to Wantage, over the eastern shoulders of the Berkshire Downs; and in camps about Wantage, the troops seem to have waited for the return of the farther travelled contingent. Meanwhile, the left wing had again turned away, driving northwest through the Lambourn gap of the downs to Shrivenham on the Wiltshire border. From there, it moved north-east to Faringdon and Kingston Bagpuze, before turning south to link up with the right wing at Wantage. Only a few miles now separated the Normans from the Thames; and in the last days of the month, the tired host struck the right bank of the river near Sutton Courtenay and followed it to Wallingford, where the duke *brought his men safely across the river, and commanded them at that place to lay out a camp.*[12]

*   *   *   *   *

It is impossible to believe that the Norman advance was not watched by English scouts; but still no plans had been laid by the English magnates to counter the operations of the Norman duke. Under the unsure and purely nominal direction of the youthful king-elect, the councils in London were divided; and as the harrying and burning spread through southern England, and refugees from the wasted regions crowded into the already crowded city, morale weakened. Dissension grew to a climax in the last week of November, when it became clear that William intended not merely a limited campaign in eastern and central Wessex, and the invaders pushed northwards from Winchester; and it reached breaking-point when the duke's forces crossed the Thames, to set foot for the first time on Mercian soil. It seems certain that some of the English leaders were prepared to carry on the struggle to a finish, trusting to the huge resources of the kingdom to overcome the challenger in the end. Among these were most probably Edgar himself and Ansgar, and possibly Waltheof and Archbishop Stigand, supported by the burgesses of London. The latter could in no way have relished the pro- spect of submitting their hard-won and jealously guarded privi- leges to the will of a foreign conqueror. On the other hand, the development of events must have strengthened the opposition of those who had given only a grudging assent to the election of the atheling. Later happenings suggest that Wulstan, Bishop of Worcester, and Walter, Bishop of Hereford, may have been of this party, though, as Englishman and Lotharingian, their motives may have differed. And it implies no treason to suggest that William, the Norman bishop of London, may have exerted his influence in the interest of his namesake and fellow-national.

The key-figures in the debate were the earls of Mercia and Northumbria, Edwin and Morkere. The grandsons of Leofric were next in temporal rank only to Edgar, and they spoke among the witan with greater authority than the atheling. After the fall of the Godwinssons, the earls were the most powerful noblemen in England; and the most substantial military force presently available to the defenders of the realm was the northern fyrd which the earls had brought tardily to the assistance of the south, and which they had promised to wield on Edgar's behalf. During the allied offensive against London, the men of the north had helped to beat off every enemy attack; and while Wessex bore the brunt of the Norman terror, the northerners were ready to afford what protection and support they could give to the fleeing West Saxons. When Duke William gained Wallingford, however, his future movements became unpredictable, and he stood on the threshold of Edwin's own earldom. North of the river, Mercia lay vulnerable, with Northumbria beyond, equally denuded of guardians. Though William's primary objective was necessarily the subjugation of London, a powerful and resolute defence of the city would drive the duke almost inevitably northwards, to the easy plunder of the midlands and the rich valleys of Yorkshire. The dilemma facing Edwin and Morkere was insoluble : their first duty was to the king-elect; their first allegiance was to the people of their earldoms. The arguments must have been bitter and coloured by the resurgent separatism which had been stifled by Harold at the gemot of York.[13] But there could be only one ending. *While many were preparing to go to the fight, the earls withdrew their assistance and returned home with their army.*[14]

Despite the losses in the battles of the late months, the strength of England was far from being broken; but there was now no Harold to unite the separate parts of the nation against the common enemy. Before the next month was out, Edwin and Morkere would surrender themselves to the mercy of the invader; and the hurried retreat of the earls at the end of November, 1066, would not protect their lands from the wrath of the Norman king in the dread winter of 1069. So much might have been achieved, if one mind and one spirit had directed the whole power of England in the interregnum after Senlac. But for the kingdom divided there was no hope. *Thus, the English who, joined together in one sentiment, could have repaired the ruin of their country, while they would not choose one from among themselves, let in a stranger.*[15] English resistance to William the Bastard ended effectively with the withdrawal of the northern fyrd from London; and though many still refused to accept it, the final submission of the realm was only a matter of time. There were those who saw more clearly than the Mercian and Northumbrian earls, or the increasingly isolated knots of diehards who continued to oppose the accession of the Norman duke. Among them was the possessor of possibly the keenest political brain in England : Stigand, archbishop of Canterbury, and, his calling notwithstanding, the least visionary of realists.

* * * * *

From the crossing at Hampton, the reconnaissance squadron had moved away from the muddy shore and marshy surrounds of the Thames, broader then than in the twentieth century. Advancing cautiously, they had probed north-west through Feltham, Stanwell and Horton, with the Berkshire forest now closing in on their left, beyond the river. A mile or two farther to the west, the detachment crossed the river again, to raid the royal seat of Windsor; but here the trees clustered almost to the water's edge, and the forest offered more danger than gain to tempt the pillagers. Regaining the left bank, the Normans continued their advance to the north-west. On both sides of the Thames, the passage narrowed as the beech-woods of Buckinghamshire drew in towards the river. It seems likely that at Taplow the raiders found the crossings to Maidenhead defended, and after a foray north to Wooburn begun to withdraw to the south-east. The attempt to open a route for the main army from the west was abandoned. After a march of some two hundred and fifty miles from Hastings, the mass of the allied host lay encamped on the great manor of Bensington east of the Thames and north-east of the ancient town of Wallingford, where the Romans had set a fortress and King Edward had maintained a garrison of housecarls. But while Duke William awaited in vain the arrival of the survey detachment from the east, another traveller made his way through the valley of the Thames to the Norman camp. At the castle of Wallingford, William *was joined by Stigand, the metropolitan archbishop, who did homage to the duke and swore an oath of fidelity to him, abjuring the atheling whom he had lightly set upon the throne.*[16]

DECEMBER

ACROSS the darkening landscape of winter, the darker shadow of capitulation to the Norman terror spread. As the last month of the year began, the fear that had come with the defeat and death of King Harold, and which had lifted briefly before the gates of London, paralysed the will of the defenders of the nation. The withdrawal of the earls had opened the way to a Norman victory; the apparent defection of the archbishop signalled its acceptance. Like Earl Godwin himself, Stigand had risen through the favour of Canute; his elevation to Canterbury in 1052 had been thrust upon the reluctant King Edward by the great earl of Wessex; and since then, the fortune of the primate had been linked inseparably with that of the house of Godwin. With the virtual extinction of that house, the archbishop had lent his now vulnerable authority to the forging of a new centre of English resistance; but the success of his efforts had depended on the unity and steadfastness of those about him. Though he was the senior statesman and the first counsellor in the realm, Stigand could not muster the fyrd : the archbishop proposed, but the military commanders disposed. Given time and resolute leadership, the forces of England might still have swept the invaders into the sea. But neither the time available nor the resolve of the English captains was adequate; and without the active support of Mercia and Northumbria, there could be no sustained defence against the invading army, powerfully augmented since it had recoiled in frustration from the November assault on London. Few could have been swifter to recognise this than Stigand; and few could have accepted more immediately that now the only realistic course, for himself and for the people of England, was to obtain the best terms negotiable for total submission.

The known history and conjectured characer of Archbishop Stigand contain nothing which makes it impossible to believe that he decided privately to surrender to Duke William, and that he rode to Wallingford in furtherance of that decision. How-

ever, there are allusions in the Norman accounts of the last days
of English freedom which may indicate that Stigand came to
the duke as the bearer of a larger mission.[1] The churchman
cannot have been alone in realising that the short kingship of
Edgar Atheling was doomed : within a fortnight at most, the
prince was to accept the fact himself. And it may well have been
that the English primate arrived at the enemy camp as the
appointed emissary of the witan in London, to initiate peace-
talks and to discover the conditions under which there could
be arranged a treaty satisfactory to both the English and the
Normans. If Stigand acted as a private individual, he presumably remained with William throughout the later phases of
the duke's campaign; if, on the other hand, he acted in an
official capacity, either he or an accredited member of his train
must have returned to London with the terms which the duke
was prepared to ratify. Whatever the truth of Stigand's purpose,
it is certain that, early in December, the witan was assembled
by Ansgar and the other English leaders to discuss capitulation.
In a seemingly unanimous verdict, the notables and the populace
of London approved the advice of the council and voted to reject
the young king they had elected little over a month earlier, and
to deliver up the city and themselves to the invader. Couriers
left to carry word of the referendum to the Norman, and to the
earls whose actions had precipitated the debate.

*   *   *   *   *

The Norman reconnaissance squadron had retired from the
forest-encircled valley of the Thames and was busily harrying the
villages and manors of north-west Middlesex, from Hayes to
Rickmansworth, from Harefield to Harrow. It seems likely that
the English commanders in London either could not now spare
troops to hunt down the ravagers, or no longer dared to provoke
William by reprisals against his agents. Over the ruined lands
where the raiders had passed, the couriers of the witan hurried
westwards, to Goring, where part of the allied army had forded
the river from Streatley, and Wallingford, where the bridge had
been left unguarded to the main forces of the duke. But the
English messengers came too late, and the encampment at Bensington was deserted. Whether the invaders had exhausted the

foraging of the surrounding countryside, or Duke William was still too cautious to leave anything to chance in forcing the surrender of London, the army was moving again, north-east, past the western slopes of the Chilterns and the southern skirts of the forest which enfolded the city on the north. In the opening stages of the march, William appears to have pursued his earlier policy, advancing in two columns and pillaging the localities close to the lines of advance. The right wing harried Princes Risborough and pushed on into the country between Aylesbury and Wendover. From here, an attempt seems to have been made to penetrate the Chiltern forest, through Aston Clinton and Tring in the direction of Berkhampstead and London. However, the wooded hills proved too awkward a terrain, and the attempt was abandoned beyond Tring; Berkhamstead remained undamaged, the exploring detachment rejoined the division, and the whole force veered northwards towards Leighton Buzzard and Bletchley. Meanwhile, the lighter left wing had wasted Thame and moved on to Fleet Marston, where the Normans found and followed the track of the old Roman road to Towcester, through the woods of north Buckinghamshire, to Claydon and Padbury.

Beyond the northern fringes of the wood, the left wing swung north-east again, along the way to Stony Stratford; and when the two wings of the army debouched into the open, rolling country of north-east Buckinghamshire and Bedfordshire, the duke relaxed the discipline of his advance. By now, it was clear that the English had lost the will to resist, or at least to challenge the power of the invaders in the field. The couriers, too, following the destruction-marked trail of the allied host, may already have delivered their message and carried back the duke's reply to the witan. Yet William still had no intention either of curbing the plunder-greedy soldiers under his command, or of allowing the English leaders any respite from the pressure which the brutality of his march brought to bear on them. In the next days, the advance became more diffuse, each column throwing off wide-ranging raiding parties. The devastation spread through Bedfordshire, north and east into Huntingdonshire and Cambridgeshire and south through Hertfordshire. Despite the fluidity of this phase of the Norman campaign, an overall pattern can be discerned. The left wing was the farther travelled. From

Stony Stratford, it pushed north to Olney and Lavendon, and then turned south-east towards Bedford. Some miles beyond the county town, the column seems to have divided, part striking due east through Sandy and Potton to Wendy in Cambridgeshire, the other section sweeping north to Eaton Socon, and east across the southern tip of Huntingdonshire into Cambridgeshire. Coming within sight of Cambridge at Trumpington, the northern section swung south-west to reunite with the other division of the column in the neighbourhood of Royston. The right wing was heavier and more slowly moving. From north-east of Bletchley, it thrust east to Ampthill, where it also divided, a strong detachment heading off south through Silsoe, while the main body continued east to Baldock in Hertfordshire.

East of the Chilterns, the forest thinned; and southward through Hertfordshire lay the ways to London for which the duke had searched. Less than forty miles from the Norman headquarters at Baldock was the prize and the country through which William would ride to seize it was gently contoured, cut by rivers and scattered with woodland, but ideal for the operations of the army which the duke captained. Only distance separated the Norman from final victory: the city which had defied the attackers a month before lacked now all means to oppose them. The repulse was not forgotten. By this time, messengers must have been speeding daily between London and the allied command; but the punishment which the duke had meted out to Wessex and southern Mercia was unremitted. Plundering, burning and killing, the invaders thrust on to the south in three great divisions, converging relentlessly on to the helpless city. The right wing pushed east of south from Silsoe through the valley of the Lea in the northern foothills of the Chilterns, past Luton and on to Harpenden and the ancient and holy city of St. Albans. Twenty miles to the east, the reformed left wing moved on from Royston, south to Puckeridge and Hoddesdon, some six miles north of Harold Godwinsson's church at Waltham. Between the wings, the Norman centre followed a course that paralleled roughly the march of the right wing. The most powerful of the three columns, led by Duke William himself, the central division drove southwards from Baldock to Stevenage, Knebworth and Tewin to come at last to Little Berkhampstead, where the southernmost rise of the low hills of Hertfordshire look down towards London.

*   *   *   *   *

The final messages from the north, before the advance of the enemy disrupted communications, had made it clear that London could look for no aid to the earls Edwin and Morkere. The allied army swept south to within twenty miles of the city; the details of the peace-treaty were established; and the act of submission could no longer be postponed. On a day in mid-December, the leading men among the defenders came to the duke's camp at Little Berkhampstead. Surrounded by his captains, and with Archbishop Stigand beside him, William received the delegates. They made a numerous, if subdued, party: Edgar, a king deposed before he was crowned; Eldred, archbishop of York and the most honoured churchman in England; the bishops, William of London, Wulstan of Worcester, and Walter of Hereford; the chief citizens of London, and others of the English magnates. It is unlikely that Ansgar had travelled with them: apart from the wounds and the illness that crippled him, his presence at Senlac had attainted him and his possessions were forfeit to the invader. The last hero of the English resistance disappears from history after the gemot which voted surrender to William; and he may already have been gone from London when the suitors to the duke rode north. In flight, there would be no lack of company. The Danes and foreign mercenaries could look for small mercy from the Norman, and with ships waiting at the docks they did not linger in the city which they had helped to defend, but which could offer them no protection. Englishmen fled also, to Denmark and Flanders, and beyond. Eadric, who had commanded the fleet, was among those who escaped to the sheltering court of Swegen; and in the next years, English exiles made their way across Europe to Byzantium, to serve in the court of the emperor, and in the Varangian guard.

It was the ultimate act of defeat, set almost within sighting distance of the minster where King Harold had prayed before his southward march to defeat. Though Duke William came to meet the deputation, and *gave grateful kisses to those left with the boy,*[2] no courtesy could hide the humiliation of the English leaders. They besought forgiveness of the adventurer who in one battle had brought England to its knees, and *bowed to him for need, when most of the harm was done*.[3] The Englishmen had accepted the inevitable. As they had pledged their duty to Harold eleven months before, and to Edgar after Senlac, they now swore oaths of fealty to William and gave hostages for their behaviour. The charade was to be played out to the full. No power in the kingdom could keep the Norman from the crown; but William had long ago determined that his accession would be legally un-challengeable. The brief reign of Harold was to be set aside by his successor as if it had never happened; and King Edward's com-mendation of 1051 was rehearsed in England as it had been in Normandy. One step towards the throne remained to be taken in justification of the duke's claim : the assent of the witan was necessary to the election of the chosen heir of Edward, son of Emma, great-aunt of William. The English magnates at Little Berkhampstead knew their part. Speaking before the duke as the representatives of the people, *the bishops and the other great ones begged him all together to accept the crown, asserting that they were accustomed to obey a king, and that they wanted a king as lord*.[4]

The immediate response to the entreaty might have been pre-dicted by those who knew the influence on the duke of his closest counsellor, the sometime prior of Le Bec, now lately appointed abbot of St. Stephen's, the duke's own foundation at Caen. Though Lanfranc had remained in Normandy, the Italianate whisperings of the devious monk might almost have been sound-ing in the ear of his patron. With the fruits of his ambition at last firmly within his grasp, William affected to doubt the wisdom of his course. The judgment of an angry God had been given against Harold and the iniquities of the kingdom; and there was a trail of wasted fields, burned homesteads and slaughtered peasants through twelve counties of England to prove it. With the victorious and rapacious army of the claimant at the north gates of London, the chiefs of the English had realised their error, and hastened in abject eagerness to plead with Ethelred's great-nephew to take his rightful place among them. But William now questioned that right. He would question it again, on his death-bed, then probably with more sincerity.[5]

Now he needed the sure confirmation of his followers. *Delibera-ting with those Normans who had come in his suite, and whom he knew to be of tried wisdom and loyalty, he exposed to them the motives which deterred him from yielding to the English entreaties.*[6] The situation in England was still extremely con-fused. It was very true. Canterbury, Winchester and London had submitted to the duke but his mandate reached only as far as his plunderers could ride. Moreover, said the duke, there were rebel-lious elements in the land, and he preferred the peace of the realm to the crown. It would be inappropriate to make undue haste at the very moment of attaining the admitted goal. Besides, he was not the slave of a passion to rule, and if God granted him this honour, he would wish his wife to be crowned with him.

William understood his audience. Unanimously, and pre-sumably with more genuine feeling than the English suitors, the Normans begged their commander to take the crown. The deci-sive argument was given, however, not by one of William's own subjects, but by his powerful and eloquent ally, Aimeri of Aqui-taine, viscount of Thouars in Poitou. The viscount paid tribute to the modesty and condescension of the duke. Rarely had simple knights been admitted to such a debate, to speak their minds freely on a matter touching so nearly the honour of their lord. There was no need to deliberate at length a wish that all there trusted would soon be implemented. To make William a king was the purpose for which the soldiers of the allied army had crossed into England, for which they had braved the dangers of the sea and of battle. Yet this was not the will only of the invaders, a trophy bought with their blood. The best men in England were joined with the duke's supporters in the plea. The Frenchman carefully ignored the relative circumstances of the late enemies. Such men, he said, would not seek to raise the duke to the throne, if they had not recognised his fitness to govern their country. The English saw in William a leader under whose rule advantage and honour would come to the kingdom and to themselves. William weighed the argument and was persuaded. As king he might end dissension in the realm. When he had begun to reign as a consecrated monarch, he might hope that those Englishmen who still opposed his crowning would lower their banners and accept his sovereignty. The coronation was fixed for Christmas Day and while the duke remained in the safety of the camp, some of his followers rode with the returning embassy, to build a fortress in the city, and to see to the preparations necessary for the enthroning of the king.

*　　*　　*　　*　　*

The crown for which William the Bastard had fought was his. The possibility had been remote thirty-eight years before, when in the Norman town of Falaise, Herleva, daughter of Fulbert the tanner, gave birth to her first child, the illegitimate son of Robert I, duke of Normandy. It seems probable that the duke and the tanner's daughter also had a daughter; but within two or three years, Robert married off his mistress to a complaisant nobleman, Herluin, viscount of Conteville. The marriage with Herluin was fruitful, and to the viscount Herleva bore the half-brothers who were to ride by William's side at Senlac, Odo of Bayeux, and Robert of Mortain. Though the association had not lasted, Duke Robert was grateful to the girl who had given him a son : Fulbert became an official of the ducal household; and Herleva's brother, Walter, was to father a daughter who would marry the rich and powerful Ralph of Tesson. In 1034, the duke suddenly decided to make a pilgrimage to Jerusalem; and when the Norman magnates, led by Robert's uncle, the archbishop of Rouen, objected that his death would leave no heir, the duke produced for their acceptance his bastard son by Herleva. Grudgingly, the Norman lords guaranteed the succession to William and swore oaths of allegiance to the young prince. Soon afterwards, the duke departed for the East, and his son went to King Henry of France to do homage as his father's successor to the overlord of Normandy. The fears of the barons had been justified. In July, 1035, at Nicaea on his homeward journey from Jerusalem, Duke Robert died; and at the age of seven, William of Falaise was duke of the Normans.

The years of the duke's childhood were years of trouble and rebellion in Normandy. In later ages, William was styled 'the Great', or 'the Conqueror', or perhaps 'the Purchaser';[7] but to his contemporaries he was unequivocally 'the Bastard'. That he survived his accession was owed to the strength of the guardians whom his father had chosen : Robert, archbishop of Rouen; Alan, count of Britanny; and Osbern, seneschal at the Norman court. Within a few years all three were dead. The archbishop died in March, 1037, and was succeeded in his chair by Mauger, a half-uncle of the duke, and brother of William, count of Arques. In 1040, Alan of Britanny was killed, possibly by poison; and in the same year, Osbern was butchered in the bedchamber of the duke, William himself escaping only through the prompt care of his maternal uncle, Walter. Within a few months, Gilbert, count of Brionne, who had replaced the Breton count as principal guardian of the prince, was likewise assassinated by hirelings of Ralph of Gace, his cousin, and son of Archbishop Robert. The struggle among the members of the duke's family for the possession of his person was unrelenting. Revolt and counter-revolt chequered the decade that followed the death of the archbishop, until 1047, when Henry of France entered the contest on behalf of his vassal and crushed the western viscounts under Guy of Burgundy, William's cousin, at the battle of Val-ès-Dunes. William was then eighteen and for the first time master in his dukedom. It was a significant year, marking not merely the finish of the duke's minority. In October, at Caen, the prelates of Normandy proclaimed the Truce of God, under which those present vowed to wage no private wars between Wednesday evening and Monday morning, and during Advent, Lent, Easter and Pentecost.

Despite the victory and the holy truce, William's future was not yet assured. Throughout thirteen subsequent years, he was almost constantly at war; and not until 1054 was he certain even of survival. After Val-ès-Dunes, the duke was left by France to deal with his defeated subjects. Guy of Burgundy had escaped to Brionne; and the taking of his stronghold proved so difficult that only in 1050 was William able to return to Rouen after the surrender and banishment of his cousin. Until the autumn of the next year, the duchy was more or less peaceful. During these quiet months, William paid his fateful visit to England, to receive the commendation of the Anglo-Norman king. It was probably in the same period, too, that Baldwin V of Flanders

married his daughter Matilda to the young duke, over the interdict of the pope and the strenuous objections of Lanfranc. It
was, however, an alliance on which the duke had set both his
heart and his head; once the prior of Le Bec was brought to see
the folly of his opposition, his advocacy was as strenuously
directed to the cause of his earthly benefactor. But William's
marital bliss was soon interrupted. The Norman was summoned
to the aid of France against a new enemy, Geoffrey Martel,
count of Anjou, lately the conqueror of Maine. In the autumn
of 1051, the duke invested the fortress of Domfront held by an
Angevin garrison just beyond the frontier of Normandy. Before
the winter was out, a southward advance by King Henry had
forced Geoffrey Martel to quit Maine; Alençon, which stood on
the border of William's own territory and was also occupied,
had been taken in a surprise assault; and the garrison of Domfront had surrendered, horrified by the barbaric maimings which
had been inflicted by the duke on the defenders of Alençon.

Again it might have seemed that William could look forward
to a peaceful possession of his duchy. However, at some time
during the investment of Domfront, William, count of Arques
and brother of Archbishop Mauger, suddenly renounced his
vassalage to the duke and retired to his castle in Upper Normandy. Possibly the most powerful subject in the dukedom, and
contemptuous of his bastard half-nephew, the count of Arques
could expect support for his challenge to the duke both inside
and outside Normandy. He was the brother-in-law of the neighbouring count of Ponthieu; and he launched his rebellion when
the growing independence of Duke William was beginning to
perturb his French overlord. By the summer of 1052, King
Henry had won the allegiance of Geoffrey Martel; and the king
saw in Arques an effective counterpoise to the formidable prince
of the Normans. The count appealed for aid to the king and
attacked the forces loyal to the duke in Upper Normandy. Duke
William retaliated immediately; and in the autumn of 1052, the
count was already under siege in his castle. Like Brionne, the
fortress proved too strong to be taken by storm, and it was still
in rebel hands, when, a year later, King Henry marched to its
relief. But, in October, 1053, the invaders were seriously weakened in an ambush near St. Aubin, in which the count of

Ponthieu was killed; King Henry managed to infiltrate reinforcements and provisions to the defenders of Arques, but the losses in the ambush forced his withdrawal from Normandy. Late in 1053, the castle finally surrendered; the lives of the garrison were spared, and Count William fled to exile in Boulogne. Soon afterwards, his brother, the archbishop of Rouen, was deposed by an ecclesiastical council, and the last revolt headed by elders of the ducal family was ended.

The French king's defeat had only served to whet his determination to bring Normandy to his feet. By February, 1054, Henry was ready to invade once more, now in coalition with the count of Anjou and his ally, the count of Aquitaine. Two enemy armies entered the duchy: in the south-east, led by the king and Geoffrey Martel, the allies devastated the county of Evreux; the other force, commanded by Odo, brother of the king, harried the north-east near Aumale. The fall of Arques, however, had freed William from treason within the dukedom, and he was able to gather troops to oppose both attacks. While the duke himself faced King Henry, the count of Eu, a loyal kinsman of William, and several of the premier barons of Normandy advanced to meet the north-eastern threat. In the south no battle developed; but north of the Seine, the Normans achieved a complete surprise. At the small town of Mortemer, the scattered right wing of the invaders was routed. The Frenchmen were massacred; Odo escaped with difficulty; and Guy of Ponthieu, the successor to the count killed in the preceding year, was taken prisoner. The victory was so overwhelming that when word of Mortemer reached the southern wing of the allied army, King Henry abandoned the campaign and withdrew from Normandy. It was a major turning-point in Duke William's history. The duke's rule was never to be challenged by such a powerful combination of enemies again. The duchy was firmly in William's hands; the warlike zeal of his nominal overlord was dampened; and when Count Guy was at last released, Ponthieu had sworn allegiance to the duke, and the county would stand as a buffer on the border of Upper Normandy, against subsequent inroads from northern France.

The next years saw the consolidation of William's authority in his dukedom. The rising barons were largely William's men. His position was also strengthened through his immediate family About 1050, the duke's half-brother, Odo, had been appointed to the rich bishopric of Bayeux. Some five or six years later, the count of Mortain was arbitrarily stripped of his fief, and the county was made the portion of William's other half-brother, Robert. In the same period, the power of Normandy spread gradually outwards. Though Geoffrey Martel remained an implacable foe, and his control of Maine lasted throughout his lifetime, the border-lands of the count's conquest were whittled away by Normandy, and the rightful heir to Maine concluded a treaty with William by which, if the heir proved childless, the succession was willed to the duke. Late in 1055, the duke negotiated a reconciliation between himself and the French king, to the profit of the duchy. Nevertheless, eighteen months later, Henry again formed an alliance with the count of Anjou; and in August, 1057, an allied army was once more advancing into Normandy. The attack now came from the south, through the Hiémois towards Bayeux and Caen. William gathered an army near Falaise, making at first no move against the invaders. But at a ford of the Dives, near Varaville, when the allies were crossing, laden with loot, the duke suddenly attacked the rearguard and baggage-train. The incoming tide had cut off the main part of the army from coming to the rescue and an impotent King Henry had to watch the slaughter of his followers on the far side of the river. As at Mortemer, the losses were so heavy that the French were compelled to retreat. It was Henry's last invasion. The war dragged on desultorily; and in August, 1060, when peace talks were in progress, the French king died. With the death of Geoffrey Martel in November, the western dominance of Normandy was assured.

The winds that blew William a kingdom in 1066 were merely the latest in a series of chances that might have inclined his commentators to name the Norman duke, 'William the Fortunate'. Though William may in later years have flaunted his bastardy almost as a banner, his birth, recognition and accession were all more attributable to luck than to any historical precedent. The very dangers that threatened his childhood and adolescence emphasise the combination of special circumstance and good fortune that enabled him, or his protectors, to overcome them. No ill stars touched the marriage he made with Matilda of Flanders: it was happy in its condition, and in its consequences, to a measure which William could not have predicted when the daughter of Count Baldwin first came to him. When he needed the help of his overlord, France was friendly; when King Henry turned against him, he was already strong enough to contemplate resistance. The might of the coalition of 1052 was more than sufficient to subjugate Normandy; but when the duke's external enemies finally united against him, he had been allowed time to eliminate treason within the duchy. At Mortemer, the barons of Upper Normandy found the invaders dispersed, unready even for their own defence; if the massacre was owed to the folly of the French commanders, William was lucky in their choice. The flooding of the Dives at Varraville might conceivably have been expected by the Norman: he could not have expected it to happen when the passage of the river had been completed only by the main fighting force of the king and the count. In 1060, within four months, the duke's two most dangerous enemies were removed. The death of Geoffrey Martel was the signal for anarchy and civil war in both Anjou and Maine. Henry of France's successor was a child, and the boy was placed under the regency of Count Baldwin of Flanders, father-in-law to Duke William.

After 1060, William could look forward to many years of increasing Norman influence in western Europe under his leadership. The duke was still in his early thirties, tall in body and powerfully built, tending to corpulence, but not ungainly. He was temperate in his habits, his style of living was moderate, his marriage vows were binding and at last accepted by Rome; and in his religious practices, he adhered closely to the disciplines of his youth. His voice was harsh, his speech was fluent and persuasive. His mind was shrewd rather than brilliant, but in the appraisal of a political or military situation he was masterly. Never a great captain, William was none the less an able tactician, swift in seizing the advantage of favourable circumstances, neither dismayed nor irresolute in adversity. His courage was beyond question and he undertook every enterprise with unswerving determination and energy. There were darker facets of the duke's character: forced growths sprung from the violence and insecurity of his childhood, and cancers of later development, corruptions bred by power. He was inflexible in the prosecution of his will. If he never forgot a kindness, he neither forgot nor forgave an insult or an injury. Ends were justified by his desiring them and means were to be judged solely by their effectiveness. Once set upon a course, he would pursue it to the finish, with a ruthlessness that shrank from no chicanery, no cruelty, no barbarity. At Alençon, thirty-two prisoners were brought before the duke: they were not killed, and they were not blinded; these were the only attributes of humanity and of manhood that were not lopped from them. There were places in Sussex and elsewhere in England that would never recover from the pillaging of 1066. In later years, the harrying of Northumbria would ruin a province and leave scars that would endure through centuries; half of Hampshire was wasted to make a hunting forest for the Norman king.

King Henry and Geoffrey Martel were dead and fortune continued to smile on Duke William. In March, 1062, the heir to Maine dispossessed by Anjou also died, without issue. William immediately claimed the county and war with a rival claimant followed. The Norman invaded and by the beginning of 1064 Maine had become a fief of the dukedom. William now turned his attention to Britanny, where since 1057, Count Conan[8] had ruled, and had recently taken up the mantle of Geoffrey of Anjou as challenger to the eminence of the Norman duke. In the same year, Harold Godwinsson came to Normandy on the mission that was to defame his memory when it was distorted by the duke's advocates. The Norman and the Englishman marched together against the Breton count and retired after a campaign that was little more than a gesture. His mission a seeming success, Harold returned to the kingdom that was already his in all but name. Conan of Britanny turned his attention away from the north-east towards disturbed Anjou. The last year of the long peace in England began, and in Normandy too there was peace. Summer passed, and autumn. Winter came; Northumbria rose to murder the servants of Earl Tostig; and the favourite of the dying king crossed to angry exile at the court of Baldwin. The year 1065 ended; and on a January morning, a messenger came to the hunting-park of Quevilly, bringing word to Duke William of the death of Edward and the crowning of Harold.

*   *   *   *   *

On Christmas Day, 1066, the bastard grand-son of the Norman tanner came to his coronation. There are later legends of continued opposition to the invaders after the surrender at Little Berkhampstead, of trees dropped across the path of the duke's march to London. But there were at most isolated incidents; and though certainly the king-elect allowed his men still to harry the countryside around, the English resistance was moribund. On the seventh day before the end of the year, William was consecrated in the minster where Harold had been enthroned six days after the year had begun. The Norman was anointed according to the ancient rites of England, in a ceremony that departed only in detail from that which had been observed by his predecessor. The same hands placed the crown on the head of the king; for though Stigand took an honoured part in the ceremony, Canterbury was again passed over in favour of the surer ecclesiastical position of York, and Eldred performed the sacrament. If the archbishop of York was scarcely *of saintly life and flawless reputation*,[9] and if the threats of Tostig had been needed to bring him the pallium, at least he could officiate now with no stigma of unorthodoxy to obscure the sanctity of his actions. Yet one doubt may have clouded the acceptance of the honour by the primate of Northumbria : Eldred could in no way have been certain that the people of his own province would approve or confirm the service he undertook this day.

The procession formed outside the palace on Thorney Island. The morning was peaceful, and there were no disturbances. But the new masters of England were taking no chances : the approaches to the minster and the church itself were guarded by soldiers, armed and on horseback. Inside St. Peter's, everything was ready, and the building was crowded with spectators, both English and Norman. The procession moved towards the minster, the monks and priests who led it walking two by two and singing songs of praise. First came the lesser clergy, bearing crosses, and these were followed by the bishops. Duke William, with Stigand and Eldred on either side of him, walked behind the bishops,

surrounded by the leaders of his army and of the kingdom which
he had won. The duke entered the cathedral; the singing was
silenced; and the shouting of the people died. William took his
place before the high altar and the Te Deum was sung, as it had
been sung over Harold. The coronation had begun. There were
additions to the liturgy, brought from Normandy : acclamations
of, and salutations to the king, in the names of the Virgin,
St. Michael and St. Raphael. No descent of the royal dignity
from father to son could be claimed by William; but in keeping
with the policy from which the Norman never deviated, the
'hereditary right' of the duke was brought forward yet again.
This was, however, a uniting of two races, a meeting of two
tongues; and when Eldred demanded in English whether the
assembled men of England would have the candidate before
them as their king, Geoffrey, bishop of Coutances, repeated the
question to the Normans. The shouts of 'Yea, yea, King
William!' rang through St. Peter's church, and the consent of
both nations had been given to the crowning.

Outside the minster, there was sudden confusion. Hearing the
clamour of the English and Normans within, and the great cry
in an unknown tongue, the horsemen on guard about the church
hurried to the assumption that treason had been done to the
duke and his supporters. For no intelligible reason, the sentinels
made no attempt to rescue the supposed victims, but instead, set
fire to the houses about the bridges that led to the city. Confusion now erupted inside the cathedral; the shouting of the soldiers and the neighing of their horses broke through the ritual,
and the glare of the burning buildings lit up the inner walls of the
minster. The doors were dragged open, and men and women of
all ranks rushed out to find what had happened and to help
quench the flames. William was left alone with the monks of the
abbey and the archbishops, bishops and priests officiating in the
ceremony. Perhaps for the first time since the terrors of his childhood had passed away, fear struck at the heart of the Norman,
and the duke trembled : in the last minutes before its achievement, an uncomprehended danger had arisen to menace the
fulfilment of his highest ambition. But the coronation went on.
Eldred administered the oath, and William swore that he would
defend the church and keep just laws, and *that he would rule*

*this people as well as any king before him best did, if they would
be faithful to him.*[10] In the almost deserted cathedral, solemn
amid the tumult, the duke gave himself up to the rites that made
him a king. The holy oil was poured, and William was dressed.
The sword was fastened about his waist. Eldred took the crown
that had been fashioned for the occasion, of gold studded with
gems, and set it on the brows of the Norman. The sceptre and
the rod were brought; and William the Bastard sat enthroned
as king of the English.

*   *   *   *   *

The claim that William had asserted with such little apparent
hope of success had been acknowledged by the people he had
vowed to govern. Shortly after the coronation, the king left
London and moved to Barking in Essex, some miles to the east.
There the remaining chiefs of the English made their submission.
With the crowning of the king, Edwin and Morkere had been
persuaded that their best opportunity for continued influence
lay in surrender: *they implored pardon for having risen up
against him, and they handed themselves over, their persons and
their property, to his clemency.*[11] The earls were confirmed in
their titles. Another who submitted, and who was to profit from
the coming of the Norman king, was Copsig. Tostig's deputy
and most probably a fugitive since Stamford Bridge. The
removal to Barking was a pointer to the future: William went
there while fortifications were being completed in London
which would enable the Normans, if need be, to control the city
by force. Among the king's early measures was the issuing to the
Londoners of a writ which recognised the status and certain
rights of the borough. It was brief and in the vernacular, and is
a key document in the development of the city. *William the king
greets William, bishop of London, and Gosfrith the portreeve,
and all the burgesses of London friendly. I give you to know that
I will that you be worthy of all the laws you were worthy of in
the time of King Edward. And I will that every child shall be
his father's heir after his father's day. And I will not suffer any
man to do you wrong. God preserve you.*[12] But already the laws
that would change the structure of English life were being drawn
up; the taxes that would drive Englishmen into bondage were

being imposed; the gifts abroad that would strip the churches of England of the treasure of centuries were being allotted.

The last day of the old year was a Sunday. The bells called the people to mass and the subjects of the king, English and Norman, made their way through the dark, winter morning to the minsters and the chapels on this seventh day of the Feast of Christ's Nativity. There was a king in England, crowned and anointed, and if as yet his rule reached through scarcely a quarter of the realm, the other provinces would feel it in time. In the years ahead, the laws of King William would be extended gradually, but implacably, to the farthest bounds of his kingdom, until all the land bowed to one master. William would try at first to govern, as Canute had governed, with the acceptance of the English, but Norman ways were alien, as Danish ways had not been. Within two years, the king's occupation of the country that was his by 'right' would be changing to a conquest. But it was not what William had desired and the term 'Conqueror' would be in itself a defeat for the Norman prince who had claimed England as his heritage. The years would pass and one by one, the offices of power in England would pass with them, into the hands of strangers. The dispossessed would meet many ends; and among those who fled into exile would be Edith Swan-Neck, who would find a last oblivion in a small town of central France, La Chaise-Dieu in the Auvergne. The bells of Sunday stilled, and the long winter night settled over Anglo-Saxon England.

AFTERWORD

ACROSS the devastated lands of eastern Wessex, the cortège wound its slow way. On the desolate cliff above the grey waters of the Channel the monks had gathered. The slab of rock had been raised and laid aside and the remains, still showing the marks of the weapons that had hewed deeply, had been wrapped in rich cloths. The monks prayed and sang hymns as they walked. They passed the ridge at Senlac where the golden banner now sent to Rome had waved and moved on by the hoar apple-tree on Caldbec Hill to the deep shadows of the Andredsweald. By devious ways they went, out of Sussex and northwards through Surrey, until at last, a little way beyond the Essex border, they came to the minster. The brothers assembled and took their charge from the travellers. They bore it into the dim quiet of the church, beneath the great cross where the Christ-figure hung with lowered head. The service that had been denied before was read, and in a place of honour by the high altar of the minster of the Holy Cross at Waltham, the canons of the foundation laid to rest the body of Harold the king.

JANUARY: NOTES

1. This combines the titles given to Harold as earl by Florence of Worcester (Flor. Worc.); they were exceptional in the eleventh century.
2, 3. Anglo-Saxon Chronicles (A.S. Chron.).
4. The events and reported speech in this and the following paragraphs come from the Vita Ædwardi Regis (Vit. Æd.).
5. With the king was also possibly his physician, Baldwin, a Frenchman and abbot of Bury St. Edmunds.
6. Vit. Æd.
7. Saga of Edward.
8. Flor. Worc.
9. Vit. Æd.
10, 11. A.S. Chron.
12. Flor. Worc.
13. History of Evesham.

FEBRUARY: NOTES

1. Vit. Æd.
2. De Inventione S. Crucis (De Inv.).
3. Roman de Rou (Wace).
4. Heimskringla (Heimsk.).
5-7. Vita Wulfstani.

MARCH: NOTES

1. A.S. Chron.
2. Bayeux tapestry.
3, 4. William Malmesbury (Wm. Malm.).
5. It was a precedent that would cause trouble in the future to the kings of Christendom.
6. Imposed by Ermenfrid, a papal legate, during a visit to England in 1070.
7. Vit. Æd.
8. Skule and Ketel: Heimsk.
9. Vit. Æd.
10. Wace.

Notes

APRIL: NOTES

1. Vit. Æd.
2. Heimsk.
3, 4. A.S. Chron.
5. Principally by the Cinque Ports, which had guaranteed naval support in return for certain juridicial privileges, and by specified areas of the country, which were required to provide one manned and equipped ship for every 300 hides.
6. A.S. Chron.
7. As distantly as Italy and Poland.
8. Orderic Vitalis (Ord. Vit.); William of Jumièges (Wm. Jum.); Benoit of St. Maur (Benoit).

MAY: NOTES

1. The 'witch-cults' of pagan England survived widely. William Rufus, the second Norman king, may owe his unjustified ill-fame among the Church historians to a personal support of the older religion.
2. E.g. mild ale, clear ale, Welsh ale.
3. The presence of grit in the ground meal increased the coarseness considerably.
4. At Jerusalem, by St. Helena, mother of Constantine the Great.
5. Even larger vessels are known to have existed, such as the 'great ships' of Canute, with more than a hundred oars.
6. A.S. Chron.
7. Geoffrey Gaimar (Gaimar) records the landing of Tostig at *Wardstane*, a place-name unidentifiable as such, but probably to be located in Wight. Of the Anglo-Saxon place-names in Wight capable of corruption to Wardstane, the most likely is *Weristestone*, a large manor in the east of the island, extending towards the coast in the neighbourhood of modern Shanklin, and commemorated by the village of Winstone, some 2 miles west of Shanklin.
8. A.S. Chron.
9. Vit. Æd.
10. Damage eastward from Chichester harbour is recorded in Domesday; some, however, may be due to later devastation by the Norman invaders.
11. See map of 'The Norman March through England'.
12. The naval equivalent of housecarls.
13. A.S. Chron.
14. Thanet rises west to east, to the cliffs of the North Foreland.
15. A channel remained until the seventeenth century and is shown on the Speed map of 1611, but its usefulness to shipping had ended by the fourteenth century.

16. Applied to any regional body of armed men, but particularly to the national army.
17. A.S. Chron.
18. The lines of demarcation between the lesser nobles and the richer peasants were distinct, but narrow.
19. Other qualifications were, of course, necessary.
20. Earl Thorfinn, died about 1064, had submitted to Norwegian overlordship under Magnus or Hardraada.
21. The south-eastern extension of Watling Street from London to Dover.
22. A.S. Chron.
23. Ord. Vit.
24. The importance of *Brunnan-mutha*, or Brunnemuth, declined gradually in later centuries; it was still of importance in the thirteenth century and is shown on the Speed map of 1611. The present Overy Staith may occupy its site.
25, 26. A.S. Chron.

JUNE: NOTES

1. In 1066, Whitsunday was June 4th.
2. Flintshire, the Vale of Clwyd, northern coastal areas stretching into Caernarvonshire, Radnor and Monmouth.
3. John of Oxenedes.
4. Domesday Book, Norfolk.
5. The story of Hardraada is taken substantially from Heimsk.
6. Runeindskrift: Piraeus. Inscription Runique du Pirée, interprétée par C. C. Rafn, et publiée par la Société Royale des Antiquaires du Nord. Copenhague, 1856.
7. The Mora is described by Wace et alia, and it is pictured in the Bayeux tapestry.
8. The descendants of the Norman colonists under Robert Guiscard.
9. This will appear in the description of Hardraada's invasion force.

JULY: NOTES

1. The term *thing* was used to mean both a regional parliament in Norway and the area of jurisdiction of that parliament; the invented term *thing-land* is used here to distinguish between the two meanings.
2. The title *jarl* was equivalent to *earl* in England; a *lenderman* was roughly equivalent to a *baron*.
3. The quotations in this and the succeeding paragraphs are taken from Heimsk.
4. The successor of Ulv was Styrkar, whose name is known only from the account in Heimsk. of the battle of Stamfordbridge.
5. Now the Oslofjord.

6. Orkneyingers' Sagas.
7. His son, Robert, invaded England with the duke and later played an important role in both English and Norman history.
8. Snorri Sturlasson quotes a scurrilous story of how, when William was mounted and about to leave, Matilda approached him, angering the duke so that he struck her on the breast with his spurred heel. The duchess is then said to have died of the wound received. The legend is evidently apocryphal.
9. Which he later resigned.
10. The quotations in this and the succeeding paragraphs are taken from William of Poitiers (Wm. Poit.).
11. This paragraph and the one which follows attempt to unravel and make intelligible a highly confused and confusing passage from Wm. Poit.
12. Heimsk.

AUGUST: NOTES

1. This is clearly indicated by Wm. Poit.
2. Harold could have little exact knowledge of Tostig's movements after May (see bibliographical note on A.S. Chron.).
3. In 1087.
4. William's favourite oath.
5. The only relevant sources suggest the opposite.
6, 7. Heimsk.
8. The river was strongly tidal certainly as far as Varaville, where William had defeated the last French invasion of Normandy.
9. This estimate accords with most of the known or calculable factors in a consideration of the Norman armada.
10. This estimate is derived from the assumed totals of the ships and personnel in the invasion force, allowances being made for the accompanying equipment and animals.
11. Some authorities list as few as 15.
12. With a listing of several hundred 'companions of the Conqueror', the Roll of Battle Abbey notoriously illustrated this practice.
13. Well known at the court of Henry I of England.
14. Ord. Vit.
15. Cartulary of Carisbrooke Priory, Isle of Wight.
16. See Genealogy Table 4.
17. Guy of Amiens (Carmen).
18. By sources not accounted of the first rank.
19. A high official of the king's household.
20. Wm. Poit.
21. Orkneyingers' Sagas: Hemingssaga.
22. In his struggle against Macbeth.

SEPTEMBER: NOTES

1. For this estimate of the sailing speed of the Norse fleet I have to thank Captain G. P. D. Hall, R.N., who has made a special study of the naval movements of the period.
2. Oswulf was the son of a previous earl of Northumbria, murdered by Earl Siward.
3. A.S. Chron.
4. See August: Note 15.
5. *The English Channel* (J. A. Williamson).
6. Carmen.
7. This will appear later in the account of the Norman movements in England.

8. The information contained in this paragraph is taken from *The English Channel.*
9. Orkneyingers' Sagas: Hemingssaga.
10. Heimsk.
11. This is clear from Wm. Poit. on the effects of the later move to St. Valery.
12. Wm. Poit.
13. Domesday, Essex (ii, 14b).
14. Domesday, Norfolk (ii, 200). Previously mentioned under June.
15. Cartulary of the Holy Trinity, Rouen. See August.
16. Aethelred of Rievaux; Vita Haroldi.
17. A.S. Chron.
18. Wm. Poit.
19. Ingulf.

20. Carmen.
21. Wm. Poit.
22. The presence of an English fleet at Tadcaster depends upon an ambiguous passage in A.S. Chron. (C). It is, however, reasonable to assume that Morkere would command a small naval force.
23, 24. Heimsk.
25. A.S. Chron.
26. Particularly Heimsk. and Orkneyingers' Sagas.
27. Heimsk.
28. This must have been the route taken, if the last phase of the battle is to be comprehensible.
29. Wm. Poit.
30. Heimsk.

31. Until recently, this exploit was commemorated annually on a day near the anniversary of the battle by the baking and eating of 'spear-boat pies'.
32. Heimsk.
33. This was the standard pattern of battle in the wars of the Saxon and Norman kings of England. The key to an understanding of any of their military operations lies in appraisal of the conditions relative to that particular operation. It is a key which has been almost consistently ignored by the historical theorists of the past hundred years; and the study of late Anglo-Saxon warfare has been bedevilled by the dicta of quasi-authorities dissertating upon the art of war without perception of its basic principles. The first of these is that the intention of military action is the destruction of an enemy; in the achievement of this, throughout history, whatever means have been provided by nature or art suitable for the killing of men have been put to that purpose. The utilisation has not always been sophisticated; but

Notes

to suggest that, for example, the horse was not used as a battle-arm by the Anglo-Saxons is to belittle the skill and intelligence of captains at least as knowledgeable in war as their detractors.

34–38. Heimsk.
39. Orkneyingers' Sagas: Hemingssaga.
40, 41. Heimsk.
42. Skule and Ketel returned to Norway with Olaf, and were granted lordships there; Copsig became an earl under William; Godred Crouan fled to the Isle of Man, which he later ruled, together with the Viking territory of Dublin.
43. Gaimar.
44. Heimsk.
45–47. Wm. Poit.

OCTOBER: NOTES

1. Flor. Worc.
2. Wace.
3. Carmen.
4. A report of a report in Wm. Malm.
5. Carmen.
6. Wm. Malm.
7–9. Wm. Poit.
10. Carmen.
11. Neustria Pia, ed. A. du Monstier; Regesta Regum Anglo-Normannorum, Vol. I, ed. H. W. C. Davis.
12. Wace.
13. Carmen.
14. Brevis Relatio (Brev. Rel.).
15. Wace.
16. Wm. Poit.
17. Wace.
18. De Inv.
19. Gaimar.
20. Wm. Jum.
21. Saga of Edward.
22. Wace.
23. Heimsk.
24. Orkneyingers' Sagas.
25–27. De Inv.
28. Wace.
29. Flor. Worc.
30, 31. A.S. Chron.
32. Carmen.
33. Wace.

34. Wm. Poit.
35. Carmen.
36. Baldslow, Ninfield and Hailesaltedc (Lemmon, C. H.. *The Field of Hastings*).
37. Wace.
38. Wm. Malm.
39–41. Wace.
42. Wace; Wm. Malm.
43. There is something almost supernatural about the influence of the weather on the events of 1066; but before conclusions are drawn about 'divine intervention on the side of right', it would be worth considering the parallel with the 'Hitler weather' of the early 1940s.
44, 45. Flor. Worc.
46–48. Wace.
49. Or possibly Heathland; on a 1625 map, the eminence is named Standard Hill, and local tradition claims that here William raised the papal standard.
50, 51. Chron. Battel Abb.
52. Wm. Poit.
53. Benoit.
54, 55. Wace.
56. The Wessex Dragon was flown in battle by Edward III.
57. Wace.
58. Gaimar.
59. Wm. Jum.
60. Wm. Poit.
61. Wace.
62. Benoit.
63. Wace; Henry of Huntingdon (Hen. Hunt.).
64, 65. Wm. Poit.
66. Wm. Poit.; Carmen.
67. Wace.
68. Hen. Hunt.
69, 70. Wace.
71. Wm. Malm.
72. There has been much controversy about the identification of the 'evil ditch', but Oak Wood Gyll is its most likely setting: the topographical features are consistent with the chronicle indications of Wm. Poit., Wm. Jum., Ord. Vit., Wm. Malm. and Chron. Battel Abb., and about 1300 the locality was referred to in an extant deed as Manfosse, a more than possible corruption of Malfosse.
73. Wm. Malm.
74. Wace.
75. Carmen.
76. See November, *1066*.
77. De Inv.

78. Wm. Jum.
79. The upper slopes of Caldbec Hill are still known as Mountjoy, and the vanished cairn was probably raised on the summit.
80. Wace.
81. Baudri.
82. Wm. Poit.
83. Wm. Poit.: this is a conjectural identification of a location otherwise unidentified, but the conjecture is supported by the following argument: the present West Gate was erected in the 14th. century on the site of an earlier edifice, at least part of which had served as a hospice for visiting dignitaries in former years; stones of the preceding structure would certainly have been used in the building of the West Gate, and the existent fabric includes identifiably Roman remains; very little stonebuilding was carried out in Saxon times, but Canterbury had been an important centre under the Romans, and they built predominantly in stone; the Roman masons built to last, but even so, a tower dating from the early centuries of the Christian era would certainly be in disrepair, if not 'broken', by 1066; the 'Broken Tower' was clearly well enough known not to require special identification to Wm. Poit.'s contemporaries, and few structures would be likely to be better known than an extant and still used building of Roman origin.

NOVEMBER: NOTES

1, 2. A.S. Chron.
3. Liber Monast. de Hyda.
4. Wm. Poit.
5. The various divisions of the Norman army and the routes followed up to the English surrender are based on the Domesday records of wastings attributable to the passage of the invaders, the established geography of 11th. century England, and military probability. The records were analysed seventy years ago by F. H. Baring (see bibliography), but the analyst did not relate his findings to woodland density, etc., or to the military needs of the allied command; his conclusions, therefore, required considerable revision. This does not materially reduce the value of Baring's work, however, and the map prepared for *1066* illustrates clearly the importance of his analysis: it explains the chronicled account of the capitulation of Winchester in realistic terms, affords support to the Carisbrooke cartulary history of the actions of fitzOsbern after Senlac, makes more believable the 'forced' surrender of London in mid-December, and settles very graphically the controversy over the site of the surrender, quoted in the chronicles only as 'Beorhamstede' and here identified as Little Berkhampstead rather than the better known Berkhampstead further

to the west; it also eliminates the paradox inherent in the standard histories of the Norman progress, of the otherwise incredible variations in the rate of the advance.

6. Wace.
7, 8. Wm. Poit.
9. A. S. Chron.
10. See August, *1066*.
11. Wm. Malm.
12. Wm. Jum.
13. See February, *1066*.
14. Flor. Worc.
15. Wm. Malm.
16. Wm. Poit.

DECEMBER: NOTES

1. Collating Wm. Poit. and Carmen.
2. Carmen.
3. A.S. Chron.
4. Wm. Poit.
5. Ord. Vit.
6. Wm. Poit.
7. 'Conquaestor', commonly translated as 'Conqueror', is more correctly 'Acquirer', or, in the legal sense, 'Purchaser'.
8. See March, *1066*.
9. Wm. Poit.
10. A.S. Chron.
11. Wm. Poit.
12. Eng. Hist. Doc., Vol. II, p. 945.

SELECT BIBLIOGRAPHY

The list which follows is concerned primarily with the sources used in any way in the writing of *1066*. As the book has been based as far as possible only on chronicles and other documents originating near to the period, this means that the bibliography of modern works is necessarily restricted. A secondary index is accordingly appended of parallel works which may be of interest to the reader, for comparative or critical study, or for extended illustration.

I. PRIMARY SOURCES

A. Chronicles and Histories

No one history can be relied upon in isolation. Allowance must be made for the religious, political and regional prejudices of the compilers, for the purposes for which they wrote, and for the conditions under which they worked; the limits of the possible knowledge of each chronicler must also be borne constantly in mind, and the distortions of subsequent editing are always to be expected. In general, the significance of each source varies from event to event with the nature, time and place of the happening described; and the historical probability of any particular event or sequence of events must be evaluated from an examination of all the relevant sources.

Except where cited, particular editions or translations of the sources listed were not used solely and are accordingly not separately mentioned. Brief descriptive notes are supplied in the references to the more important sources.

(i) *English*

Anglo-Saxon Chronicles: compiled in the vernacular, usually close to the events chronicled; reasonably reliable for occurrences in England, but not elsewhere; three versions concern the period dealt with, two continuing through 1066.

Vita Ædwardi Regis qui apud Westmonasterium requiescit (ed. F. Barlow, Edinburgh, 1962): written probably in 1067 by a monk

303

attached to the royal household, an adherent of the Godwinssons; reliable for events, circumstances and relationships intimately concerning the house of Godwin.

Bayeux Tapestry: completed before 1082; the masterwork of the period, discussed in the main text.

Chronicon ex Chronicis by Florence of Worcester : written before 1118; a skilful and balanced recension of several chronicles, some now lost.

Gesta Regum Anglorum by William of Malmesbury : written about 1120; comprehensive and well composed, but generally overvalued by later writers.

Historia Anglorum by Henry of Huntingdon : written before 1154; pedestrian in style, but with inclusions of value.

Chronicle of Battel Abbey: written before 1176; generally unreliable, but useful for local traditions.

De Inventione S. Crucis apud Waltham Historia: written before 1177; romanticised, but invaluable for matters concerning Waltham.

Historia Novorum in Anglia by Eadmer (ed. M. Rule, Rolls Series).

Historia Regum by Simeon of Durham (ed. T. Arnold, Rolls Series).

Vita Haroldi (ed. W. de G. Birch, London, 1885).

Vita Wulfstani by William of Malmesbury (ed. R. R. Darlington, London, 1928).

(ii) *Norman*

Carmen de Hastingensi proelio by Guy of Amiens : written about 1067; garishly coloured, very unreliable, but with inclusions of great worth; apparently used as source-book by William of Poitiers.

Gesta Normannorum Ducum by William of Jumièges : written about 1070; very brief.

Gesta Willelmi Ducis Normannorum et Regis Anglorum by William of Poitiers : written before 1077; the most accepted Norman account, but violently prejudiced, deficient in construction, rhetorical, and composed with the avowed intention of depicting William the Bastard as a 'hero' in the worst Greek sense of the term.

Brevis Relatio de Willelmo nobilissimus Comite Normannorum : written in early twelfth century; unoriginal.

Historia Ecclesiastica Angliae et Normanniae by Orderic Vitalis : written before 1138; more balanced than most Norman accounts and providing information unavailable elsewhere.

L'estorie des Engles by Geoffrey Gaimar : written about 1145; poetic, but including detailed information seemingly based on lost English sources and unavailable elsewhere; consistently undervalued by later students.

Roman de Rou by Robert Wace : written about 1160; the most elaborate and literate Norman account, but highly fictitious and preserving only a few acceptable traditions.

Chronique des Ducs de Normandie by Benoit of St. Maur : written in late twelfth century; useful more for its descriptive passages than for its matter.

Draco Normannicus by Stephen of Rouen.

Historia Croylandensis by Ingulf.

Poem addressed to Adela, daughter of William the Conqueror by Baudri of Bourgeuil.

Vita Herluini by Gilbert Crispin (ed. J. A. Robinson, Cambridge, 1911).

Vita Lanfranci by Milo Crispin (ed. J. A. Giles, Oxford, 1844).

(iii) *Norwegian and other*

Heimskringla by Snorri Sturlasson (transl. S. Laing, ed. P. Foote, London, 1961) : written about 1230; a careful and critical recension of sagas, histories and scaldic verse; the principal source for all matters concerning Norway.

Orkneyingers' Saga (trans. Sir G. W. Dasent, Rolls Series) : lacking the critical balance of Snorri, but preserving important Norse traditions.

Gesta Danorum by Saxo Grammaticus (ed. J. Olrik, H. Raeder, Copenhagen, 1931).

Various other national and monastic chronicles of England, Wales, Scotland, Ireland and western Europe were consulted and used, either directly or through references in other sources, but too briefly to warrant inclusion in this bibliography.

B. Charters, Writs and Other Documents

All but one of the documents noted in the preparation of *1066* were quoted in the texts or footnotes of other works and source-collections listed elsewhere in this bibliography. The single unquoted document was :

Cartulary of Carisbrooke Priory, Isle of Wight.

Select Bibliography

C. Modern Works and Source-collections

Anglo-Saxon Charters (ed. A. J. Robertson, Cambridge, 1939).
Anglo-Saxon Wills (ed. D. Whitelock, Cambridge, 1930).
Anglo-Saxon Writs (ed. F. E. Harmer, Manchester, 1952).
Baring, F. H., 'The Conqueror's Footprints in Domesday' (*English Historical Review*, Vol. XIII, 1898).
——, 'William the Conqueror's March through Hampshire in 1066' (*Papers and Proc. Hants. F.C.*, 7, ii, 1915).
Barlow, F., *The English Church 1000–1066* (London, 1963).
——, *The Feudal Kingdom of England* (London, 1955).
Brooks, F. W., *The Battle of Stamford Bridge* (York, 1956).
Darby, H. C., 'Domesday Woodland' (*Economic History Review*, 1950).
Dawson, C., *History of Hastings Castle* (London, 1909).
Domesday Book: Liber Censualis Willelmi Primi (ed. A. Farley, H. Ellis, Record Commission, 1783–1816, with translations by counties in *The Victoria History of the Counties of England*).
Douglas, D. C., *William the Conqueror* (London, 1964).
English Historical Documents, Vol. II (ed. D. C. Douglas, G. W. Greenaway, London, 1953).
Feilitzen, O. von, *The Pre-Conquest Personal Names of Domesday Book* (Uppsala, 1937).
Freeman, E. A., *The History of the Norman Conquest of England* (Oxford, 1867–1879).
Glover, R., 'English Warfare in 1066' (*English Historical Review*, Vol. LXVII, 1952).
Hollister, C. W., *Anglo-Saxon Military Institutions* (Oxford, 1962).
Lemmon, C. H., *The Field of Hastings* (St. Leonards-on-Sea, 2nd ed., 1960).
Loyn, H. R., *Anglo-Saxon England and the Norman Conquest* (London, 1962).
Maitland, F. W., *Domesday Book and Beyond* (introd. E. Miller, London, 1960).
Oleson, T. J., *The Witenagemot in the Reign of Edward the Confessor* (Toronto, 1955).
Poole, A. L. (ed.) *Mediaeval England* (Oxford, 1958).
Schramm, P. E., *A History of the English Coronation* (Oxford, 1937).
Searle, W. G., *Anglo-Saxon Bishops, Kings and Nobles* (Cambridge, 1889).

Select Bibliography

Stenton, F. M., *Anglo-Saxon England* (Oxford, 2nd ed., 1947).
Wilkinson, B., 'Northumbrian Separatism in 1065 and 1066' (*Bulletin of the John Rylands Library*, xxiii, 1939).
Williamson, J. A., *The English Channel* (London, 1959).

2. SECONDARY INDEX : GENERAL

Andrieu-Guitrancourt, P., *Histoire de l'Empire Normand et de sa civilisation* (Paris, 1952).
L'Art de Verifier les Dates (Paris, 1783–1787).
Blair, P. H., *An Introduction to Anglo-Saxon England* (Cambridge, 1956).
Bouard, M. de, *Guillaume le Conquérant* (Paris, 1958).
Brønsted, J., *The Vikings* (London, 1960).
Bryant, A., *The Story of England: Makers of the Realm* (London, 1953).
Burne, A. H., *The Battlefields of England* (London, 1951).
Chambers, R. W., *England before the Norman Conquest* (London, 1926).
Clemoes, P. (ed.) *The Anglo-Saxons* (Cambridge, 1959).
Corbett, W. J., *Cambridge Mediaeval History*, Vol. V, Ch. XV (Cambridge, 1922).
Creasy, E. S., *The Fifteen Decisive Battles of the World* (London, 1908).
Darby, H. C. (ed.) *Historical Geography of England* (London, 1936).
Fuller, J. F. C., *Decisive Battles of the Western World*, Vol. I, (London, 1939).
Green, J. R., *A Short History of the English People* (London, 1929).
Haskins, C. H., *Norman Institutions* (Cambridge, U.S.A., 1918).
Hodgkin, R. H., *A History of the Anglo-Saxons* (Oxford, 3rd ed., 1953).
Lot, F., *L'Art militaire et les armées au moyen âge en Europe et dans le Proche Orient* (Paris, 1946).
Oman, C., *A History of the Art of War in the Middle Ages* (London, 2nd ed., 1924).
——, *England before the Norman Conquest* (London, 9th ed., 1949).
Ramsay, J. H., *The Foundations of England* (London, 1898).
Round, J. H., *Feudal England* (London, 1895).
Slocombe, G., *William the Conqueror* (London, 1959).

Spatz, W., *Die Schlacht von Hastings* (Berlin, 1896).

Stenton, F. M., *William the Conqueror* (London, 1908).

——, (ed. with others) *Bayeux Tapestry* (London, 1957).

Tait, J., *The Mediaeval English Borough* (Manchester, 1936).

Trevelyan, G. M., *History of England* (London, 1952).

Vinogradoff, P., *English Society in the Eleventh Century* (Oxford, 1908).

GENEALOGIES

Notes : 1. Names in capitals are of individuals actively concerned in the narrative of the year, 1066.

2. The abbreviations used in the tables are :

Emp.—emperor; K.—king; D.—duke; C.—count; E.—earl; archbp.—archbishop; bp.—bishop; d.—daughter; s.—son; m.—married; ob.—died; c.—about.

309

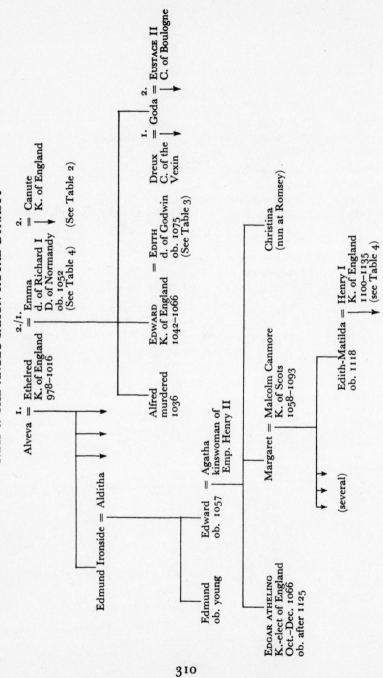

TABLE 1. THE ANGLO-SAXON ROYAL DYNASTY

TABLE 2. THE DANISH ROYAL DYNASTY AND ENGLISH ASSOCIATIONS

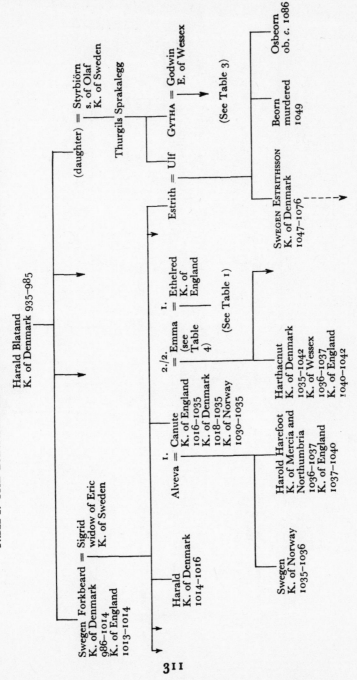

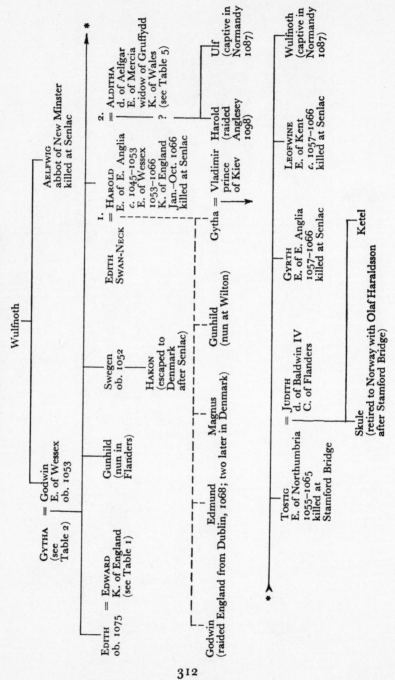

TABLE 3. THE HOUSE OF GODWIN

Wulfnoth

GYTHA (see Table 2) = Godwin E. of Wessex ob. 1053

AELFWIG abbot of New Minster killed at Senlac

EDITH ob. 1075 = EDWARD K. of England (see Table 1)

Swegen ob. 1052

HAKON (escaped to Denmark after Senlac)

Gunhild (nun in Flanders)

1. HAROLD E. of E. Anglia c. 1045-1053 E. of Wessex 1053-1066 K. of England Jan.-Oct. 1066 killed at Senlac

EDITH SWAN-NECK

2. ALDITHA d. of Aelfgar E. of Mercia widow of Gruffydd K. of Wales ? (see Table 5)

Gytha = Vladimir prince of Kiev

Harold (raided Anglesey 1098)

Ulf (captive in Normandy 1087)

Godwin (raided England from Dublin, 1068; two later in Denmark)

Edmund

Magnus

Gunhild (nun at Wilton)

TOSTIG E. of Northumbria 1055-1065 killed at Stamford Bridge = JUDITH d. of Baldwin IV C. of Flanders

GYRTH E. of E. Anglia 1057-1066 killed at Senlac

LEOFWINE E. of Kent c. 1057-1066 killed at Senlac

Wulfnoth (captive in Normandy 1087)

Skule (retired to Norway with Olaf Haraldsson after Stamford Bridge)

Ketel

312

TABLE 4. THE DUCAL HOUSE OF NORMANDY

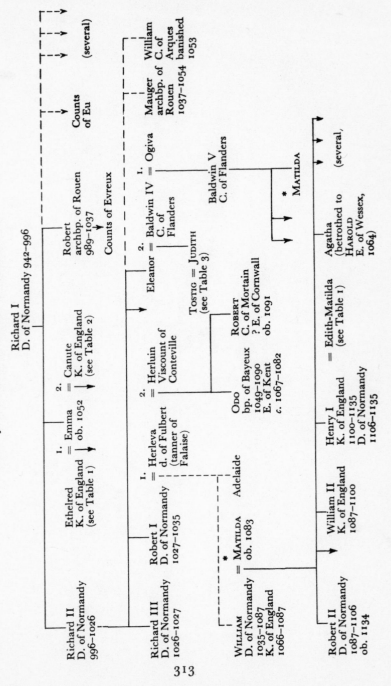

TABLE 5. THE HOUSE OF LEOFRIC

Leofric
E. of Mercia
ob. 1057
= Godiva
sister of Thorold
of Bukenhale

Aelfgar
E. of E. Anglia
1053–1057
E. of Mercia
1057–c. 1062
= Alveva

Edwin
E. of Mercia
ob. 1072

Morkere
E. of Northumbria
(captive in
Normandy, 1087)

Gruffydd
K. of Wales
assassinated
1063
= 1.
Alditha
= 2.
Harold
K. of England

?

Lucia = Ivo Taillebois

(daughter) (see Table 3)

TABLE 6. THE NORWEGIAN ROYAL DYNASTY

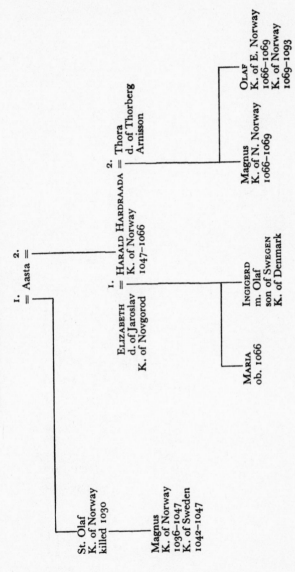

= Aasta =
1.   2.

St. Olaf
K. of Norway
killed 1030

Magnus
K. of Norway
1036–1047
K. of Sweden
1042–1047

ELIZABETH
d. of Jaroslav
K. of Novgorod

1.

HARALD HARDRAADA =
K. of Norway
1047–1066

2.

Thora
d. of Thorberg
Arnisson

MARIA
ob. 1066

INGIGERD
m. Olaf
son of SWEGEN
K. of Denmark

Magnus
K. of N. Norway
1066–1069

OLAF
K. of E. Norway
1066–1069
K. of Norway
1069–1093

315

TABLE 7. SCHEMATIC SUMMARY OF TABLES 1-5 SHOWING INTERRELATIONSHIPS

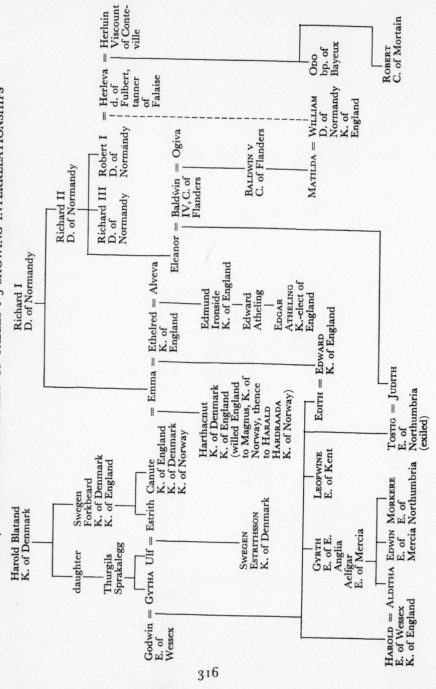

316

GENERAL INDEX

General Index

(N.B. This is a select list only, of places important to the narrative of the year, 1066.)

General Index

C. ITEMS OF SPECIAL INTEREST

THE BATTLE OF SENLAC:

14th October, 1066

Archers
Footmen
Knights

Watch Oak

Caldbec Hill

Hoar Appletree

Trackway

Oak Wood Gyll

Oak Wood